Other books by this author

The Busy Person's Guide to British History
Deus Vult: A Concise History of the Crusades
The British Empire in 100 Facts
The Napoleonic Wars in 100 Facts
The Romans in 100 Facts
The American Presidents in 100 Facts

You can find me on social media as @HistoryGems on Twitter
and as the same name (with the @) on Facebook and YouTube.

FORGOTTEN
HISTORY

FORGOTTEN HISTORY

HISTORY

Unbelievable Moments
from the Past

JEM DUDUCU

AMBERLEY

Dedicated to Uncle Bill and Aunt Toni: consider this to be the perfect read for the pause that refreshes.

This edition published 2017

Amberley Publishing
The Hill, Stroud
Gloucestershire, GL5 4EP

www.amberley-books.com

Copyright © Jem Duducu, 2016, 2017

The right of Jem Duducu to be identified as the Author of this work has been asserted in accordance with the Copyrights, Designs and Patents Act 1988.

ISBN 978 1 4456 7135 2 (paperback)
ISBN 978 1 4456 5635 9 (ebook)

British Library Cataloguing in Publication Data. A catalogue record for this book is available from the British Library.

Typesetting and Origination by Amberley Publishing
Printed in the UK.

CONTENTS

INTRODUCTION

Several years ago, when I was working as a trainer in a FTSE 100 company, I was continually being asked, 'What should we do about social media?' by the company's sales force. As a married father-of-two, Twitter and Facebook just hadn't been on my radar, but I was getting enough queries to know I needed to have a view.

So I set up some accounts to fiddle around with, just to see how everything worked. I quickly realised I would have to pick a topic – a subject on which I could provide regular posts. I am not a sports fan, so that was out, but I have always loved history. I was one of the last people to get a GCSE in Medieval History, and I have a degree in Archaeology and Medieval History, so I settled on history as my subject matter. Using a lame play on my first name, @HistoryGems on Twitter and @HistoryGems on Facebook were born in 2011 (yes, I am aware I should not have used that name for the Facebook page, but like I said, I was learning; years later I wish I could change it). Little did I know then how many other people also love history and how many would find their way to my posts and tweets.

As I'm sure was true of a lot of people when they started out on social media, the only ones who 'followed' or 'liked' me were my immediate family and a few curious friends. But I persisted, and at the time of writing I have around 5,000 followers on Twitter and more than 30,000 likes on Facebook. And just for the record, I don't work for the FTSE 100 company anymore.

I learned the hard way that Facebook doesn't store all of the posts, and Hootsuite, which is an essential tool, has limitations on the number of words per post. This means that many of my favourite posts have been lost in some kind of electronic backwater. It was the idea of both saving and expanding posts that inspired a good old-fashioned book – the one you're reading now – so you could say that not only was this book inspired by social media, but also that *Forgotten History* has taken more than four years of research to produce. I have had great fun finding the weird and wonderful stories that enrich and enhance what we already know and remind us that history is not dull. If it ever seems that way, it's the way it's presented.

Even if you have perused all of my social media presence, you will find more here. A book simply means that as well as introducing new topics, I have been able to expand and elaborate on a few old favourites. Here you can dip in and out of over 180 different stories, which are of varying importance to history and, therefore, of varying lengths, from just a few paragraphs to a few pages. Some of the subjects are provocative; others are truly despicable, and a few are just plain fun. I hope you will find all of them to be interesting and informative.

I have split the book into four loose time frames: Ancient History (although we start in prehistory), Medieval, Early Modern to the Victorians and the Twentieth Century. Of course the term 'medieval' is anachronistic for those anecdotes pertaining to any civilisation beyond Europe, but it was a convenient way to group together disparate stories from roughly the same period of time. If you finish up and wonder why there wasn't more on Napoleon or the Romans, that's because I wouldn't want readers of my other books to feel cheated by repeating copy. For those who are new to my work, please have a look at my back catalogue for more books packed with historical facts.

In *Forgotten History* we travel from the Stone Age to the age of satellite technology, from death in battle to death by disease, from great women to mad rulers. The point is simply that truth is stranger than fiction, and once you step off the well-trodden path of familiar historical accounts, it doesn't take long to unearth something truly appalling, amazing or bizarre.

I hope you enjoy the journey!

ANCIENT HISTORY

Let's Start with Some Prehistory

The Earth is about 4.5 billion years old, but for billions of years it was too hot, too toxic or too regularly slammed by meteors to foster life. Some of the oldest fossils on the planet are sedimentary rocks that were once living organisms. Western Australia is famous for both living and fossilised examples of these early Earth inhabitants. The best known of these microbial structures are called stromatolites, and they grow in a wide range of environments: underwater, on the shoreline, on salt flats and inland.

The ecosystems that generated Earth's oldest stromatolites also produced other sedimentary structures. It's here that fossils of single-celled organisms called microbes have been found dating back a colossal 3.49 billion years. It would be BILLIONS of years before the planet would start to see fish or vertebrates, so the microbes that built these ancient sedimentary structures are the oldest fossils ever identified. It's interesting to think of them as our oldest ancestors.

Jumping forwards some 3 billion years plus, we arrive at the Permian–Triassic extinction, generally referred to by geologists as the 'Great Dying'. It occurred about 252 million years ago, so we can't blame humans for it.

This event forms the boundary between the Permian and Triassic geological periods and is the Earth's most catastrophic extinction episode. Nothing else in history or prehistory comes close to this level of loss of life on our planet. The estimated numbers are truly terrifying, with up to 96 per cent of all marine species and 70 per cent of terrestrial vertebrate species becoming extinct. If that sounds bad, nature's survivors, the insects, didn't do well either, as it's the only known mass extinction of these invertebrates. It is estimated that, in total, about 57 per cent of all families and 83 per cent of all species became extinct during this era.

So who was the culprit? It was climate change and a dramatic increase in CO_2 in the atmosphere (I won't comment on current similar concerns). The pattern of mortality is consistent with what is known about the effects of hypoxia; this is a shortage, but not a total absence, of oxygen. The probable cause has been identified as supervolcanoes spewing out noxious gases, something that, in theory, could happen again tomorrow – and there would be nothing we could do about it. A few geologists have found some possible evidence of a meteor impact around the same time, but this is controversial and unverified.

The Earth's atmosphere has changed many times. There were eras of much larger oxygen concentrations, which led to colossal forest fires. But on the occasion of the Permian–Triassic extinction, because so much biodiversity was lost, the time it took for different species to became established and blossom again was significantly longer than after any other extinction event – up to 10 million years.

While this mass extinction is fascinating in its own right, the effects of wiping the slate clean led to the rise of the dinosaurs. Just as the mammals needed the meteor strike of 65 million years ago to come to prominence, so it is true for the dinosaurs: no Permian–Triassic extinction, no dinosaurs.

This is another reminder of how random evolution really is. Most evolutionary biologists agree that if we turned back the clock some 500 million years and ran evolution again, almost certainly we would not end up with the same outcomes – and humans are in no way an inevitable outcome. There are just too many variables. Things like changes in temperature or the chemical composition of air, widespread flooding or fires or meteor strikes ... all of these are unpredictable and uncontrollable and have created us and our world.

The statistical chances of our existence are too slim to be calculated.

How Do You Know the Date?

It's a simple question that has a complex answer because, all too often, the relevant information is manipulated by groups with political, nationalist or religious agendas, who create an atmosphere far more volatile than should ever exist over a question as simple as 'when did it happen?'

For the last thousand years or so, most events have good historical records to support them. For example, there can be no doubt that that Battle of Hastings happened in 1066 because separate sources from a number of countries all corroborate a date of 1066. The further back you go, the trickier it gets to cross reference these records, but many areas around the Mediterranean, the Middle East, the subcontinent and China have accounts that go back 3,000 years or more, with some very early civilisations (like ancient Egypt and Babylon) able to corroborate events to a surprising degree. However, we can run into problems even here.

Literal believers in the Bible have a problem with Herod the Great, a major villain in the New Testament, who orders infanticide in an effort to stop Jesus before his mission has even begun. The problem is that this story has no source other than the Gospels, which were written at the end of the first century AD. None of the records from the time (around AD 1) mention any such memorable event and, even worse, using the same dating method that was used in the first century in the Middle East (including during Jesus's life), Herod would have died in 4 BC, so he can't have done anything in AD 1. Some Biblical scholars try to move the timelines to make things fit, but it's a bit like pushing a ruler around a desk: no matter where you put it, it's still thirty centimetres long. There have also been attempts to validate the Gospel's version by saying the Herod dates are wrong and the Bible is right. But which is more likely to be correct: the official records of a kingdom or a spiritual text written 100 years later by no official record keeper? You can argue omission or bias, but there was no reason for the record keeper to get his dates wrong ... unless he did it to annoy Christians a generation before Jesus was preaching, which is unlikely.

When texts get more fragmented, scholars have to rely on science to help out. Numismatics, occupation layers, dendrochronology and carbon dating are all tools which help to date early events. The last one is the most famous, so the others first.

Numismatics is the study of coins. Find a ditch with a coin that's from, say, AD 973, and the ditch can't have been dug before that point. The coin has set a start date. If there is an occupation layer above it, with a coin from AD 1135, then you know the lower layer was active no earlier than 973 and no later than 1135. This is not helpful if you want to know whether the site was key to the events of 1066, but at least you can say it's a possibility. Using evidence in layers of occupation is called stratification.

Dendrochronology is really clever. Some very smart people have worked out that the width of tree rings (the annual growth of a tree) creates a unique signature per tree type in a certain region; in other words, all oaks in northern Europe have the same pattern of tree rings. By bringing together all kinds of wooden finds, it has been possible to detect the unique patterns made by tree rings for most deciduous (not evergreen) trees in northern Europe; therefore, if you find something made of wood, you can get some incredibly accurate dates, going back thousands of years. For example, the Sweet Track is a Neolithic wooden pathway in Somerset, England, which they know was built in 3,807/6 BC. They have the date to within twelve months from over 5,000 years ago.

Then there's radio carbon dating – C14 dating. Not being an expert in quantum physics, I just have to believe those who know when they say that while all living creatures have carbon in them, every now and then the carbon atoms get their structure a bit wrong and end up with 14 electrons – C14. This is a radioactive isotope which starts to degrade as soon as organic matter dies. It's a rather helpful atomic clock because if you can measure the degradation, you can get a relatively accurate idea of how old something organic is, usually to within an eighty-year period (although, sometimes controversially, the sample will be destroyed in the dating process). Similar techniques can be used on stone, but the method is only suitable for very early finds from the Palaeolithic period or earlier.

So, by using a number of these techniques, archaeologists and historians can date a site with varying degrees of accuracy.

The Opening Line of J. R. R. Tolkien's The Hobbit *is …*

> In a hole in the ground there lived a hobbit. Not a nasty, dirty, wet hole, filled with the ends of worms and an oozy smell, nor yet a dry, bare, sandy hole with nothing in it to sit down on or to eat: it was a hobbit-hole, and that means comfort.

Hobbits are, of course, fictional. At least, that's what everyone thought until there was an amazing discovery in Liang Bua Cave on Flores Island, Indonesia, in 2003. It was here that a new type of *Homo genus*, a species of hominids, was discovered. The mature adults stood about one metre high, roughly the height of a hobbit, and they seemed to live in caves … like hobbits. They were also intellectually sophisticated enough to use stone tools, but there the similarities end. Clearly the caves they lived in were not subterranean rural-England-style cottages, nor is there any evidence of clothing.

What was discovered was a new branch of the hominid tree: human-like individuals, who would have lived at the same time as both *Homo sapiens* and the last Neanderthals. Not much more is known about this type of early man, and the remains of only nine individuals have so far been found. However, the discovery of *Homo floresiensis* (as this hominid group is known) has rewritten archaeological textbooks, as the species lived in this area of South East Asia from around 94,000 to 13,000 years ago.

It is a bit of a head-scratch that an imaginary creature turned out to be a real part of our evolutionary story.

The Yeti, Bigfoot and … Gigantopithecus

Humans are one of the great apes, and just by looking at a chimpanzee or gorilla it's easy to spot the similarities between us. However 100,000 years ago (at the dawn of *Homo sapiens*), there was another great ape, and this one was really BIG. Based on fossil evidence, the adult male Gigantopithecus is estimated to have stood about three metres tall and weighed as much as 540 kilograms, making the species two to three times heavier than today's gorillas and nearly five times heavier than the orangutan, its closest living relative. Large males may have had an arm span of over three metres. All of this has been extrapolated from a few teeth and one lower jaw find. It's hard to know anything more, so there's even debate as to whether it walked on two legs or more like a gorilla, using its arms to support its upper-body bulk.

Considering that Gigantopithecus lived in South East Asia, where the Yeti is said to have been sighted, it is not impossible that the last few Gigantopithecuses might have survived long enough to become legends in local communities.

For the record, I am not suggesting there are a bunch of them roaming around the Himalayas. It is more likely that early groups of humans encountered them and passed down the stories that have become the Yeti legends of today.

Cavemen Were Communists

Let's forget, for a moment, contemporary political associations with the word 'communist' and have a look at how hunter-gatherers survived. They lived in small groups, which worked together to protect the tribe from multiple external threats, whether enemy tribes, large predators or natural disasters. When food was collected, it was shared. Killing a mammoth took cooperation, so the team and their families would equally share the spoils of the hunt. (Side note: there seems to have been two ways to kill large mammals like a mammoth or bison. The first was the very hard and dangerous way of surrounding it and hurling spears at it. The other method was the more cowardly but more efficient way of provoking them into panic by means of fire and stampeding the herd over the edge of a cliff, letting gravity do the rest. I get the feeling that I'm descended from one of the guys who preferred the cliff-gravity option.)

It seems the men worked together to hunt animals, which allowed for a protein-rich diet, while the women looked after the young and scavenged for nutritious nuts, berries and herbs (the sort of food that is unlikely to attack). When we consider that the hunter-gatherers shared both the work and the resources of the group, we have the very definition of a 'socialist commune', not that those words would have meant anything to our early ancestors.

The communist ideal is just that – members of the community working together, sharing both the effort and the reward. It is a worthy concept, but there's just one problem: after the Stone Age, it doesn't work.

Once humans stopped roaming and settled down to farm crops, establish permanent communities and create 'civilisation' (whatever that is), specialisation developed, and some specialisations had a higher value than others, which is where inequality comes in. The warrior caste, which protected the group, had more value, status and skill than that of manual labourers, therefore the warriors claimed more of the resources. Fast forward through to today, it simply takes more time to become a surgeon than to learn to operate a fast-food till, so is it any surprise that one earns substantially more than the other? Of course not. Discrepancies in pay are explained in terms of what the surrounding culture values. Any modern attempt to implement a communist concept of equal sharing is, ultimately, folly. But it's fair to say that Marx would have been proud of Palaeolithic mankind.

The Mysterious Göbekli Tepe

It is a well-established fact that humans did not start building large structures until the invention of agriculture ... but then archaeologists found Göbekli Tepe in south-east Turkey. It was first thought that these structures were started about 6,000 to 7,000 years ago, on the very edge of agricultural civilisation, but it turns out that Göbekli Tepe is closer to 12,000 years old. It is an early Neolithic sanctuary located at the top of a mountain ridge, and includes massive stones carved over 11,000 years ago by people who had not yet developed metal tools or even pottery. It is thought that workers used flint points to cut through the bedrock, located approximately 100 metres away, and from these pits the slabs were transported to their hilltop site.

These early buildings range from ten to thirty metres in diameter. Their most notable feature is the presence of T-shaped limestone pillars, evenly set within thick interior walls, which are composed of unworked stone. Four such round structures have been unearthed so far; geophysical surveys indicate that there are sixteen more, enclosing up to eight pillars each, amounting to nearly 200 pillars in all.

Stone benches line the interior, and two taller pillars are positioned at the centre of each circle. Many of the pillars are decorated with enigmatic pictograms and carved animal reliefs. The pictograms may represent commonly understood sacred symbols, some of which are recognisable from Neolithic cave paintings elsewhere. The reliefs show lions, bulls, boars, foxes, gazelles, donkeys, snakes and other reptiles, insects and birds (particularly vultures). The complex makes Stonehenge look like a modern pile of minimalist blocks.

The discovery of the breathtakingly old Göbekli Tepe has forced us to rewrite what we know about early civilisation.

The Problem with Milk

The one thing animals spend most of their time doing is finding food. For early humans, the imperative to hunt was the same as the necessity to eat: one drove the other. However, the establishment of an agricultural society and the domestication of animals made access to food a whole lot easier and gave our early ancestors time to start creating civilisation.

While butchering tame goats or pigs was easy enough, it took much longer to master the collection of that other great source of nutrients, milk. Obviously human milk is fine for us – a mother's milk has all the nutrients and proteins a growing human needs. The same is true for other animals whose milk is designed for their young. But the milk of one species is not necessarily easily digested by others, and *Homo sapiens* started out as lactose intolerant.

Over time, humans have adapted to lactose, and as a result we now have access to a source of nutrition that can be consumed as liquid milk or turned into yoghurt, cream or cheese. The development of cheese was particularly useful as this meant that a nutritional food could be carried around. In the Chinese Taklamakan Desert, ancient burial sites discovered in the 1930s revealed clumps of yellow matter on the necks and chests of mummies from as early as 1615 BC. These clumps turned out to be the earliest cheese ever discovered (although long past its sell-by date). The fact that it was deposited with the dead shows its importance in that society.

It is thanks entirely to the sheer bloody-mindedness of our ancestors, who, generation after generation, endured stomach cramps, gassiness, and even diarrhoea, in the pursuit of their goal to consume milk from animals such as cows, goats and yaks, that most of us are able to drink the milk of other animals today.

I'll conclude with a question raised by Charles de Gaulle (former President of France):

How can anyone govern a nation that has 246 different kinds of cheese?

We've come a long way.

How Old Is the World's Oldest Paved Road?

The Romans were famous for their roads, so maybe 2,000 years old? No. The Persian Empire needed roads, so 3,000 years? The answer is an astonishing 4,500 years old and it is to be found in Egypt.

This paved road is now referred to as the Widan Al-Faras Quarry Road, and, as the name suggests, it wasn't a road to connect towns but an access road for a basalt stone quarry. Because we can trace the origins of stone, we know the route the stone would have taken to get to its destination. This highway was built to move blocks of basalt from the Widan Al-Faras mines to the shore of the ancient Lake Moeris, the bigger ancestor of the modern Lake Qarun.

The road itself is about two metres wide and about eleven kilometres long. Ancient Egyptian workers used not only slabs of limestone and sandstone but also logs of petrified wood to construct and stabilise the road, which was constantly threatened by shifting sands.

The road ended at a quay not far from an Old Kingdom temple that is still standing, north of Lake Qarun. From there, the basalt was moved to the Nile and, from this point, to the Giza Plateau, where it was used to build sarcophagi and the floors of mortuary temples around the Giza Pyramids. The fact that the world's oldest paved road was nothing more than a convenience to get stone blocks to the areas of real innovation and building perfectly symbolises the incredible feats of engineering achieved by the Egyptians, who were then on the very edges of the early Bronze Age.

While it is on a list to be designated as a UNESCO World Heritage Site, it has been on that list for ten years. There are no signs to show its location, but neither has there been any attempt to protect the road from either trophy hunters or the elements. It is slowly crumbling away as you read this.

The History of the Swastika

You may be wondering why the symbol of the Nazis has made it into the Ancient History section. Shouldn't it be with the Twentieth Century section, somewhere at the back? It is nothing short of shameful that the swastika has become indelibly connected with a fifteen-year period of political activity by a group of German fascists when the symbol has been used for thousands of years by Hindus.

In Sanskrit, 'swastika' means 'it is good'. This is a positive statement and therefore, unsurprisingly, it can be seen everywhere in India. I have even seen a brick maker stamp a swastika on every single brick he and his workforce produced 'for luck and security'.

The earliest swastika was found in Ukraine and dates back to around 10,000 BC; however, the Stone Age Vinca culture in central India (dating back to around 5,000 BC) is where it really took off. The symbol is one of such simplicity that it has been used in numerous (and unrelated) cultures at different times around the world. Everyone from the Ancient Greeks to the Vikings was using it long before German fascism was something people could spell.

It was in the nineteenth century, however, that the swastika began to be linked to the 'Aryan race', and so, when the Nazis were looking for a symbol for Aryan purity, 'untainted' by

Judaism or Christianity, they picked this ancient cross. It is important to pause and consider the Eurocentric bias in this. The Nazis had little impact in India, and as such, the people of India continue to associate the emblem with beneficial links to their gods, rather than with the horrors of the Nazi regime. It's really only in the West that the swastika has come to symbolise evil.

It is unfortunate that a sign that has represented something positive for millennia has been turned by the western world into something that signifies racism, hatred and violence.

There Really Was a 'Scorpion King'

While today the Scorpion King is probably best known as a terrible baddie in the 'Mummy' films (and the subsequent spin-off *Scorpion King* movies, but let's not go there), there is evidence of a pre-dynastic Egyptian monarch who used a scorpion as the symbol of his rule.

The fact that he pre-dates the pharaohs is an indication that we are talking about the very edges of 'history'. It's also worth pointing out that while pharaoh and king are essentially interchangeable titles, pharaoh literally means 'great house' (or hall) and implies the monarch is so mighty you cannot name him, you have to refer to his abode instead.

It could be that some of the first pharaohs had multiple names, in which case it may be that the Scorpion King and one of the first pharaohs, called Narmer, were the same person. Indeed, a mace head in the Ashmolean Museum in Oxford shows the Scorpion King in a very similar way to this pharaoh, who also wears the white crown, which shows he ruled the Upper Nile region. On later pharaohs, the head gear displays an image of a serpent and a vulture, showing they ruled both the Upper and Lower Nile regions.

Whatever he was called (and personally, I think Scorpion King sounds cooler than Narmer, don't you?), he ruled at a time when trade and agriculture were starting to bind the disparate facets of Egyptian society into a larger entity that would become the foundation of the Egyptian dynasties for millennia. It was also the time when the first writing appeared, which means we can set the period to around 3,200–3,000 BC. Whoever he was, he was an important and formative figure, and it is frustrating that so little evidence of his identity and his reign exists. He's a hot topic of discussion amongst Egyptologists, with many theories and counter-arguments swirling around the few relevant artefacts. More than 5,000 years later, historians are still debating his legacy, which, in some ways, makes him one of the most important rulers in history.

The Wheel Was Not Mankind's Earliest Invention

The wheel is often regarded as the earliest and the single greatest invention in human history. Whether it's the most important is debateable (it's certainly up there), but proof of its existence in human society is unexpectedly late. The first evidences occur simultaneously in several locations in the Near East and parts of Asia, around 3,500 BC. About this same time there are indications of carts in southern Poland.

It's shortly after this period that the early civilisations of Babylon and Egypt developed. Both of these utilised fast-moving war chariots to build their empires, essential because horses had not yet been bred to carry the weight of a man. In other words, the chariots of this era were the cavalry of later antiquity and were rightly feared on the battlefield.

So what came before the wheel? Well, quite a lot: clothing, tools, the bow and arrow, spears and other weapons, agriculture, fishing, art, pottery, boats, writing and permanent settlements, to name a few. It's also worth pointing out that some hugely complex civilisations never had the wheel. The Inca, for example, were able to build an entire empire without it. The wheel was a great leap forward, but it was by no means there at the start of civilisation.

It's a little odd that in popular culture, fire, the wheel and writing are regarded as the greatest of the early inventions. True, they are all impressive, but perhaps the least necessary is the wheel. Agriculture, irrigation and communication are far more important to the development of civilisation, but everybody loves wheels!

What Is the Magical and Sinister 'Grimoire'?

The term 'grimoire' comes from eighteenth-century French, but it describes something as old as writing itself. A grimoire is a book of magic. It has nothing to do with religion, but is, specifically, a book of magical knowledge, including spells and potions. The earliest extant written incantations come from ancient Mesopotamia (modern Iraq). They aren't in book form, but are written on clay tablets 2,500 years old.

However, ancient Egyptian burial charms are far older; they were being added to bodies 4–5,000 years ago. This can be at least partially explained by the fact that the Egyptians had a god of magic, Heka, and this is where magic and religion get muddled. To this day, the relics of saints in many European churches are believed to be imbued with miraculous properties, able to heal or perform miracles. Looking at them another way, they are 'magic'.

Books of spells may sound like black magic, but a number of non-canonical Jewish, Muslim and Christian texts, such as the Book of Enoch, have spells and messages allegedly written by angels. A number of these books are, in fact, early chemistry books, but the results were attributed to God or magic, rather than what we would now call a chemical reaction. The grimoires in this instance contained what was regarded as secret knowledge and were used by the priesthood to prove God's power through miracles. They had nothing to do with evil.

It's in the medieval era that spells and magic became associated with witches and devil worshippers. In the 1790s in France, the tale of the 'Grand Grimoire' introduced the idea of a pact with the Devil – a sinister concept that really took off in the late nineteenth century. This was a period of fascination with the paranormal, and the notion of hidden knowledge reflected the fears and preoccupations of contemporary society.

All of this makes grimoires an exciting area of primary source research because there's no getting around the feeling that you are reading forbidden and powerful knowledge.

How Long Have Women Been Using Cosmetics?

The short answer is, presumably, since prehistory. Primates groom each other, and while this is a means of social bonding, it is an act of hygiene, too. In the case of humans it is also an attempt to arrange the hair in a manner which the other party finds pleasing.

It has been mooted by anthropologists that early human females may well have tried to enhance their looks by pinching their cheeks to look rosier or by crushing berries to improve lip pigmentation. The fundamental reason for all of this? The healthier the female looks, the more likely she will be to attract a mate. In the case of a community of primates, the healthiest-looking females will have more choices of mates than others. Makes you think, doesn't it?

Moving into the historical era, aristocratic Mesopotamian women were probably the first to wear lipstick, about 5,000 years ago.

They crushed gemstones and used them to decorate their faces, mainly on the lips and around the eyes. Of course the images from ancient Egypt reveal that both men and women used black eye make-up. It's worth remembering that while the marketing of cosmetics to men today seems innovative, there are numerous instances of them using make-up in different civilisations in the past.

Cosmetics are, of course, a trick used to camouflage imperfections and enhance desirable features. Their usage reached a certain logical conclusion in 1770, when the British Parliament passed a law which annulled a marriage if the woman wore cosmetics before her wedding day (presumably this would come under the heading of 'false advertising').

It is more than a little ironic that in this same period men wore powdered wigs and white lead foundation, and beauty spots for both sexes were common in the courts of Europe.

Throughout most of nineteenth-century Britain, the obvious use of cosmetics was considered to be unacceptable for respectable women. It was associated with marginalised groups such as actors and ... erm ... working girls. Until the end of the nineteenth century it was considered uncouth to wear make-up in Western Europe.

Ancient Egyptians Strike Action

Going on strike, you would assume, is closely linked to the history of industrialisation and the formation of trade unions. Wrong! While it was, of course, the industrialisation of economies that led to better-organised work forces, the idea of putting down tools because of a dispute goes back a very long way.

The very first strike recorded in history started in 1152 BC, on 14 November. This was during the reign of Rameses III in ancient Egypt.

It is a common misconception largely created by Biblical stories that much of the work on ancient Egyptian monuments was carried out by slaves. While the Egyptians did have slaves, they were by no means the main workforce. Craftsmen, artisans, designers and builders were paid men who took pride in their work. The evidence is in the quality of the structures, many of which have stood for more than 3,000 years.

In November of 1152 BC, trouble was brewing during the construction of a royal necropolis – a group of tombs and crypts – at Deir el-Medina. The workers not only felt they were underpaid, but were concerned that their wages were in arrears, so they organised a mass walkout and halted construction.

The response was interesting. You might assume that a pharaoh would bring out the whips or cut off the heads of the ringleaders, but after a round of negotiations their wages were paid. In fact, their wages were increased, and the workers returned to finish the job.

The necropolis still stands to this day.

Ancient Chinese Writing

China has quite a lot of history. Just getting the different dynasties straight can be a headache for westerners.

Most people in the West have heard of the Ming Dynasty and, possibly, the Han or Qing dynasties, but one of the longest running was the Shang Dynasty, which lasted for more than 500 years, from (roughly) 1600 BC to 1046 BC. Quite amazingly, this was a working dynasty and administration 500 years before the Persians met the Greeks at Thermopylae and centuries before Rome was even a village.

It is, however, disingenuous to think that Shang territory was the same thing as 'China'. The Shang Dynasty ruled a large territory, but it was only about a fifth of modern-day China. And there were several periods, centuries after the Shang, when 'China' was a region of warring nations and monarchs. With those caveats, the archaeology associated with the Shang is impressive. Work at the ruins of Yin (near modern day Anyang), which has been identified as the last Shang capital, has uncovered eleven major royal tombs and the foundations of palaces and ritual sites containing weapons of war and the remains of both animal and human sacrifices. Tens of thousands of bronze, jade, stone, bone, and ceramic artefacts have been uncovered and classified. The workmanship on the bronzes attests to a high level of civilization.

The Anyang site has yielded the earliest known body of Chinese writing: not histories or official court documents, but mostly divinations inscribed on oracle bones. More than 20,000 were discovered in the initial scientific excavations of the 1920s and 1930s, and over four times as many have been found since. Di Xin was the last Shang king, but he was mad, suffered a series of military defeats and committed suicide, which is why the dynasty faded. In their prime, however, the Shang were perhaps the most advanced culture in the world.

The Battle of Kadesh Is Important for a Number of Reasons

The Battle of Kadesh is thought to have been the biggest chariot fight in history, with between 5,000 and 6,000 of them rattling around the battlefield in modern-day Syria. It is also one of the first conflicts for which historians have contemporary records outlining the tactics used. And finally, it's an early provable example of political propaganda.

In 1274 BC the Egyptians were fighting the Hittite Empire for supremacy over Syria. What seems to have happened was that, in his haste to capture Kadesh, Ramesses II committed a major tactical error: he increased the distance between his Amun Division and the remaining Re, Ptah and Seth divisions, thereby splitting his combined forces. When they were attacked by the Hittites, Ramesses II blamed the failure of his officials to dispatch scouts to discover the true location of the Hittites and report to him.

The ensuing battle was closely fought, and it was only the arrival of the dispersed Egyptian forces that saved the day. The result was a negotiated peace settlement between the two empires. However, the Hittites claimed that the Egyptians were defeated, and subsequent Hittite expansion shows that Egyptian power had waned.

However, that is not the way Ramesses II recorded it. As pharaoh for about thirty-five years (dying in his eighties), he had plenty of time to work up a version that suited his god-like status:

No officer was with me, no charioteer, no soldier of the army, no shield-bearer.

Only with help from the gods did Ramesses II personally defeat his attackers and return to the Egyptian lines:

I was before them like Seth in his monument. I found the mass of chariots in whose midst I was, scattering them before my horses.

Just as we understand that you can't believe everything on the internet, this is a good example of why primary sources must also be treated with caution.

A Statue Was Put on Trial ... for Murder

Theagenes of Thassos is an excellent example of an over-achiever. An outstanding athlete, he is said to have won a total of 1,300 crowns in the Olympian, Pythian, Nemean, and Isthmian games.

He was so successful a rumour spread that he was the son of Hercules. He could run, wrestle and throw the discus; he was the ultimate all-round athlete.

It was boxing, however, that was to give him a bizarre legacy. The story goes that following his death, the people of Thassos erected a statue in his honour. While little is known of Theagenes beyond his list of titles, it seems he died when still able to compete. This can be inferred from the fact that a rival boxer, who had been hoping for a rematch, apparently became so annoyed by Theagenes's untimely death that he attacked the statue with a stick (it is not recorded if alcohol was a contributing factor to the evening's incident).

Theagenes claimed an unintended posthumous victory when the statue fell on the angry boxer and killed him (obviously the citizens of Thassos were better at producing athletes than they were at erecting sturdy monuments). The people of Thassos found the crushed man under the statue the next morning, and it was decided that the sculpture of Theagenes should be put on trial. The statue was found guilty, which was hardly surprising, given the presumed lack of a good defence. As a 'punishment', the statue was thrown into the sea.

But it wasn't over. The Oracle of Delphi got involved by predicting disaster and famine if the statue was not returned to its rightful place. So the islanders raised the sculpture from the depths, and the statue eventually became the focus of devotion for a hero cult. Although the original has long since been lost, many statues of Theagenes could subsequently be found throughout the ancient world.

Can the God Ba'al Sue?

The most mentioned god in the Bible, after ... y'know ... God, is Ba'al (the lord), who gets numerous mentions in the Book of

Kings and the Book of Judges. There's plenty of archaeological evidence to show he had a widespread following around the southern Mediterranean and the Near East in the first millennium BC. He was so popular with both Semitic and non-Semitic communities that early monotheistic Jews saw him as an obvious threat, and every time he or his priests are mentioned in the Bible, it's in a negative context. After all, you're not going to cast the competition in a positive light, are you?

This theme is echoed in the Qur'an, which also mentions Elijah (Elias) arguing with the priests of Ba'al. The name is distorted into Beelzebub, meaning 'lord of flies', and is a slightly obscure name for the Devil. This was picked up by nineteenth-century occultists, and Beelzebub is occasionally referred to as the true name of the Devil or as having other nefarious or black-magic connotations. This is downright libellous for a god once associated with nothing more sinister than the weather.

Let's be clear: Ba'al wasn't the god of bad weather or floods, just normal weather. If you wanted rain, you'd pray to Ba'al. Need the weather to be a little cooler? Ba'al was the god who got the offering that week. He was part of the pantheon of the many gods that existed in that part of the world at that time.

Ba'al was not among the mightiest of the gods, not was he evil in any way, and followers of the group of gods, which included Ba'al were not devil worshippers. In fact, all the existing iconography of him shows him in a benevolent god-like state rather than portraying him as a source of wickedness. However, the cult gradually died out, and there's nobody left to defend him. Thanks to his legacy in Jewish, Christian and Muslim communities, he is remembered as an ancient evil, best forgotten. Poor old Ba'al.

The Chinese Money that Could Make a Killing ... Sort of

China may have invented paper currency and produced high-quality coins, but, for a time, there was a type of currency that has become known as Chinese 'knife money'. It was created during the Zhou Dynasty, which lasted continuously from around 1046 BC to 256 BC, making it the longest dynasty in Chinese history. It was during this era that Chinese bronzeware reached its pinnacle and included knife-shaped tokens that were used as forms of money. They came in different shapes and sizes and lasted from around 600 BC to 200 BC. Practically shaped metal money was clearly the fashion during this period because there was another currency in northeast China, called 'spade money', which looked like small bronze spades.

Nobody is quite sure why the currency ended up being shaped like a knife, but one story about a prince either etching payments on his soldiers' knives or accepting their knives as a form of payment for minor fines seems to have been the kernel of the idea.

Standard metal coins predate knife money, which fell into disuse with the unification of China under the first emperor. Based on coins previously used in his Qin region, Qin Shi Huangdi introduced uniform copper coinage throughout the new empire.

The Remarkable Ancient Greek Tunnel of Eupalinos

In sixth-century BC Samos, a Greek mathematician and architect known as Eupalinos came up with the plan for an underground aqueduct 1,036 metres (3,399 feet) long. Although this is the second known tunnel to be excavated from both ends (the first was in Babylon), it was the first with a geometry-based approach to its construction.

So what does that mean? Digging a tunnel from just one end means it's always guaranteed to be in alignment; starting at both ends risks one section missing the other, or, if you've done the maths incorrectly, the two ends could meet laterally but miss each other due to depth miscalculations. When the two ends met, Eupalinos was off by about twenty centimetres: a remarkable achievement in an era of Bronze Age technology.

The tunnel was not only an architectural achievement but also proved that Eupalinos knew his numbers. He was a genius, who used geometric concepts that weren't finally codified until Euclid (often referred to as the 'father of geometry') came along two hundred years later.

Having an underground aqueduct (it runs under a series of hills and mountains) meant that an attacking army would find it virtually impossible to cut off the city's water supply, so the project was of huge strategic importance. Even the source of the water, an inland spring, was covered over to ensure the supply was protected.

The aqueduct was used for over a thousand years, and is so well hidden that it wasn't rediscovered until the 1880s – and only then because Herodotus thought to mention it in his writings.

It's a Myth that Afghanistan Has Never Been Conquered

It's also a myth that 'it's easy to get in but hard to hold onto', an Afghani saying. 'Afghanistan has never been conquered' is a statement often used in the West to support a generally held belief that NATO should never have invaded the country in 2001. However, rather than taking 'received wisdom' for granted, let's look at the history.

It is true that the first-ever attempts by an imperial force to invade the area ended badly for the Persian invaders. Afghanistan is mountainous, providing the perfect terrain for ambush. It is also arid, so it's hard to sustain a large army because of its relatively meagre agricultural land. Taking these factors into account, how likely is it that other empires really wanted this fairly harsh region? Yes, it was on the Silk Road, but it was simply easier and more profitable to hold the key trading cities than to waste men and money conquering mountains, which had, literally, no value.

All of that said, Alexander the Great arrived in the area in 330 BC and did what he did best. Among the places he conquered were Herat and Kandahar, cities that occasionally hit the headlines today, although usually for the wrong reasons. There are still tribal groups in Afghanistan with blue eyes, who proudly claim they are the descendants of Alexander's Macedonian troops.

Alexander died young, at which point his empire split, and the area that included modern-day Afghanistan was then conquered by and incorporated into the expanding Mauryan Empire. This was an empire that covered most of modern-day India, Pakistan, Bangladesh and, eventually, Afghanistan. Theirs was an invasion from the south and was (using anachronistic terms) an Indian-run Afghanistan – a state of affairs which continued for over a century.

So far, so very 'BC'. Let's move on about 1,000 years to the Islamic caliphate. Today Afghanistan is *very* Muslim (the Taliban certainly think so), and this is because the Islamic caliphate successfully invaded the region and implanted an alien religion that had originated in Arabia. So, you could say that the existence of the Taliban is proof that Afghanistan has been successfully invaded in the past (but probably best not to if they have you in captivity).

In the early thirteenth century, Genghis Khan arrived and attempted to conquer the region by means of extreme violence – and it worked. Then, in the late fourteenth century, Emir Timur (better known in the West as Tamerlane) tried to conquer the area and, once again, achieved his aims by means of extreme violence – so it worked again. At one point, when some local warriors hid in mountain caves, Timur sent troops to the top and lowered them in baskets to reach the entrance of the caves, where they started fires which smoked out the occupants or roasted them alive. That worked, too.

In both of these cases, the armies involved used terror tactics and tolerated no resistance. They were willing to throw men and money (and baskets) into the capture of mountains in order to have sole control. In both instances, rebellions were snuffed out before they began; there was no resistance after the first shockwaves of invasion.

In the early sixteenth century, Timur's descendant, Babur, started the Mughal Empire, which (like the Mauryan Empire) would go on to rule Afghanistan, Pakistan, Bangladesh and a large part of India. This time, however, the invasion started from Afghanistan in the north and headed south into India. So, in reality, there have been many successful invasions of Afghanistan over the millennia. It's only in the last 200 years that the country has become a military nightmare for its invaders.

Drinking Like a Greek

Much is made of the modern practice of drinking to excess, but ever since the invention of alcohol (an Arabic word, somewhat ironically), humans have consumed too much and lived to regret it the following morning.

An ancient example of this excess comes from 2,500 years ago in Hellenic Greece, with a drinking game called *kottabos*. It appears to have been the custom that while attending symposia, elite men of all ages would be invited to the host's home, where they reclined on cushioned couches lining the walls of the men's quarters. Here they would have lively conversations and recite poetry; they might even have discussed the thorny philosophical issues of the day. Most certainly they were entertained by dancers, musicians and courtesans.

So far all of this sounds like other familiar descriptions of ancient Greek dinner parties, but then the scenario descends into something less classy. The men proceeded to get drunk on wine and, in the name of competition, hurled their dregs at a target in the centre of the room to win prizes such as eggs, pastries and even sexual favours (remember, this was an all-male party). After the game of *kottabos* was finished, it was the slaves who cleaned up the mess.

What's particularly brilliant about this topic is that a professor and students from West Chester University in Pennsylvania have had a go at *kottabos* (with or without the sexual favours is unspecified), and in the words of Heather Sharpe, an Associate Professor of Art History from the university,

> Trying to describe this ancient Greek drinking game, *kottabos*, to my students was always a little bit difficult because we do have these illustrations of it, but they only show one part of the game – where individuals are about to flick some dregs at a target, I thought it would be really great if we could try to do it ourselves. It took a fair amount of control to direct the wine dregs, and interestingly enough, some of the women were the first to get it. In some respects, they relied a little bit more on finesse whereas some of the guys were trying to throw it too hard.

To all those who say that history is dull, I say, beat this with an afternoon of lectures.

Truth and Lies Behind the History of Cinnamon in the West

Cinnamon is extracted from tree bark and, in its natural state, looks like a stick. Until the eighteenth century, virtually all of the cinnamon in the world was found in Sri Lanka. The word comes from the ancient Greek *kinnamomon* and shows that there was a taste in the West for this exotic spice, probably for centuries.

Cinnamon is mentioned in the Old Testament, showing that even then it was an important and, probably, expensive spice. Make no mistake about it, cinnamon was enjoyed by the rich and powerful only. The cost of shipping it from Sri Lanka to somewhere like Athens was huge, and that cost was further inflated by its legend.

Herodotus is the first extant source of the myth that these sticks were part of the nest of a monstrous bird. Aristotle added that the birds brought the sticks from the edge of the world – an area unreachable by humans. It was the poor cinnamon harvesters who risked life and limb to get even the tiniest amounts of the spice away from these terrifying giant bird-serpent things. (Don't blame me; the description is vague, but the idea is that they're terrifying giant bird monsters ... okay?)

It was the first-century AD Roman philosopher Pliny the Elder who was one of the first to doubt the veracity of the tale of giant birds sitting on nests made from cinnamon sticks, but this legend persisted for millennia as no trader was going to disabuse his client of a notion that made their product glamorous, desirable and difficult to obtain.

In Europe, spices in general were often more valuable than gold. Many came from the so-called 'Spice Islands' of Indonesia and were fought over by the Portuguese, Spanish and Dutch. These feuds were bloody, but at the same time none of the trading nations involved encountered giant bird monsters; so the legends were disproved, and it became common knowledge that cinnamon came from trees. Eventually specimen trees were taken from Sri Lanka and planted elsewhere in similarly suitable conditions, which, as supplies increased and shipping costs decreased, brought the price down and made the spice more widely available.

Who knew that what we regard as an everyday spice could have so much history attached to it?

Where Does the Term 'Pyrrhic Victory' Come from?

There was once a kingdom on the Balkan coast called Epirus. It faced the heel of Italy in what is now modern day Croatia and was a prosperous neighbour to the rising Roman Republic. In 280 BC these two neighbours went to war. The Romans were led by Consul Publius Valerius Laevinus (this was before the era of emperors), and the Epirians were led by their King Pyrrhus.

The first major battle was a decisive victory for Pyrrhus, but in 279 BC he fought the even bloodier Battle of Asculum, which was significant because Asculum is on the eastern side of the Italian peninsula and showed that Pyrrhus was taking the fight to the enemy. At the time of the battle Pyrrhus not only had the resources to match Rome's army, he also had over a dozen war elephants – a truly terrifying sight on any ancient battlefield. Pyrrhus won this battle, too.

The war rumbled on for several more years, during which Pyrrhus captured lands from the Romans and, later, took the Macedonian crown too. However, his expenditure on all these campaigns had exhausted both his treasury and his supply of manpower, and all of his gains evaporated after his death, when Rome absorbed the region of Epirus into its own territory.

Pyrrhus was a capable military leader and ruler. He held his own against a Roman power that was soon to go up against the mighty Carthaginians and beat them. So what of Pyrrhic victories? Well, we can all blame Plutarch, the first-century AD Greek writer who wrote about an alleged conversation after the Battle of Asculum. Plutarch states,

> Pyrrhus replied to one that gave him joy of his victory that one more such victory would utterly undo him.

This sealed the idea of a victory that's simply too costly – a concept that has resonated down the generations. However, Plutarch was born about 300 years after the events he is describing and is perhaps unfairly putting Pyrrhus's name to an interpretation of events that require hindsight. So this now-forgotten king, who beat the Romans on multiple occasions, is only remembered as a warning that there are situations where great effort may produce no clear gain. It's an important concept, but it's not what happened to Pyrrhus.

Who Was Herod the Great, Really?

As Herod is a major figure in two monotheistic religions, I have to be careful with this one. First interesting fact: Herod died in 4 BC, so if Jesus was born in AD 1 (there is no year 'o') they missed each other by half a decade. It's another fact that Herod was responsible for many bloodthirsty acts, and they are well documented, but the wholesale Massacre of the Innocents, based on a supposed tip that among those innocents would be the prophesied Messiah, isn't mentioned anywhere except the Bible – and the Gospels were written well after the event.

In general, Biblical scholars agree that the massacre is mentioned to fulfil messianic prophecy or to echo Moses' infancy rather than to be regarded as historical 'truth'. After all, if we know about his other crimes, why would chroniclers miss this one out? But that doesn't stop Herod being called a 'baby killer', known primarily for a horrifying crime that never happened.

Herod was a fascinating man. He was a close associate of Augustus, and outside of Jerusalem he was very much the Romanised king. However, he was not only assiduous in his observance of Jewish rituals in the Holy City, but also the king who rebuilt the Temple in all its glory – this is the same Temple whose creation is mentioned in the Bible and which was accidentally destroyed at some point in the AD 70s. The Wailing Wall, with its gigantic ashlars (blocks), is the only part of either the original Temple or Herod's reconstruction that exists today. The remains show how rich he was to be able to create something so vast, and this wasn't his only architectural marvel (his tomb, the Herodium, is another example of building on a massive scale).

However, not killing babies and being really good at building things doesn't automatically make you a nice guy, and although he can be acquitted of infanticide, there were many spasms of violence in his reign. Even his family members weren't safe: sons were murdered, his mother-in-law was executed, and he even had his wife killed (although he felt so guilty about it he had her preserved in honey and was seen wandering around the palace lamenting her demise). He died from some sort of terrible affliction (possibly caused by a series of organ failures), covered in boils; after swelling to a grotesque size, his body and penis burst, exuding foul-smelling liquid from his wounds. It was a really disgusting way to go. Some believe it was poetic justice.

Before Reading This Item, Have a Look at This

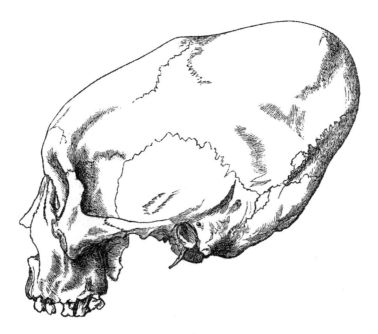

An elongated skull. (Courtesy of the Wellcome Library)

Is this a human skull? Or is it from some hominid? Is it evidence of aliens?

All of the above questions have swirled around these skulls found in Peru. As odd as it may sound, after DNA tests and anthropological research, we can definitively say that they are human skulls. And there are loads of them, all with this strange elongation of the cranium.

What happened? Well, it seems that the people of the Paracas culture had their heads bound from infancy, so over the course of their natural lives their skulls developed these unusual shapes. Children's skulls are very soft, so it would not be hard to alter their shape. It seems to have been what was aesthetically pleasing to the people of that society.

The Paracas existed in central Peru from around 800 BC to around 100 BC; however, there is increasing evidence to show that rather than dying out, it is possible that this civilisation evolved into the Nazca culture, which created the famous Nazca lines (more on those later). This is another feature often associated with alien theories.

To add to the puzzle, there are finds of extremely complex textiles and high-quality ceramics, but while they are unique in design, they were not, in terms of know-how, unusually advanced for the era (sorry, alien theorists). Relatively speaking, the Paracas were probably more sophisticated than the Celts of Europe but not as advanced as the Romans.

One question that remains unanswered: the shape of the skull would have changed the shape of the brain, so did they think differently?

Why Jesus's Title 'King of Kings' Means More than You Might Think

The term 'king' is a variation on the Anglo-Saxon word 'cyng'. The Latin for the equivalent title is 'rex' (where the term 'regal' comes from). In Persia and India the word is 'shah'. A 'king of kings' is, of course, a supreme leader, such as an emperor or, in the case of Jesus, a leader of all humanity. However, the specific term 'king of kings' was first used in Persia, where it translates as *shahanshah*. The Assyrians in the thirteenth century BC, and later in the sixth century BC, saw the rise of the first true empire under the Persians; these were also the first genuine *shahanshahs*.

Using the term for Jesus conveys multiple messages. The first is the previously stated 'none higher than he' concept. In Judaism (which was influenced by the Babylonians during the period under their rule), the term was used specifically for God because God's real name could not be uttered by mere mortals.

Further, the use of 'king of kings' is a deliberate association with the biggest empire the world had ever seen by the first century AD. Rome's major enemy at that time was Persia, so the title is perhaps hinting that Jesus's power could take on the Romans (who were persecuting Christians at the time the Gospels were being written). There are other links between Jesus and Persia: the 'three wise men' were not kings but 'magi', a Persian word, and 'they came from the East', where the Persians were, rather than from the West.

'King of kings': three little words that have more meaning and complexity than you might think.

A Brief History of Guerrilla War

The term 'guerrilla' means 'little war' in Spanish and has been used to describe this type of asymmetric warfare since the eighteenth century. Ironically, the idea of hit-and-run tactics by small groups against larger ones is first described in 3100 BC, so the concept can be traced back through the millennia.

Groups of small hostile forces hiding in larger local communities have been a problem ever since the era of the Persian Empire, but in reality small bands of 'freedom fighters' could inflict relatively little damage on something like a Roman garrison.

Guerrilla warfare (now often called insurgencies) is not to be confused with rebellions, which were much bigger. Rebellions could topple dynasties and change the fate of nations; guerrilla warfare was a great way to resist on the fringes of things, but no guerrilla war has won a decisive victory over a nation.

The concept only came into its own in the age of gunpowder. During the Napoleonic Wars, French forces in Spain faced a vicious insurgency. The mutilated corpses of French soldiers were deliberately placed where they would be found by their comrades; it was a ploy to get the French to leave the area and sometimes it worked.

Perhaps the most famous guerrilla campaigns were conducted in the twentieth century when a relatively small number of Boers in South Africa managed to stall the 500,000-man British Army for years, but it shouldn't be forgotten that, by fair means or foul, the British Empire won that war.

Vietnam in the 1960s is another classic example of the tactics used in guerrilla warfare. In this case, a small farming class of irregular fighters, called the Viet Cong (VC), held their own against the might of the United States. Yes, America lost the Vietnam War, but the guerrillas had to be supported by the North Vietnamese Army after the VC were all but wiped out in the Tet Offensive.

Generally speaking, while guerrilla fighting can be a major destabilising factor, it needs the weight of a supporting conventional army to win. Ambushes and booby traps kill a few troops, but against a much larger force, such tactics aren't going to lead to strategic victory. Using a more recent example, the Taliban in Afghanistan weren't defeated, but they didn't cause any serious ISAF (International Security Assistance Force, a NATO-led force) defeats either. However, the DNA of modern insurgencies can be traced back to those fighting the Persians thousands of years ago.

The Peasants' Revolt – Chinese Style

The English Peasants' Revolt in the fourteenth century was an indication that people power was on the rise, but ultimately it ended in failure. China had its Peasants' Revolt more than a thousand years earlier, and it was a much bigger deal.

The conflict became known as the 'Yellow Turban Revolt' (so named because the peasants wore yellow scarves on their heads). The uprising started in AD 184 in central China, which was then part of the Han Dynasty. The causes were the usual peasant complaints of poverty, corruption in government, and rising taxes. So far, so similar to the events in England. However, there's a saying that's worth repeating: the histories of Russia and China are easy: they're the same as everybody else's, just a lot more people die. This was certainly true in the case of the Yellow Turban Revolt, as it resulted in a twenty-year war between the peasant classes and the ruling dynasty. The death toll can only be estimated, but it's thought to be between 3 and 7 million (so give or take a mind-blowing 4 million).

For decades, millions of peasants effectively kept imperial forces on the back foot, defeating them in a number of pitched battles. The revolt's original leader was the now legendary Zhang Jue, who called himself 'the great teacher' and, among other things, claimed to be a powerful sorcerer ... because, well, why not? He was supported by his brothers, Zhang Bao and Zhang Liang, and between the three of them they led the peasants on the 'Path of Heaven'. They came to power as healers, tending to the sick, including those who could not pay for their services. All they asked was that the patients spread their names and news of their work, and soon their form of Taoist spirituality was sending shockwaves through the ordered world of the Han Dynasty.

The rebellion broke out over a number of areas, and initially Han forces were more worried about protecting the capital than they were about what was going on in the countryside. However, once the capital was secure from rebellion and coups, Han forces

Ancient History

marched against the Yellow Turbans and were defeated in a number of epic engagements.

Eventually, with a change of generals, the imperial forces started pushing back the rebels, and in the first year the Zhang brothers were all killed. The rebellion had lost its charismatic leaders and was now no match for the Han forces.

But the Han Dynasty never recovered from the war. The corruption that had long existed at the top led to its collapse just a few years later. The rebellion had left many regions denuded of their imperial framework of governance, and once loyal Han generals became increasingly independent warlords, ruling over their individual fiefdoms. By AD 220 hundreds of thousands of people had died. Unfortunately, despite the fact that there was now a new imperial family, the peasants were still roughly where they had been in the first place.

The Other 'Hadrian's Walls'

Built in the second century AD, Hadrian's Wall is internationally famous and has become a UNESCO World Heritage Site. However, this was by no means the only frontier fortification the Romans built.

As the empire expanded, there was no need to build border defences because the legions were always ready to march beyond whatever current borders existed to conquer new lands for the glory of Rome. But as the empire reached its zenith, there was a growing realisation that any further expansion wouldn't be effective and that most of the empire's borders now needed to be defined and protected. Hadrian's Wall is merely the most famous of many fort networks and barriers erected by the Romans to say, 'This side is ours, the other side we don't care about.' Roman writers used the collective term 'limes' (which could mean boundaries, but also paths) for these frontier defences, but they varied enormously. Some were ordered by Hadrian, but others came later and were built under the orders of other emperors.

In the Germanic regions, the River Rhine served as the usual delineation between Roman and barbarian lands, and the Rhine was reinforced with a network of forts. It was a similar story in the Middle East: in the arid areas that separated the Romans from the Persians, there was a string of frontier forts to keep an eye on the enemy and to protect Roman realms. Once again, a major river was used as a border, in this case the Euphrates.

More walls were built along the edges of the Sahara Desert to create a physical barrier between the sub-Saharan African empires and desert raiders. These walls are in modern day Tunisia, about 100 miles inland from the coast. If Hadrian's Wall was located on the rain-swept northern edges of the empire, these sun-soaked walls in Africa were on its southernmost edge.

In the very late second and early third centuries, the emperor Septimius Severus ordered expeditions even further south, until even the Berber capital city of Garama was captured, but these were short-lived acquisitions, regarded as simply not worth the effort, and the legions invariably turned back to earlier frontiers (both here and in other areas such as Caledonia – modern Scotland).

The Martyrdom of a Young Mother

St Perpetua was a twenty-two-year-old married noblewoman and mother. She was martyred in Carthage in the Roman province of Africa during the early third century AD.

There is a truckload of Roman martyrdom stories, so this is more or less a normal start to an unusual tale. What makes Perptua unique and her story so deeply moving is that while she was in prison she wrote an account of her ordeal that has survived as 'The Passion of St Perpetua'. This poignant account is her first-person description of events leading not only to her death, but to the deaths of many of her fellow Christians, with the conclusion written by an eyewitness.

The story opened at a time when Christians were widely persecuted for their beliefs, and Perpetua was in conflict with her father, who wanted her to recant her faith. She refused and was imprisoned. After a bribe, she was allowed to move to a better part of the prison, where she cared for her child, who was able to remain with her (remarkably, she never revealed the gender or name of her child, possibly to protect his or her identity).

Eventually she was brought before a court, where she and her fellow Christians refused to repudiate their faith. Because of this they were condemned to death in the arena.

Perpetua is unambiguous about a powerful vision she had, reflecting a commonly held conviction at the time that there was nothing unusual about God communicating directly with the faithful. In a second vision, she saw her brother, who had died unbaptised at the age of seven. She prayed for him and later had a vision of him being happy and healthy.

The day before her martyrdom, Perpetua envisioned herself defeating a savage Egyptian and interpreted this to mean that in the arena she would battle not only wild animals but the Devil himself (a racist interpretation, but given the times, we'll let it go).

On the day of the games, the martyrs were led into the amphitheatre. As the crowd demanded, they were scourged (beaten and whipped) in front of a line of gladiators. The men in the group were then set upon by a boar, a bear and a leopard; a bull attacked the women. Wounded by the wild animal, Perpetua gave her slave Felicita (who had converted to Christianity and remained with her mistress throughout the imprisonment) the kiss of peace before they were both put to the sword by gladiators.

It's a sad and emotional story which brings the immediacy of Roman persecution to the modern reader. It's also an important account of one Christian woman's steadfast faith before the time of Constantine, when Christianity became the fashion. Although remarkable by today's standards, it's interesting that she feels there's nothing unusual about having visions or healing her brother with prayer. The fact that God communicated with and carried out healing through a woman would have raised a few eyebrows even then, but such acts would not be considered credible after the Council of Nicea.

Constantine the Great's Greatest Mistake

The Roman Empire is often portrayed as a realm of peace and tranquillity that kept the barbarians out of civilised areas. However, you only need to dig a little deeper to understand that this is a ludicrously inaccurate reading of events. In reality, the Roman Empire frequently erupted in civil war, and quite often they weren't just minor skirmishes. Thousands died in disputes over power. Constantine came to power by means of civil war, and unfortunately his children ended up doing the same.

Before Constantine the Great died, he did something that may have seemed counter-intuitive. After all his campaigns to unify the Roman Empire, he split it. Specifically, he recreated the Western and Eastern Roman Empires, each ruled by one of his two older sons (there were three). After his death, the two empires rapidly disintegrated into mini empires, each ruled by a member of Constantine's family.

Constantine's oldest son was Constantine II, who initially ruled most of the Western Empire, including Britain, France, Spain, Portugal and an area of north-west Africa. Constantine II had been marked out for great things from an early age – emphasis on 'early'. In AD 317, the elder Constantine made the younger 'Caesar' when Constantine Junior was just a year old.

Constantine took Junior on campaigns from the age of seven. At the age of ten, he was commanding the forces in Gaul (presumably he had some help). Then at fourteen he was given the title 'Alamannicus', which implied a victory in Germany. Not much is known about this, but if he went on the campaign, he would more than likely have had support from experienced generals. Whatever the specifics, it is significant that the teenage son of Constantine the Great had been on campaign regularly for nearly a decade before he hit the age of twenty.

At the time of his father's death, Junior was overlord to his younger brother Constans (son number three), who had been given the prized areas of Italy and North Africa in the Western Empire. Although a ruler in his own right, because of his minority age he had to do what his big brother ordered. So in AD 337, when Constantine the Great died, all bets would have been on Constantine II to become the dominant power. However, the unifying force of the father passed with his death, and the empire descended into *Game of Thrones* levels of internecine feuding.

Enter son number two: Constantius II (the fact that they are all called almost the same name is confusing) ruled the Eastern Roman Empire, except for Thrace and Greece. These were ruled by his cousins, Dalmatius and Hannibalianus, but it was only shortly after they'd assumed power that they were murdered by their own soldiers – which suited Constantius II.

Meanwhile, in AD 340, Constantine II amassed his forces and moved on Italy. If he could capture Rome, he would be the new Caesar and have the resources to thwart his two brothers; the victory would establish his authority as the head of the family and the entire empire.

Constans may have been the youngest brother and may not have had the benefit of his oldest brother's mentoring, but he was clearly a chip off the old block. He knew he had only one chance to counter Constantine's plans, so he sent out an ambush party to find and stop him. It reached Constantine in Aquileia (a city in north-east Italy, near the Croatian border), caught him by surprise, and killed both him and his retinue. The great heir was dead; the Caesar you would have put money on to win the family feud was killed aged twenty-four. Constans lasted another ten years before he, too, was assassinated, and it was Constantius II; who was to have a long reign (and the last laugh).

The Death of a Genius

Early Christianity is often accused of being anti-learning. This is not fair. There are many examples of the Church encouraging scientific endeavour, and it is often forgotten that Alexandria was, at one point, an epicentre of literature, philosophy, medicine and Christian theology. However, in Alexandria in the fifth century AD there was an incident that shows Christians can behave just as cruelly as anyone else.

Tensions in the city (over the establishment of Jewish communities) had been rising between the firebrand Christian community, led by the bishop Cyril, and the Roman governor Orestes. There had already been mob violence, when in AD 415 Orestes invited Hypatia, a famous philosopher and mathematician, to intervene and calm the situation. Hypatia had a formidable intellect. She was a Neoplatonist philosopher and a member of the intellectual school, which encouraged logic and mathematical study in place of empirical enquiry. She is today seen as one of the key female figures in the study of classical mathematics.

Because of her wisdom, oratory skills and Christian pedigree, Hypatia seemed to be the perfect person to bring calm to this stormy period of religious unease. However, as is so often the case, while smart people look for peaceful solutions, hysterical rabble rousers want conflict more than anything else.

A rumour spread in the Christian community that blamed Hypatia for Orestes' unwillingness to reconcile with Cyril. Led by a Christian fanatic, a mob formed, and they kidnapped Hypatia. They took her to a church, stripped her and then murdered her by tearing off her flesh using either tiles or oyster shells (the word used could mean either). It was a truly repellent act of barbarity – and all of this was done in a church.

The early Christian chronicler Scholasticus wrote an account of the event, which ends with this:

> Surely nothing can be farther from the spirit of Christianity than the allowance of massacres, fights, and transactions of that sort.

Aliens vs Smart Humans: the Nazca Lines

The Nazca Lines in Peru are thought to have been created by the local Nazca culture about 1,500 years ago, between AD 400 and 650. Although the massive images they form are only visible from above, this is not enough to prove alien landing strips (which have been suggested).

The lines themselves are nothing more complex than shallow furrows made by removing the reddish pebbles on the surface to uncover the greyish ground beneath. They would be useless as a runway for alien space craft. Why they were created is a mystery, and perhaps it is their mystery which makes them so fascinating.

The hundreds of patterns range in complexity from simple lines to stylised hummingbirds, spiders, monkeys, fish, sharks and lizards. Some of the pictures are so massive that they are measured in miles. The fact that the images aren't distorted has led some to believe that the Nazca had advanced knowledge, but earth-based archaeologists think the patterns are more likely to have been staked out, using ropes, to ensure that the patterns were completed as planned. A basic understanding of maths and geometry, and the use of cords fixed to posts would allow anyone to create a giant image on the relatively flat, arid plane where they are to be found.

We can probably thank the fact that the area had no agricultural value for their preservation for over a millennium. By comparison, the 'sacred landscape' in southern England, linked to the sites at Avebury and Stonehenge, has been ploughed out many times, and over the millennia some of the ritually placed stones have been broken up to become building materials. Had the Nazca chosen to create these patterns in the middle of fertile fields, these gigantic images would have been lost forever.

The Truth about Leprosy

There was no greater scourge in ancient and medieval times than leprosy, but modern medicine has greatly demystified what was once considered to be a terrifying and shameful disease.

Today it is known as Hansen's disease. It is not 'god's curse' as previously believed, but a chronic infection caused by bacteria. It is a disease of the peripheral nerves and the upper respiratory tract; skin lesions are the primary external sign. Left untreated, leprosy can be progressive, causing permanent damage to the skin, nerves, limbs and eyes, even causing blindness. Although it damages the victim's appearance, leprosy does not cause body parts to fall off; it is secondary infections that can result in tissue loss, causing fingers and toes to become shortened and deformed as cartilage is absorbed into the body. The result of this is disfigurement, which can make it appear as if parts of the body have rotted away, and all of this is because the body's defences have been compromised by the primary disease.

In times past it was an unreasonable fear of lepers which resulted in the creation of colonies where victims were isolated. This was a pointless exercise as 95 per cent of people are naturally immune, which explains why the nuns and priests who worked with lepers rarely caught the disease. It wasn't God who was doing the protecting, but their own immune systems. To this day it remains unclear exactly how leprosy is transmited, but it is difficult to catch and, with modern medicine, has become increasingly rare.

The History of the Rottweiler

With a name like Rottweiler, you could be forgiven for assuming the origins of the breed are German, and probably nineteenth century. This was a time in Germany when a lot of dog breeding was taking place – when the Doberman and German Shepherd were first bred – but the modern Rottweiler has evolved from a Roman herding dog first introduced from Italy to Germany in the first century AD.

The Romans used these dogs to herd cattle, and they were justifiably regarded as being smart, loyal and reliable, not to mention that their muscular build meant they made predators (and bandits) think twice about trying their luck with the livestock.

It was, however, the town of Rottweiler in southern Germany, an important centre of trade, that became associated with the breed. The descendants of the Roman cattle dogs were used by travelling butchers in the Middle Ages to guard their money pouches, which they tied around the dog's neck. These dogs eventually came to be called Rottweiler Metzgerhunds, 'butcher dogs', because of their close association with the butchers who traded in the Rottweiler market. Once railroads became the primary method for moving stock to market, the need for the breed declined.

It was the First and Second World Wars that saved Rottweilers because they were recognised as being the most suitable breed for use as police dogs. To this day, they are still regarded as excellent guard dogs.

An Interesting Dilemma

Roman lead (as in the metal) is increasingly sought after, but perhaps not quite in the way you would expect. Archaeologists and physicists compete fiercely for this highly prized ancient element for vastly different reasons.

Very old lead is pure, dense and much less radioactive than the metal in its newly mined form, so it is ideal for use in the extremely sensitive experiments that hunt for dark matter and other rare particles vital to the study of quantum physics. But archaeologists object strongly to the melting down of 2,000-year-old Roman ingots, which can tell us about Roman know-how and practices in the past. Once the ancient metal is repurposed, it loses any historical significance.

Most of the Roman lead available to us today comes from shipwrecks in the Mediterranean. The law surrounding these finds is murky. The 2001 UNESCO Convention on the Protection of Underwater Cultural Heritage prohibits commercial exploitation of historic shipwreck artefacts. Whether that applies to physics experiments, however, is unclear. After all, the physicists aren't using this lead to make a quick buck but to broaden our understanding about the very nature of the universe itself. So it boils down to this: is destroying some of our past worth unlocking knowledge about our future?

The Last Pagan Emperor

The last pagan Roman Emperor was not the one just before Constantine the Great, but one of the ones after. Emperor Julian was a vigorous and successful emperor who came from the Constantine Dynasty. While he was still in his twenties, he rose to prominence by crushing Frankish and Germanic invasions in Gaul in the AD 350s. His military successes were particularly impressive as the empire was then in serious decline, and he did not have the resources that had been available to past emperors.

This was the era of two emperors, one in the East and one in the West, and Julian went to war with Constantius II (of the Eastern Roman Empire), who was also his cousin. However, when Constantius died, Julian became Augustus and the sole emperor of the Roman realm. Julian, unlike his cousin and many of his subjects, was a pagan and proud of it. He recognised the empire was in serious trouble; whereas Constantine had thought to use Christianity as the glue to bind the disparate nations of the empire together, by the AD 360s this was no longer working. So Julian decided to return to the ancient gods, like Jupiter and Sol. This would later earn him the title 'Julian the Apostate'.

However, Julian is a reminder that it's easy to be beguiled by the idea of 'inevitability' in history. After the Roman Empire was Christianised, people assumed there would be no backsliding, and there was a stampede of pagans to come over to the 'true' faith. When Julian returned to the old ways and the old gods, the result for fourth-century Romans was a dilemma over clearly competing religious beliefs. Julian was neither a pagan brute nor an ill-educated barbarian: he was a successful, thoughtful and powerful man who wanted to return to a familiar religion. While he was a proud pagan, he did not persecute the Christians.

Like Constantine, Julian regarded religion as a tool to be used to galvanise the empire.

However, fate had a hand to play, and in AD 363 Julian was fighting the Sassanids (essentially, the Persians) in the east of the empire. He lost a battle and, deciding that speed was better than protection, left the battlefield without any armour. A Sassanid spear pierced his side, and he later died from the wound. This is an intriguing moment in history. Had the Sassanid soldier missed or had Julian been wearing armour, would he have ruled for another twenty-five years? Would he have been able to turn back the clock or, at least, have facilitated pagan beliefs to achieve the same status as Christian ones? If that had happened, what kind of religious beliefs would have evolved in Europe?

All of this is, of course, impossible to answer. As it was, Julian's rule was relatively short – not long enough to make a lasting impression on the religious evolution going on in the empire at that time.

The History Behind Sinbad the Sailor

Sinbad is a popular folk hero in both the West and the Middle East. In the original story it says he lived in Basra, which is in modern-day Iraq, however, the name Sinbad is Persian and means 'Lord of the River Sindh' (Sindh is another name for the Indus River, so he could be from modern-day Pakistan or India). The tales are specifically set in the time of the fifth Caliph of the Abbasids, Harun al-Rashid, which means the stories come from the late eighth and early ninth centuries.

In Europe his legends have become intertwined with fables from the *Arabian Nights*. These, however, are Persian and come from a very different folkloric tradition (a bit like saying the tales of Robin Hood are the same as those of King Arthur). The feats of Sinbad are possibly the fanciful and exaggerated tales of a real merchant (there is conjecture that the stories could have been inspired by Suleiman Siraf, who travelled from Persia to southern China at this time).

The original tales describe the seven voyages of Sinbad, and in them he is (among other things) shipwrecked and escapes the clutches of giant birds. Some of his adventures suspiciously echo the *Odyssey*, but the fabulous journeys, which can be seen as just entertainment, show the importance of trade between the Persian Gulf and the wider world. For thousands of years, merchants in the area have found it easy to navigate to India and the east coast of Africa, and many would have returned with true tales of the exotic and the dangerous.

The stories live on today, both in books and in Ray Harryhausen's glorious Sinbad films.

Vortigern Asks for Help

After the Roman legions left Britain at the start of the fifth century AD, Britain had no army and was feeling somewhat vulnerable. According to a story by the Venerable Bede (who didn't always get the facts right and wrote this at least 250 years later), Vortigern, King of the Britons, asked twin brothers from the northern coasts of Europe to come to his aid.

The account is repeated in a number of chronicles, all of which were recorded much later and may just be repeating Bede's story. The *Anglo-Saxon Chronicles* record the year of their arrival as AD 449. The account continues that these twin brothers were called Hengest and Horsa, and when they came to Britain they were so impressed with its lands and riches that, rather than defend the country from invasion, they became the invaders and helped themselves to Kent.

This event is often seen as the start of the Anglo-Saxon invasion of England, and it's interesting to note that it doesn't start with naked aggression but an invitation. Admittedly, it is a bit like asking to dinner someone who then refuses to leave, saying instead that they now own your house. The Britons did their best to repel this onslaught from the Germanic invaders, but as more and more of Hengest and Horsa's kin arrived, the less chance the Britons had for victory, and as Britain didn't have an army to begin with, it could only rely on amateur fighters to protect it from hardened warriors.

By AD 600 the Britons were associated with Wales, and the eastern areas of the island were now the land of the Angles, or Angle Lund ... England. Even though Vortigern was attempting to protect his country, his actions resulted in its demise. Nice one, Vortigern.

The Hagia Sophia Is the Most Important Building in the World

In the early sixth century AD, Emperor Justinian ordered the construction of a new Hagia Sophia to be built on the ruins of an older, smaller structure. What rose out of the ground in Constantinople was the largest ancient dome ever built and a structure that wasn't to be matched for over a millennium. For nearly a thousand years this was the world's largest church – a record that's still unbeaten. The church is also the pinnacle of late antiquity architecture and a sign that the early Byzantine Empire was every bit the match of the fallen Western Roman one.

The reason Russia is Orthodox Christian, rather than Catholic Christian, is that the envoys sent from the Rus capital of Kiev said that when they walked into the church it was as if they were walking into Heaven itself. Had Hagia Sophia been smaller, Rome might well have swayed this potential eastern ally.

In 1054, in this very building, papal legates excommunicated the entire Eastern Orthodox Church, which resulted in the 'Great Schism', a fracturing of the two largest church groups, which continues today (more on that later). Then, in 1453, Constantinople was defeated by the Ottoman Sultan Mehmet II, and this great church was turned into a great mosque. In fact, to the modern eye, Hagia Sophia looks like a mosque. Prior to 1453 there had been some mosques with domes, but most ancient mosques only had open courtyards (there was no need for a roof to keep out the rain in Saudi Arabia). However, after the conquest, this beautiful structure heavily influenced architecture throughout the Islamic world, so mosques were made to look like an ancient church, not the other way around.

When the Ottoman architect Sinan recognised that the building needed additional support, he built buttresses, which is why it still stands today. Following its illustrious history as a church, Hagia Sophia spent 450 years as one of the largest and most venerable mosques in the Islamic world. After Ataturk came to power in Turkey in the 1920s, the structure became a museum, and, quite fittingly, it remains so to this day.

This one structure has been home to two major religions and has influenced architecture in countless countries. The Hagia Sophia has got to be the most important building in history.

Japanese Aborigines
It has been said that the Japanese are the most racially pure people in the world. The nation has rarely been invaded, and there have been whole centuries when it has deliberately cut itself off from the outside world. Because it is a nation that has valued its seclusion and guarded its identity, it is not generally known that Japan has its own aboriginal race on its northern islands.

The Ainu people could in no way be mistaken for 'Japanese' (their ethnic term is Wajin). The men generally have heavy beards and traditionally the women wear what looks like exaggerated lipstick. Their culture is a mix of those of the various groups from northern Hokkaido and the Kuril Islands. Although their exact origins are a mystery, they are thought to have settled in the area in the tenth century AD.

Unlike other aboriginal groups, they were not hunter-gatherers but successful traders, who were often the middle men between China and feudal Japan, where trade was regarded as a dubious activity and merchants were viewed with suspicion (rather like the Jews and money lending in Europe). So these social outcasts were well placed to do the job nobody else wanted to do. They were always a niche community which, even today, doesn't number more than 200,000. They have always been considered 'other' by the insular Japanese culture and, at times, have been treated as slaves by the Wajin Japanese, with occasional violence breaking out between the two races.

It wasn't until 2008 that a bipartisan resolution was approved by the Japanese Diet (parliament), calling upon the government to recognise the Ainu people as native to Japan and urging an end to discrimination against the group. The resolution recognised the Ainu people as 'an indigenous people with a distinct language, religion and culture' – and not before time.

The Dome of the Rock in Jerusalem Is Unique

The Dome of the Rock on the Temple Mount is one of the very first examples of Islamic architecture. It's also the only religious building in Islam that is not a mosque. The building surrounds a stone, which has always had a sacred connotation. According to Jewish tradition, the stone (the Foundation Stone in Judaism) is the place where Abraham prepared to sacrifice his son Isaac; most Muslims believe it was Ishmael, not Isaac, who was to be sacrificed. Other Judaeo-Christian beliefs state that Adam's skull (as in Adam and Eve) is buried under the rock. According to Islamic tradition, however, the rock is the spot from which the Prophet Muhammad ascended to Heaven, accompanied by the Angel Gabriel.

Though Muslims now pray towards the Kaaba in Mecca, they once faced the Temple Mount. The Dome of the Rock, which was originally grey, was initially completed in AD 691 on the orders of Umayyad Caliph Abd al-Malik. Gold gilt was only added in the twentieth century by the King of Jordan.

Problems arise because the building encompasses the so-called Foundation Stone of the Jews, who regard the stone and its surroundings as their holiest site. However, the site was not deliberately chosen to offend Jews; early Muslims picked a location which, at the time, was a disused spoil heap. (The Wailing Wall was visible, but it was not then a holy site for Jews. That tradition took root a millennium later.) So what could have been a structure to symbolise the close relationship between Judaism, Christianity and Islam, is sadly one of the most controversial religious buildings in the world.

Please Count Aloud the First Ten Numbers in the Number Line

... Done it? Did you just count 1, 2, 3, 4, 5, 6, 7, 8, 9, 10? In which case, your count was wrong. 0 is the first positive number, and it's an oddity as numbers go. For example, if you look at a calculator, you'll see it starts at 0, but it's set on its own relative to other numbers grouped above it. Look at a keyboard, however, and you'll see that starts with 1 – 0 is at the other end after 9, which is not where it should be. No other number is treated so ambivalently as zero, and there's a reason for this.

Roman numerals work for lower numbers but become increasingly unwieldy the higher the count. For example, MCMLXXIII is the Roman for 1973. Which would you rather write? To make things even more complicated, the Romans had no value for 0.

And when you get to Christian Europe, zero is associated with a null point or void. The void is where the devil lurks; you can't have a demonic value, so the humble zero was banned for centuries. It's also why our calendar is wrong. You can't have Jesus born in the year 0, so he was born in year 1, and the year before was 1 BC (ignoring completely any need for a year 0). Zero is an important value, needed in everything from accountancy to codebreaking, but it's a hard concept to understand, which is why infants get books with three dogs or seven fish; there's no book for kids that uses the number zero.

'Here you go, Johnny. This is what zero frogs look like.'
'But, Mummy, there's nothing there!'
'Exactly.'

The figure 0 originated from India and came to Europe via Islamic scholars, and all of our numbers are based on Arabic numerals, not Roman ones. Don't believe me? Look at an Arabic clock, and you can see the similarities, although their 0 is more of a dot, and 5, to the European eye, looks more like a 0 than anything else. The point is that repeating values, based on a decimal system, come from the Middle East, not the Romans. The fact that the 0 arrived so late in the number game explains why we have so many different names for it. We only have one name for the 1: it's one. 2 is two. However, 0 can be zero, oh, nought or, in football, nil.

It's History Pedant Time

When it comes to siege warfare, there are all kinds of exotic words and phrases, most of which have no use in modern language. So while it might sometimes sound like nit-picking, there are good reasons to be fussy about their applications. The best example of this is why a trebuchet is not a catapult.

Catapults have been around since the time of the Romans. Using tension, a throwing arm was pulled down and then released to hurl items such as rocks, diseased animals and Greek fire (ancient napalm). It was an effective weapon in its day. However, it was simply outclassed by the medieval trebuchet.

Rather than using tension, the trebuchet used gravity. The throwing arm on the opposite end had a counterweight that was usually a wooden box filled with rocks, often weighing tons. The box was winched up and, when released, hurtled towards the ground, flinging the other end forwards with breathtaking force. A catapult might get through a wooden palisade; a trebuchet could knock down stone walls.

Trebuchets were the most powerful siege artillery until the refinement of cannons under the reign of the Ottoman Sultan Mehmet the Conqueror. The cannons that existed prior to this were not as effective as the trebuchet, which were so fearsome they were given names (Edward I had one called War Wolf).

Sometimes the defenders were shown the trebuchets as a warning that, from here on in, things were going to get messy, so best to surrender now.

Warwick Castle has the largest working modern trebuchet. It weighs 22 tonnes and can hurl an 80-pound projectile nearly 1,000 feet (300 metres). This is an example of medieval engineering that was superior to Roman and/or classical designs.

THE MEDIEVAL ERA

The period in European history from (roughly) AD 900 to 1500 is generally regarded as a time of religious supremacy and non-stop brutality, probably best forgotten. While there can be no denying the power of the church or the level of violence at the time, the era has too often become a caricature of the true picture.

I thought it would be useful to start the medieval era by debunking some of the myths that surround it. Most of these originated in the nineteenth century, when writers did their best to make their ancestors look even more barbaric than they really were.

The Iron Maiden (nothing to do with the band)
These coffin-sized metal caskets, with the figure of a woman on the outside and a comprehensive set of spikes inside, were supposedly a form of medieval torture ... except that no contemporary chronicle from the medieval era mentions them.

Let's be clear about this: Torture happened a lot throughout history. Amnesty International has an easier job today than it would have had 500 years ago, but the iron maiden just doesn't work as an implement of torture. Are you going to half close it and only sort of kill the person? Or slam it shut and have a very messy death?

Executions in this era were beheadings, hangings or the slightly more religious burning at the stake. As for pain, well, thumbscrews, racks, branding with hot irons – all of these are a lot less bother than making an iron maiden. However, after these became associated with the era, every stately home and castle (especially in Germany, for some reason) felt they needed to acquire one, and a cottage industry developed to meet the demand. But for all of this, the iron maiden was a nineteenth-century invention.

Prima Noctur (or 'first night')

This is the idea that a peasant bride was compelled by law to sleep with the local landowner on her wedding night. It's not true; it's completely made up. No law from the era has ever been found that would enforce such a regulation, and even a passing knowledge of history would make it seem unlikely.

Why? The Church. The medieval church may have ignored the bit in the Bible that said, 'thou shalt not kill', and it may have dreamt up both the Crusades and the Inquisition, but it hadn't forgotten about chastity. Lustfulness was frowned upon in every level of society, so to have enshrined in law the idea that the local nobleman could work his way through the maidens of the area is to propose an idea that was contradictory to everything medieval society stood for.

Did nobles seduce any peasant girl who caught their eye? Yes, but that's not the same thing as having enshrined in law the right of a lord to have 'access' to every bride, and it is shameful that the movie 'Braveheart' uses this non-existent law as a key motivation for William Wallace's rebellion. Once again, this idea of *prima noctur* is a Victorian invention to make the past look more barbaric.

The Chastity Belt

When a crusader went off for what could be years abroad, he would lock his wife's loins in a sturdy metal device to ensure that she could not be unfaithful (even if she wanted to be). Apart from the fact that, once again, there is no contemporary evidence for such a contraption, the idea itself is laughable. Even allowing for the fact that reproductive knowledge in those days was much sketchier than today, if the husband was away for years and came home to a wife with a baby, everyone knew enough to be suspicious about the circumstances.

Even if such equipment had existed, it would have been totally impractical if only because it would have killed the wearer through poor hygiene, not to mention that, generally speaking, 'where there's a will, there's a way'. It's just another example of the kind of barbaric image the post-enlightenment world loved to project onto that of the pre-Renaissance.

There are examples of 'medieval' chastity belts in museums, but none have been dated back to the era of the Crusades. They are all, most likely, nineteenth-century fakes.

So with those clichés out of the way, let's explore real history from this era.

The First Great Piece of English Literature Is So Old We Can't Understand Its English

Beowulf is where the language we call English starts, and yet it's not immediately obvious. Here's the first line:

Hwaet! We Gardena in geardagum.

Roughly translated, it means:

Lo! We of the Spear-Danes in days of yore.

It's obvious from this that the language has moved on a bit since then. *Beowulf* makes Chaucer look positively modern.

It's hard to say exactly when the poem was written. The single copy we have (in the British Library) could be from the seventh century or perhaps a ninth-century copy of something earlier. It's down to literary guesswork, but the best estimate is that, give or take a few years, the manuscript is 1,000 years old.

The poem is a classic Scandinavian saga, full of drinking halls, heroic deeds and brave warriors. The original manuscript has no name, but over the years has taken the name of the hero of the story. Beowulf first fights a monster called Grendel, then he goes after Grendel's mother, and finally he becomes king. Many decades have passed before the final act (spoiler alert), when he fights and kills a dragon but is mortally wounded and is given a proper pagan cremation. The poem comes from a tradition of epic poetry that can be traced from Iceland to Denmark (not classic Latin/Roman stories), and like all sagas, it loves a good fight. Also in the tradition of early sagas, it portrays Christianity as something to be regarded with suspicion. This underlines the question of exactly how Christian was the early Anglo-Saxon period.

The language of the poem is not simple Old Norse. It is showing signs of evolution, which is why it's considered the first 'English' piece of literature. But Anglo-Saxon English is a long way from the language we speak now, and it's about 800 years removed from Shakespeare, all of which is reflected in the opening line.

By the medieval era, Britain had been invaded by several tribes. The area of Scotland had been conquered by Irish raiders called the Scotti, which is where the name Scotland comes from. Similarly, the name England comes from the land of the Angles, who, along with the Jutes and Saxons, invaded from northern Europe. The fact that *Beowulf* is set in Denmark, not England, demonstrates that the people of Britain were part of a society that covered all of northern Europe, so the language, laws and literature changed accordingly.

Dead Men CAN Talk

There are many strange tales from the Vatican, and one of the perennial favourites is that, in the Middle Ages, there was a Pope Joan. The story goes that a woman managed to become pope, and the deception was only revealed when she gave birth as she mounted a horse.

Let's examine the facts.

The chronology for popes is about as verifiable as it gets, especially given the worldwide importance of this powerful ecclesiastical organisation, which, even then, had been around for centuries. Any time a later source quotes a date for Pope Joan, it turns out there was a legitimate (and provable) male on the throne of St Peter. And just how easy would it be for a heavily pregnant woman to get on a horse while giving birth? This is, quite simply, a much repeated and embellished myth that started after the Reformation, when Protestant propaganda was used to ridicule the Roman Catholic Church. However, they needn't have bothered because there are far stranger stories lurking in the history of the Vatican. Perhaps the most bizarre and most ghoulish is the 'Cadaver Synod'.

Occasionally the papal numbering system got a bit muddled, so Pope Stephen VII is sometimes called Stephen VI. Either way, he obviously didn't recognise that Christian teaching about turning the other cheek. Stephen wanted revenge, and he wanted revenge principally on his predecessor, Pope Formosus. So, in 897, the dead Formosus was exhumed from the grave and put on trial for perjury (among other crimes).

There were some real world politics present in the decision. The late ninth century saw central Europe at a crossroads. In his day, Formosus, hoping for protection, had backed the old Carolingian powers in France. This was not unreasonable as, for a century or more, this dynasty had been hugely powerful and able to project its power into the Italian peninsula. However, by the time of Stephen, the Carolingians were on the wane, so when he became Pope he wanted the support of new, more local Italian powers. Stephen knew this change of allegiance would come at a price, so he determined the best way to handle the situation was to denigrate his predecessor. The idea was nothing new in papal politics and was a practice that would continue for centuries.

From the early Middle Ages until the nineteenth century, the Vatican had not only spiritual power but also temporal power. In terms of size, the composition of the Vatican states ebbed and flowed over the centuries, but for more than a millennium central Italy was under the control of the Pope. This was the focal point of the church and, as such, required armies, fortifications, an almost unlimited supply of funds and an ability to raise regular taxes. This was all worth fighting for, even dying for, but the idea of exhuming a previous pope was unique in the annals of papal history. Exactly who suggested a post-mortem synod, with a corpse in attendance, is unknown, but the fact that Stephen was actively involved in this trial is not in any doubt.

Formosus was disinterred from his resting place underneath St Peter's. The rotting corpse was dressed in fresh robes and seated in a high chair, presumably tied into position. Stephen was present during the trial in which Formosus put up a predictably poor defence. When questions were put to the deceased pontiff, a cleric stood behind the body and called out prepared statements. The whole thing was both farcical and deeply creepy. After all, a synod of this type would not have been open to the general public, so why go through the whole charade in the first place?

When in Stephen's position, previous popes had issued a writ, called a papal bull, which declared a holy revelation that nullified the old views and allowed for the change of direction that suited the new Pope. Digging up a dead man, putting him in fresh clothes and making him stand (well, sit) trial all seemed … excessive, to say the least.

After all this effort, it came as no surprise that Formosus was found guilty. Once the verdict had been reached, poor old Formosus was stripped of his sacred vestments, dressed in the clothes of a layman and had three fingers of his right hand (the blessing fingers) cut off.

The whole gruesome farce had repercussions beyond the walls of the Vatican. The guilty verdict was the perfect excuse Stephen needed to oust Formosus's followers from their appointments and consolidate his own power. In doing so he tilted the Vatican away from the Carolingian powers, which enabled him to look more locally for allies.

Following the trial, Formosus was reburied not under St Peter's but in a local graveyard for foreigners, which was, of course, a deliberate insult. Then, having had time to reflect, Stephen changed his mind, and Formosus was dug up again (this corpse really did get around). This time he was tied to weights and thrown in the River Tiber. The idea was to get rid of the problem, once and for all, but it was a botched job. The body washed up on the banks of the river, and rumours spread across Rome that Formosus had begun to perform miracles.

With this unlikely turn of events, the fiasco became public, and popular opinion no longer supported Stephen. The Vatican was quick to react, and he was imprisoned by an unknown group of clerics; a few weeks later, Stephen was found strangled in his cell. Stephen's pontificate had lasted barely a year. Who said ecclesiastical history was dull?

AD 793: the Year of Dragons

Anyone reading the contemporary sources for 793 could be forgiven for thinking they were reading an early version of *Lord of the Rings* or a particularly apocalyptic section of the Bible:

> AD 793. This year came dreadful fore-warnings over the land of the Northumbrians, terrifying the people most woefully: these were immense sheets of light rushing through the air, and whirlwinds, and fiery dragons flying across the firmament. These tremendous tokens were soon followed by a great famine: and not long after, on the sixth day before the ides of January in the same year, the harrowing inroads of heathen men made lamentable havoc in the church of God in Holy-island, by rapine and slaughter.
>
> *Anglo-Saxon Chronicle*

Yes, dragons. As if the slaughter of monks was not bad enough, fiery dragons were sighted. This was the beginning of the Viking Age.

The Vikings are a chance to show the story behind 'history', because there is real history to the way the Vikings have been portrayed. In the nineteenth century, the Vikings were all horned-helmeted psychos, quick to anger and slow to grasp anything civilised. It wasn't until the mid-twentieth century that academics thought the popular legacy was one-dimensional (and by then even the whole horned-helmet thing had been disproved). So there followed a flurry of papers pointing out what great sailors, explorers, traders and artists they were, which was all true. This was also the period when it was first revealed that the Vikings got to North America before any other Europeans. All cities in Ireland that are pre-modern were founded by the Vikings. Dublin is a slightly mangled version of the Viking name for Blackpool. They also founded Kiev, the capital of Ukraine, as a trading post at the end of the Silk Road, and served as bodyguards to the Byzantine Emperors. They really did get around.

This body of newer research took the Vikings from one extreme to the other, rehabilitating them to the point where the roots of their fame in Europe had been lost. There was now a need to refocus because, yes, they were excellent boat builders, but they built those boats to kill and enslave as many people as they could lay their hands on. And while they were shrewd traders, they were also brutal fighters whose sagas loved to dwell on grisly images of crows pecking at the bodies of their slain enemies. This was not exactly Aristotle. To paraphrase a contemporary proverb: to get to Heaven, you have to be a good, decent, upstanding individual; to get to Valhalla, you have to die a good death in battle. If you died of old age, in a nice comfy bed, you would end up in Helheim (Viking Hell). When a Viking lord died, he would be cremated in a ship, along with his favourite living slave (so he could serve his master in the next world). Brotherly love wasn't high on the Viking agenda.

A Viking longship is a thing of beauty. Their curves make the whole structure exquisitely streamlined. They are also remarkably practical: one of the few seaworthy ships able to navigate the rough waters of the North Sea and the north Atlantic, and yet their shallow draft allows them to manoeuvre up rivers, perfect for exploration and, of course, raiding. An average ship would have had thirty to forty oarsmen, which made a compact fighting force, so even three or four ships arriving out of the blue could deal with almost any martial response thrown at them. Pre-modern communication was slow, so by the time a raid had taken place and the news had reached a local power base, the Vikings were long gone. Theirs was the perfect criminal enterprise: smash and grab on a continental scale.

In mainland Europe, Charlemagne was at the peak of his power and was crowned Emperor in Rome on Christmas Day 800. He was the first person to unify most of the Western Roman Empire for over three centuries. France, the Low Countries, Germany and Italy were his to rule, and yet, with all this power, the end of his reign was marred by his inability to deal effectively with the Vikings. With all the resources at his disposal, if he couldn't solve the problem, what chance did the disunited kingdoms of Britain have?

When it came to raiding, the Vikings loved a monastery. These were (from the point of view of a pagan bandit) the perfect place for plunder and violent fun. There was always a reliable stock of good quality communion wine, some of the best booze they ever had. Then there was all the treasure: gold and silver crosses and relics covered in gemstones. They knew they could get richer faster by raiding monasteries than by scrabbling through the meagre possessions of peasant huts. But it was the monks themselves who were, in many ways, the ultimate attraction. They didn't fight and they were never armed. In the Viking chronicles there are more than a few references to the 'ravaging' of monks. Finally and helpfully, as the monks were literate, they made highly prized slaves back in the homeland. To a Viking, a holy monastery was a shopping mall full of desirable things.

Historians have long debated the reasons for this era of Viking raids. There have been in-depth discussions about population densities and even potential over-fishing of the seas around Scandinavia, but putting aside all the in-depth research on herring breeding, it could be argued that the question is being asked the wrong way round. As has been pointed out, Europe had already suffered generations of raiding and invasion by Visigoths, Angles, Saxons and, in the east, Magyars ... the list goes on and on. The Vikings were just the most recent people to engage in the traditional business of rape and pillage, but their boat technology gave them an enormous advantage and made them particularly hard to catch.

The Scandinavian influence on Britain can be traced from the end of the eighth century to the mid to late eleventh century, a period of around 300 years – far longer than the Tudor period or the Georgian era – and yet many people see them as peripheral to British history. They weren't. The further north you go in Britain, the more evidence there is, particularly with respect to place names. Any town ending in 'by' is invariably of Viking derivation and means 'farm of' or 'land of'. Grimsby is, therefore, the 'farm of Grim'.

Year after year Viking ships appeared on the horizon, their square sails announcing the arrival of violence. It was a miserable and uncertain time for the Britons and much of Europe.

Magical Mummies? Forgotten Kingdom? Want to Read More?

The Kingdom of Makuria was a Christian country in southern Egypt/Sudan, which became isolated in the seventh century when Egypt fell to the Muslims. It is an example of yet another forgotten African kingdom, which had all the trappings of a 'western kingdom', proving that African history and heritage are every bit as sophisticated as that of its later colonial overlords.

For centuries this unique Christian state flourished and coexisted peacefully with its Muslim neighbour to the north. The Arabs tried to invade it but were successfully repulsed and so chose an easier route along the North African coast to invade Spain.

In 2013 a 900-year-old crypt was uncovered in the city of Old Dongola (opposite the modern Sudanese city of Dongola, on the other side of the river). Its walls were covered with inscriptions written in Greek and Sahidic Coptic, and it contained seven naturally mummified bodies. One of the mummies (scientists aren't certain which one) is believed to be that of Archbishop Georgios, probably the most powerful religious leader in the kingdom. His epitaph was found nearby and says that he died in AD 1113 at the age of eighty-two.

The writing on the walls is inscribed in black ink on a thin layer of whitewash paint. It includes excerpts from the Gospels of Matthew, Mark, Luke and John as well as magical names and signs. Archaeologists found an inscribed prayer, attributed to the Virgin Mary, at the end of which Death appears to her in the form of a rooster (nobody knows why that symbolism is important). After Mary died, according to the text, she ascended to Heaven with Jesus.

The inscriptions likely served as protection for the deceased against evil powers. The entire site is a tantalising peek at a complex and forgotten kingdom.

Alfred the Great Shouldn't Have Been King

The problem with history is that we look at it the wrong way round. It is obvious to us that certain events seemed to be inevitable, and that's because the human brain works to find a pattern, even when there isn't one. A great example of that is Alfred the Great, King of Wessex, grandfather to the first King of England, who started life very low down the pecking order.

Alfred was the youngest child of King Aethelwulf of Wessex. In order to become king, he first had to get past this lot:

Aethelstan, King of Kent
Aethelswith, Queen of Mercia
Aethelbald, King of Wessex
Aethelberht, King of Wessex
Aethelred, King of Wessex

As you can see, he was so far down the line of succession that he didn't even have the 'Aethel' bit in his name. That's important as it is a regal prefix meaning noble (but it is sometimes translated as elf). It wasn't that Aethelwulf disliked his youngest son; it's because there was no expectation that Alfred would ever be king.

However, as the years rolled by a few of his brothers died, some in suspicious circumstances, and Alfred began to rise up the pecking order. To be clear, the culprits of the murky deaths are unknown. It could be that the brothers were getting rid of each other while Alfred remained bottom of the heap, no threat to anyone – or Alfred could have been the Anglo-Saxon version of a serial killer. We just don't know. The arrival of a massive Viking army in 865 resulted in the deaths of large swathes of Anglo-Saxon nobility, and the house of Wessex also had its fair share of young men who fell to Viking axes (more on this in the next fact).

Eventually Alfred became a co-ruler with his older brother Aethelred (the first; it was the second Aethelred, born more than a century later, who was the famous 'unready' one). When Aethelred died, Alfred was left to rule on his own, and the rest, as they say, is history.

Had power politics gone a different way, or had the Vikings chosen to attack mainland Europe rather than England, Alfred would probably have been nothing more than a forgotten Anglo-Saxon aristocrat. Instead, he is the only English monarch to have 'the Great' in his title.

AD 865: One of the Most Important Years in British History

After AD 793 and for the next two generations or more, Norsemen regularly raided across the British Isles and Ireland. Nobody knew where or when they were next going to attack. They struck with terrifying speed and brutality and left just as suddenly as they had arrived.

In 865 the Viking tactics changed, and instead of raiders, a *micel here* ('great army' in Anglo-Saxon) arrived on the shores of England. It had taken over seventy years, but the Vikings no longer wanted to raid; this time they wanted to stay. The exact size of this army is still hotly debated, but it wasn't that large: 2,000–3,000 men maximum. However, the Viking reputation for brutality and their bellicose nature meant they were able to defeat Anglo-Saxon army after Anglo-Saxon army. By 870, after only five years, East Anglia, half of Mercia (the Midlands) and most of Northumbria had been captured. No Anglo-Saxon king had been able to conquer so much territory in such a short space of time.

The Vikings didn't have chronicles, but they did have their sagas, which describe three brothers as the leaders at this time:

Halfdan Ragnarsson, Ivar the Boneless and Ubba. However, by 871 a Viking called Guthrum was leading the forces. We know this because he was the leader who would go toe-to-toe with the Anglo-Saxon king, Alfred of Wessex, aka Alfred the Great (as discussed in the previous item).

Alfred was never King of England, but what earned him his 'great' title was his ability to resist the Vikings and push them back, so that by the time peace terms were agreed about half of England was under his rule and the other half was 'Danelaw', Viking lands. It would be later generations of Anglo-Saxon kings who would defeat the Viking armies and become the first kings of England.

Aethelflaed: Lady of the Mercians and Daughter of Alfred the Great

Anglo-Saxon society was patriarchal to the point where there is no Anglo-Saxon word for 'queen'. Only one wife of an Anglo-Saxon king made it onto the coinage and that was Cynethryth, the wife of the mighty King Offa, who ruled in the late 700s.

However, there was another noblewoman who jumps out of the pages of this male-dominated era, and her name is Aethelflaed, the oldest child of Alfred the Great. She was married to Aethelred, the Ealdorman (high-ranking official) of Mercia at a time when Mercia and Wessex had allied against the Viking-held English lands called the Danelaw, which then covered about half of modern-day England. Mercia and Wessex were fighting together to try and win back lands from the Danes.

When Aethelred died in battle against the Danes in 911, the Mercians, most unusually, recognised Aethelflaed as the 'Lady of the Mercians'. She was the first woman to rule an Anglo-Saxon kingdom, but she couldn't be 'queen' because they had no word for that, and as she was not a divinely anointed ruler, she couldn't be 'king', either.

Aethelflaed, however, was very much her father's daughter and, with Wessex, continued the campaigns of expansion against the Vikings, which were largely successful. She was seen not only as a leader of armies (she won battles, always a bonus in this era), but also as a woman of culture and piety. Looking at contemporary sources, there is no doubt that she was genuinely regarded as an effective ruler. Her reputation was such that the people of York asked her to rule over them in return for protection from Viking raiders.

Aethelflaed died in 918 (for reasons unknown, but there is no suggestion of either violence or foul play) and was succeeded by her daughter Aelfwynn – the only time in Anglo-Saxon history a kingdom passed from mother to daughter. By now a full merger between Wessex and Mercia was inevitable, and Aelfwynn was deposed by King Edward, the Elder of Wessex, who was her uncle. The chronicles are biased towards Edward, but it does seem to have been a peaceful transition of power.

Aethelflaed was one of the greatest Anglo-Saxon rulers and an indication that even in a male-dominated society women can sometimes rise to the top.

'Henry the Fowler' Was the Most Impressive Henry in History

'Henry the Fowler', or, more formally, Henry I, was the King of East Francia (basically, Germany) from 919 to 936. His unusual epithet comes from the story that he was fixing bird nets when messengers arrived to inform him that he was king. Apart from among German medieval historians, Henry is little-known and rarely remembered; he's not a subject that excites social media. However, Henry is the man who founded the Ottonian Dynasty, so-called because there were three powerful rulers, one after the other, all called Otto.

The German emperors were regarded as the 'first amongst equals', and their story is a complex one. Elections were held and the crown was not automatically passed from father to son; in order to become emperor, the candidate also had to gain the favour of the Pope – sometimes with tact, other times with brute force.

Early in Henry's reign, the duchy of Lorraine rebelled, so Henry invaded and became master of a large part of it. However, Henry allowed the rebellious duke to remain in power and arranged for his daughter Gerberga (I suspect there is a good reason why the name has fallen out of fashion) to marry the duke in 928. Henry was a skilful diplomat and politician as well as a capable military leader.

It was Henry who finally confronted Germany's age-old enemy, the Magyars (Hungarians), who had been attacking from the east for nearly 150 years. Their cavalry-based forces were quick, agile and much feared. When they invaded Germany and Italy in 921, Henry and his allies managed to corner the Magyars, a position where the heavy armour of the Germans could be used to get in close and take down the lighter-equipped Magyars. Henry's forces routed them, captured one of their princes and negotiated a ten-year truce in 926. This breathing spell allowed Germany time to better fortify its towns and create a new elite cavalry force, which was the start of knights in central Europe.

Later there were more wars with both the Slavs and the Vikings and another war with the Magyars, where once again Henry fought them and won. All of this led to the unification of German Christian principalities under one elected ruler. The Holy Roman

Empire started with Henry the Fowler, making him the most impressive Henry in history.

Aethelred II and Danegeld

What do you do with extortionists? Pay them off and hope they go away? This solves things only in the short term, and until the issue itself is resolved the extortion continues. It's one thing for an individual to be the victim; it's another matter entirely when a country has a knife to its throat. That was exactly the situation that Aethelred II, King of England (forever remembered as Aethelred the Unready), faced in the late tenth and early eleventh centuries. The ones doing the extorting were, unsurprisingly, the Vikings.

Aethelred was advised by the Archbishop of Canterbury to pay them off. You can see the logic: give them what they want, they go away, and England has time to ramp up its defences. It was by such means that the Viking leader Olaf got 10,000 pounds (Roman weight) of silver, and he went home a happy man. In the meantime, Aethelred didn't do much in the way of preparing better defences, so when Olaf returned three years later, this time with Sweyn Forkbeard, they had a clear run at London. Once more Aethelred bought them off and a pattern emerged, with Aethelred caught in a vicious circle. The amounts being extorted got larger and larger, which meant more money had to be raised in taxes, and less money was available for things like defence. The navy dwindled, the burh system of fortified settlements wasn't maintained, and in the meantime the Vikings came back with alarming regularity. Why wouldn't they? Turn up, wave your battleaxe around, get the attention of the local ruler and sail off with a colossal amount of treasure. It was a low-risk, high-reward gamble, and the resulting pay-offs were known as Danegeld.

By 1002 things were grim. The Vikings were arriving regularly, the treasury coffers were being emptied, and now there were rumours of treason. Aethelred had heard that Danish settlers were willing to support a Scandinavian takeover of his throne. After ten years of draining extortion, it is highly likely that there were more than a few people hoping for a change of leadership, but Aethelred's response was appalling. On 13 November 1002, he ordered what became known as the St Brice's Day Massacre. This act deliberately targeted men of Danish decent, who were murdered on the grounds of treason. Exactly how many died is still contentious, but in the areas that were Danelaw it's not likely that the locals slaughtered each other. It was a xenophobic, irrational act that was, in many ways, the last desperate roll of the dice for a man who was losing his grip.

Many dictators try to solve unrest with massacre, but this was a rare event in Britain. Moreover, it turned rumour into fact. Now the people of Danish descent had a reason to look to the Northlands for protection.

Unfortunately, one of the victims of the massacre was none other than Sweyn Forkbeard's sister Gunhilde. So not only did this make things personal for a Viking warlord (never a good idea), it also gave Sweyn Forkbeard a moral mandate (something of a novelty for the Vikings) for another invasion. In 1003 he arrived with a large army. This time he stayed for two years until a combination of famine and bribery (in the huge sum of 36,000 pounds of silver) made the Norse king head home once again (notice how the price for peace had more than trebled since the first payment of Danegeld).

Sweyn returned in 1013 at the head of a Viking invasion fleet – one of the largest so far seen. He put an end to Aethelred's underwhelming reign and achieved what no one since the Romans had done when he conquered all of England. Aethelred lost his crown, and his reputation has been in tatters for a thousand years.

Ever Heard of Radbot?

No? Well, what if I told you he was also known as Radbot, Count of Habsburg? You might recognise the last word.

There have been many successful dynasties: the Ottomans, the Plantagenets and the Romanovs, but few can touch the Habsburgs of Europe who, from the late medieval era to the nineteenth century, dominated the monarchies of Europe. This was the family that produced the following (deep breath): a Holy Roman Emperor, a King of the Romans, a King of Germany, a King of Spain, a King of Aragon, a King of Sicily, a King of Naples, a King of Castile, a King of Hungary, a King of Bohemia, a King of Croatia, a King of Portugal, a King of Galicia and Lodomeria (also known as Austrian Poland), a King of England, a King of Ireland, a Grand Prince of Transylvania, an Archduke of Austria, a Duke of Burgundy, a Duke of Parma and, of course, a Count of Habsburg.

Obviously nobody had all of these titles at the same time, but the list illustrates how effectively the family married into the upper echelons of European nobility – and how widespread their influence became. Pretty much the only obvious title missing is the King of France.

Going back to Radbot, the irony is that almost nothing is known of him except that he built the Habsburg castle, after which the dynasty is named, and founded a monastery ... and he died in 1045. Radbot was about as minor and as unimportant as a member of the nobility could be, but it's probably fair to say that he would have been very happy with the impact his descendants would have on Europe. There are still dozens of people (some with grand titles and some with none) alive in Europe today who are his direct descendants and continue his name.

The Great Schism of 1054

The Great Schism of 1054 was the biggest event in the political history of the Church and affects more than a billion Christians to this day. By 1054 there had been a thousand years of groups vying for supremacy in matters of Christian doctrine. The origins of the competition go back to the time of the very early Church when there were five patriarchs, who were the five great leaders in the centres of Christian authority, and based in Jerusalem, Alexandria, Antioch, Constantinople and Rome. You don't need to know much history to guess that with the rise of Islam in the seventh century, three of these authorities now existed in what had become majority Islamic societies. The result was that by 700 only two leaders remained, one in Rome and the other in Constantinople. The one in Rome became known as the 'father of the Church' or 'papa', which turned into the word 'pope'.

These two centres of Christianity continually jostled for primacy. The popes in Rome argued that St Peter himself had come to Rome and that, according to the Gospels, Jesus had declared that Peter was 'the rock on which I shall build my church'. However, the patriarchs in Constantinople pointed out that for all practical purposes, the West, having suffered innumerable barbarian invasions, was in disarray and that the still-intact Eastern Roman Empire had a better and more consistent claim to be the spiritual leader of Christians.

It was six of one, half a dozen of the other, and the power of the two competing spiritual leaders ebbed and flowed with the power of their more temporal backers. However, it is important to understand that at this point they were all part of the same church, and any suggestion that they were separate was anathema to both. Ultimately they were two sides of the same coin.

However, communication and culture being what they were in the early Middle Ages, there could be no denying that the two sides of the Church were slowly moving in different directions. One example that still applies today is that Orthodox priests can marry, but Roman Catholic priests must remain celibate. The crunch came in 1054 when Pope Leo IX and the Patriarch of Constantinople Michael Cerularius heightened the conflict by suppressing the use of Greek and Latin languages in their respective domains. Further, in Constantinople all Latin churches in the city were closed, a theological act of war, so clashes, while still common, had yet to become irrevocable.

Following this latest round of ever escalating provocations, Roman legates travelled to Constantinople, where they insisted that Cerularius recognise Rome's claim to be the head and mother of the churches. When he refused, the leader of the legation, Cardinal Humbert, stormed into the Hagia Sophia (then the largest cathedral on the planet and the centre of Eastern Christianity for about 1,000 years) and excommunicated not just Cerularius, but the entire Orthodox Church. In return, Cerularius excommunicated Cardinal Humbert and the other legates.

Since Pope Leo had died, the validity of the Roman legates' act is dubious, and Cerularius's excommunication applied only to the legates personally. Regardless, this fundamental breach created more than 950 years ago has never been healed, as each side accuses the other of falling into heresy and initiating the division. There were attempts to reunite the churches, but after the Fourth Crusade's sacking of Orthodox Constantinople in 1204 any future attempts at reconciliation were consigned to failure.

Feelings still run high. When Pope John Paul II visited Greece in 2001, there were some in the crowds waving banners comparing him to the Antichrist.

The Mosque that Name Checks Jesus

The Umayyad Mosque in Syria is also known as the Great Mosque of Damascus. It is one of the largest and oldest mosques in the world. It is considered by some Muslims to be the fourth holiest place in Islam (after Mecca, Medina and Jerusalem).

So far, so Muslim, but this is also a mosque with an interesting and inclusive history. The site comes with a strong pagan heritage because it was originally the location of the temple for a local god of thunder, which later evolved into a Roman complex for the worship of Jupiter. With the Christianisation of the Roman Empire, this was modified and became the Cathedral of Saint John.

The city of Damascus was captured by the Muslims in the 630s, and the Umayyad Dynasty chose Damascus to be the administrative capital of the Muslim world. Such was the importance of the city that it even contained the main treasury. In 706, the caliph (Muslim ruler of the new Islamic Empire) commissioned the construction of a mosque on the site of the Byzantine cathedral. Prior to this, the cathedral was still in use by the local Christians, but a *musalla,* prayer room, for Muslims had been added on. The Umayyads recognised that conquest would not lead to immediate conversion and that it would take generations for the locals to go from being majority Christian to majority Muslim.

Now we fast-forward about 500 years to get to the next intriguing part of the story. In the fifteenth century, the Minaret of Jesus was finally completed (work had started and was continued under a number of regimes). It should be remembered that Jesus (called Isa in the Quran) is regarded as an important prophet in Islam, which agrees with the New Testament Bible that it will be Jesus who leads the true believers to Heaven on Judgment Day (he's even referred to as al-Masih, the Messiah). In the case of this particular mosque, it is believed that Jesus will descend from Heaven before the Day of Judgement to confront the Antichrist. According to local Damascene tradition, he will reach earth via the Minaret of Jesus, hence its name.

This minaret is a reminder that Islam and Christianity have much more in common than some think and are theologically intertwined.

Eleanor of Aquitaine: Possibly the Most Powerful Woman in Medieval History

Eleanor of Aquitaine, a formidable twelfth-century French woman, was the only woman who was Queen of France, Queen of England, and the mother of two English kings and two daughters who became queens. She was also the closest thing we have to a female crusader. She accompanied her first husband, King Louis VII of France, on the Second Crusade and was the Regent of England when her son King Richard I of England went on the Third Crusade.

Eleanor became the Duchess of Aquitaine as a child, and as Aquitaine was a huge area of France the lands made her the premier catch of the age. Naturally, the French king got to the prize first. Louis was neither a great king nor a great husband and, strangely, allowed his wife to come with him on the hugely difficult and dangerous march to Jerusalem on the Second Crusade. When they arrived at Antioch, Eleanor met her uncle Raymond, Prince of Antioch, and it was rumoured that they became lovers. Raymond and Eleanor certainly spent a lot of time together, and Louis certainly disliked Raymond. The final blow to Eleanor's marriage came when Louis shaved off his beard, and Eleanor found the new look repulsive. It took a while to get an annulment from the Vatican, but she got it.

Let's pause here to consider Eleanor's position. Women in medieval Europe had few rights; they were largely regarded as their husband's property – a situation that would have been heightened in the case of a king. Louis may not have loved Eleanor, but Aquitaine was a prize worth the hassle of an unhappy marriage, so he would not have wanted to annul the marriage. Further, if we consider how difficult both divorce and annulment are now in the eyes of the Roman Catholic Church, imagine how much harder it would have been in the era of the crusades. And yet, despite these huge obstacles, Eleanor got her way. This implies that she was possessed of formidable determination and willpower, and that she was also a skilled negotiator.

After the annulment, she turned to another hugely powerful monarch and married Henry II of England, bringing Aquitaine with her and instantly tilting the balance of power from the French king to the English one. When Henry's children rebelled against him in later life (and we're talking open warfare), she sided with her son Richard. When Richard became king and went on crusade, it was Eleanor who was appointed regent and, in effect, ran England. She even raised the taxes to pay for Richard's ransom when he was captured on his return to England at the time of the Third Crusade.

Eleanor died in Poitiers in 1204 at the age of eighty-one. Her final years were tinged with disappointment: Richard was killed in an accident in 1199, and her youngest son John became the new king of England but proved to be a disaster. Despite this, her legacy lived on through her children, who had the following distinguished titles:

Marie, Countess of Champagne
Alix, Countess of Blois
William IX, Count of Poitiers
Henry the Young King
Matilda, Duchess of Saxony
Richard I of England
Geoffrey II, Duke of Brittany
Eleanor, Queen of Castile
Joan, Queen of Sicily
John, King of England

King Richard Couldn't Stop Spending

When 'Good King Richard' went on crusade, we all know (thanks to the legend of Robin Hood) that Prince John demanded savage taxes, which put a tremendous burden on the English peasants. While it is historically true that there was heavy taxation around this time, Prince John was the last person to blame.

Crusading was an expensive business, and so when the Third Crusade was announced the Pope authorised a special tax to allow the Christian rulers to fund this campaign. The tax became known as the Saladin Tithe, and both laymen and priests had to pay it.

But Richard's taxes didn't stop there. When he was captured on his way back from the Holy Land he was held, quite literally, for a 'king's ransom'. Again the country had to cough up the cash, but again it was because of Richard's choices, not John's (as stated in the previous item, it was their mother, Eleanor of Aquitaine, who ran England while Richard was away).

Richard was so obsessed with raising money (and so disliked the country he was king of), he is alleged to have said, 'I would sell London if only I could find a buyer.'

However, even when he wasn't on crusade or in prison, Richard spent time fighting in France, trying to conquer it for himself – and he squeezed as much cash as he could from England to support his army there. His most formidable castle, Chateau Gaillard, was built in just three years but cost two years' of royal revenues to construct. Could you imagine a modern government spending two out of three years' annual budgets only on tanks?

So, while John was a disastrous ruler, Richard was too, at least economically. But he did win battles, which is why he's still remembered as Richard the Lionheart.

The Biggest Loser in History Was Ala ad-Din Muhammed II, Shah of the Khwarazmian Empire

Who? What? Where's that? Trust me, this is a good story. In the early thirteenth century, the Khwarazmian Empire was spread over most of central Asia. Parts of Georgia, most of Iran, Kazakhstan, Uzbekistan and other parts of central Asia were all included in this vast and powerful empire, which at the time was the largest Muslim empire in the world. It was about the same size as Western Europe. Its ruler was the hugely powerful and tremendously pampered Ala ad-Din. His fawning followers described him as the new Alexander the Great, and he believed the hype.

The spanner in his works was his problem neighbour, the not-exactly-mild-mannered Genghis Khan. Genghis had a simple rule: if the enemy capitulated unconditionally, it could expect mercy as long it did as it was told. Any resistance would result in total war, with killing, pillaging and destruction on an unimaginable scale. Many tried to defy Genghis, but only Ala ad-Din submitted. The result? As long as he gave Genghis the troops and money he wanted, he was allowed to remain emperor and to continue to enjoy the pleasures of palace life, with everyone telling him how awesome he was.

But then Ala ad-Din changed his mind and murdered the Mongol emissaries as an act of defiance. After all, was the emperor not the new Alexander and an awe-inspiring leader? Well, no, but as well as being the first ruler to capitulate without a fight, he was now also the first ruler to renege on a deal with a man who was possibly the most volatile in history (apologies to Genghis Khan, who was far more complex than that, but really, annoying the Mongols was never a good idea, and the deliberate offence was a serious contender for first prize for 'worst idea in history').

In 1219 Genghis sent an army of at least 150,000 (the whole of Western Europe at this time would have had difficulty scraping together an army of that size) and descended on the Khwarazmian Empire like the hounds of hell. When the city of Urgench had the audacity to hold out against the Mongols, they were eventually punished with one of the worst massacres in human history. All because their leader thought he was a greater man than he was.

One after another, the cities of the empire fell to the Mongols. Ala ad-Din found out the hard way that he was no Alexander the Great and spent the last few months of his life being chased across Asia by Mongol scouts. They never quite got to him, but the once-great shah died a broken man, on an island in the Caspian Sea. His only remaining possession was his cloak, which he was buried in by his handful of followers. He went from being one of the richest, most powerful men on the planet to a deposed and destitute ruler, who saw his empire go up in flames – in the modern parlance, a total loser. The Mongols did their best to erase him (and his empire) from history, which is why there are no surviving images and why you've probably never heard of him.

The moral of Ala ad-Din's story? Don't do anything stupid. Specifically, don't do anything to provoke a bloodthirsty neighbour. Oh, yes – and never, ever believe your own hype.

A Historic Event That Sounds Made Up

The First Crusade captured Jerusalem, the Second Crusade didn't do much, and the Third Crusade was instigated because in the 1180s Jerusalem fell to Saladin and became an Islamic city once again. The Third Crusade rolled back the Islamic advance but failed to capture Jerusalem, so only a decade later the Fourth Crusade set out to capture Jerusalem by ship, i.e. the men and equipment needed to conduct the crusade travelled part of the way by sea. Unfortunately, the crusade got side-tracked and ended up capturing Constantinople, which was Christian and about a 1,000 miles away from Jerusalem. That's quite a detour.

Moving on to the year 1219, the Fifth Crusade had arrived at the mouth of the Nile and was sieging the key port of Damietta. Since Jerusalem was now in the hands of Muslim powers, it was time to attack the new target of Egypt. If this crusade could control the Nile and Cairo, the Muslim power base would be seriously compromised, and the crusaders would be in a position to ask for whatever they wanted, including Jerusalem.

Damietta was a heavily fortified town and strategically located, so if the crusade could capture it then Egypt itself would be vulnerable. The siege had gone on for months when one of the most celebrated saints of the medieval era, Francis of Assisi, arrived at the crusader camp. Even during his lifetime he was revered as a holy person, and his arrival appeared to sanctify and bless the endeavours of the crusade.

Francis had correctly predicted that an attack on the Ayyubid camp to the south of Damietta would fail, and recently he'd had another vision in which he had converted the Sultan of Egypt, Al-Kamil, to Christianity. Because of his evident powers, he was allowed through the Christian lines to go to the sultan. If Francis could perform such a miracle then the crusade would be 100 per cent successful, and Egypt would be a Christian kingdom led by a newly converted Christian king. Surely this was a sign from God.

Francis approached the Muslim forces, and after some discussion was allowed to visit the Al-Kamil (presumably for his amusement). Sadly, none of the chronicles record the unique discourse between holy man and sultan, but Francis returned to the crusader lines having barely escaped with his life. He'd failed to reach agreement on any terms and had insulted Al-Kamil's faith in the process. Soon after that, Francis left Egypt and returned to Europe, where he was a more successful holy man. St Francis of Assisi's high hopes of becoming a missionary to convert Muslims to Christianity was an utter failure – something that echoed the Fifth Crusade.

In the end, the crusaders did capture Damietta, and the church bells of Europe rang to rejoice such a hard-won victory. However, the sultan flooded the Nile Delta, which bogged down the crusade's progress south, and it was eventually surrounded and captured. The crusaders bargained for their lives and were allowed to leave if Damietta was returned to the sultan. The deal was agreed, and the crusaders returned to an ignominious homecoming. Many in Europe thought they should have sacrificed their freedom for the sake of holding onto the prize of Damietta.

The Word 'Kamikaze' Has Medieval Origins

Kamikaze literally means 'divine wind', and for the Japanese of the 1940s the word harked back to a time in the thirteenth century when invasion by foreigners also loomed. On that occasion, Kublai Khan, the Mongol ruler of an empire that stretched from the borders of Poland all the way to Korea, had completed the conquest of China and was now looking at the isles of Japan. On two separate occasions he gathered a huge fleet that, while Mongol-led, was full of Chinese and Korean soldiers. The divided feudal society of Japan stood little chance and conquest looked certain.

However, on both occasions (the second time was worse), the Mongol landings were thwarted by typhoons. The storms smashed ships, killing thousands, and the battered invasion fleets went home, having had victory snatched away by bad weather (the fact that the vessels had been built so quickly and in such numbers meant that they weren't of the highest quality and were therefore more susceptible to storm damage). The Japanese recognised they'd avoided catastrophe only through sheer good luck, and for decades afterwards coastal lookouts kept watch for a third attack, which never came.

The winds that had saved them were called 'kamikaze' and were transformed in the popular imagination from random events into a spiritual guardian ensuring that Japan would never fall to foreign invaders. Fast forwarding to the 1940s, the Japanese conceived the idea that a man-made kamikaze could perform much the same service. After all, until 1945 Japan had never been successfully invaded, so it was easy to imagine that they were somehow protected from external threats.

Japan's kamikaze aircraft created bloody mayhem and killed thousands while also crippling massive and expensive Allied ships, all for the price of a few men and some outmoded aircraft. Cold calculations by the Japanese high command showed the missions were well worth the minimal cost (in lives and money), and the Allies developed a fear and loathing for the waves of Japanese suicide airplanes.

It is likely that the 'never surrender' attitude of the Japanese was a key factor in persuading the Americans to use nuclear weapons for the first time. Better to obliterate the enemy than to fight tooth and nail for every inch of the Japanese home islands. Not even suicidal bravery could not stop the invasion this time. Japan surrendered after suffering two nuclear attacks and came under occupation for the first time in its long history.

What Was a Teutonic Knight?

The Order of Brothers of the German House of Saint Mary in Jerusalem is better known simply as the Teutonic Knights, one of the three largest 'military orders'. These were unusual groups of men who led monastic lives, swore vows of poverty and chastity and lived in a similar way to monks. However, rather than pray to God, they fought for him.

The other two main orders (and there were dozens of small ones, my favourite being the Order of Saint Lazarus of Jerusalem, which started as a leper colony) were the Hospitallers and the Templars. While the Teutonic Knights did their bit in the Middle East during the crusader era, they always played a supporting role to the two older, larger orders. However, as their name suggests, the Teutonic Knights were, specifically, a

Germanic military order, and that meant they had non-Christians closer to home to fight.

The Teutonic Knights were founded in 1190, and at that time large swathes of northern Europe and the Baltic were still pagan. This may sound odd nowadays, but it is a testament to the effectiveness of the so-called 'Northern Crusades' that we now associate Christianity with all of Europe. It also meant that when the last Christian city in the Middle East fell in 1291, the Teutonic Knights still had legitimate 'God's work' to do, whereas the Hospitallers and the Templars looked redundant.

The Northern Crusades fought not only pagans, but Orthodox Christians too, and they lasted for centuries. Eventually the Teutonic Knights ran huge swathes of what is now Poland and the Baltic region as their own state. However, in 1410 a (Christian) Polish–Lithuanian alliance crushed the knights at the Battle of Tannenburg, and the next blow to their prestige was the Reformation. Their lands are now part of many European countries, and they have been transformed into a Catholic charitable organisation based in Vienna.

A Medieval War Crime

In 1209 the Albigensian Crusade (a crusade in France against heretics) arrived at the fortified town of Béziers, a city encompassed by large stone walls, with guard towers and well-defended gates. The crusaders were being led by the papal legate (the official papal authority on a crusade) Arnaud-Amaury, who was also the Abbot of Citeaux.

A message was sent to the town to expel its heretics, and the crusade would deal with them. The Church was particularly eager to get its hands on the Cathar heretics, who were not a separate community but part of the general population. Arnaud-Amaury failed to understand that the residents of Béziers were not going to betray each other on the orders of invaders.

Béziers was a microcosm of the wider problem with the Albigensian Crusade. People were more loyal to each other than to external authorities. The Pope might have seen the crusade as a simple way to remove heresy, but the men doing the defending saw this as the northern French trying to dominate the south, and the people of Toulouse or Béziers would do everything to resist that, even if it meant good Christians fighting side by side with heretics.

When it became obvious that the people of Béziers were not going to comply by handing over their fellow citizens, the crusade set up camp to begin a siege. However, they were surprised by the local militia, who saw this as their only chance to gain an advantage over the elite soldiers from the north. Despite this, there could be only one outcome in a fight between an inexperienced militia and veteran soldiers: the attack was quickly repulsed and the crusaders pushed through the gates.

The problem for the crusaders was that most previous crusades had been against Muslims, who could be easily identified (so it was thought) by western Christians (even though eastern Christians and Jews fell victim to crusader ignorance, which was regarded as a minor inconvenience by the crusaders). So a cry went up asking how they could tell the difference between heretics and good Catholics. Arnaud-Amaury replied,

Kill them all for the Lord shall know his own.

What happened next was a full-scale massacre; everyone the crusaders could find was butchered. The main (Catholic) church was burned down, and non-heretic priests were murdered as they sought refuge next to their altars. In Arnaud-Amaury's own words,

> Our men spared no one, irrespective of rank, sex or age, and put to the sword almost 20,000 people. After this great slaughter the whole city was despoiled and burnt.

The numbers are (thankfully) exaggerated, but it is chilling to read such an unapologetic statement from a supposed 'man of God', who should also have been a 'man of peace'.

The Holy Roman Empire: It Wasn't Holy; It Wasn't Roman, and It Wasn't an Empire

So why was it called that? Like most institutions in medieval western Europe, its roots can be traced back to the Roman era. After the fall of Rome in the fifth century AD, the Roman Empire didn't end. It was doing very well in the east, with the capital city now Constantinople. Meanwhile, after centuries of turmoil, most of Europe was again reunified under Charlemagne (not his real name but a mangling of the phrase 'Charles the Great' in Latin), who was crowned Roman Emperor by the Pope on Christmas Day 800.

Charlemagne's empire split up after his death, and the central part of Europe came under the rule of the tenth century Ottonian Dynasty (this is the one with three Ottos in a row), and it was their dynasty that revived the tradition of going to Rome to be crowned Roman Emperor. It still wasn't called the Holy Roman Empire, but the concept developed from this period.

The Eastern Roman Empire (now referred to as 'Byzantium' by everyone except the Byzantines) did not recognise the western emperors. They could draw a clear line from their rule back to the era of the Caesars. To the Byzantine emperors, the western emperors were little more than barbarians playing dress up, unworthy of the title.

However, this absurd state of affairs saw German kings trooping down to Rome every few decades, either to make the Pope crown them (if the Pope had been rebellious) or to ask nicely (if the Pope was a puppet of the German emperor). The journey also meant that for more than 500 years German armies marched over the Alps to cause trouble in Italy.

Furthermore, this strong link to the Vatican caused real problems for the Holy Roman Emperors, who often found themselves threatened with excommunication. If the Pope were to carry out this threat, rivals would have the perfect justification to start a civil war. The incongruous situation can be highlighted by events in 1077, when Emperor Henry IV had to walk barefoot in the snow to Canossa as a sign of penitence before Pope Gregory VII. A Pope had humbled an emperor over an issue of excommunication – a weapon more powerful than an army during the Middle Ages.

So, we have seen that this empire was neither 'holy' nor 'Roman', nor was it an 'empire', because the area it covered was composed largely of semi-autonomous states. At its peak it ruled northern Italy, Austria, Germany (which was then a patchwork of counties, duchies and principalities) and the Czech Republic. So to appease these vying power bases the emperor was elected. Quite often the role was passed from father to son, but a Holy Roman Emperor did not have the same right to power as, say, a Chinese emperor or a Russian tsar.

Despite waning powers, the Holy Roman Empire survived until the early nineteenth century, when it was dismantled by Napoleon after his victories in central Europe. In spite of everything against it, the empire had lasted for over 800 years.

The Mongol Invasion of Europe

In the year 1241, the devil's hordes made manifest had descended on the borders of Europe, and they appeared to be unstoppable. Europe was teetering on the brink of anarchy.

It's often forgotten what an enormous impact the Mongols had on Europe. By this time Russia was already under their control. When the Mongols thought the capital of 'Rus', at Kiev, was too far away, they created a new centre of administration at a small outpost called Moscow. By the end of 1241, Hungary was in ruins, and Poland had become part of the Mongol Empire that stretched all the way to Korea.

The assault on Europe was part of the second generation of Mongol expansion. With Genghis Khan dead, it was now up to his third son, Ogedai Khan, to conquer the world. Unlike many other rulers who claimed unlimited powers, the Mongols not only believed it was their divine right to rule the entire planet, but they were also able to enforce it. Their empire would continue to expand for a further generation, and when it finally reached its zenith it would dwarf all other empires … that is, until the British came along. But it would take another 600 years before the British Empire could match and exceed that of the Mongols, who can still claim the largest land-based empire in world history.

After invading most of China and the Middle East, the Mongols had conquered the cultural and economic giants of the known world. By comparison, Europe in the thirteenth century was poorer, more fragmented and far less of a military threat than anything they had already faced; however, it was still there to be conquered. Ogedai's plan was to order massive simultaneous assaults across huge swathes of Eastern Europe – a feat well beyond any European army at this time.

The Mongols (who, contrary to contemporary beliefs, were flesh and blood, rather than demons) had to ride from Mongolia, about 3,000 miles away, before engaging in a blitzkrieg across unknown lands; an achievement that earns respect if only in terms of sheer endurance.

The two key battles were Mohi in Hungary and Leignitz in Poland, which are 500 miles apart. In addition to their horsemanship, martial skills and fortitude, the Mongols were also master strategists and, despite the distance, were able to co-ordinate their troops.

On 9 April 1241, a coalition of Polish Teutonic Knights and Knights Templar joined the battle against the Mongols at Leignitz. These knights were the cream of the European chivalric class, and a much welcome addition to the defensive forces.

Contemporary accounts relate that the Mongols were able to create smoke on the battlefield, and at Mohi there are references to sparks and roars. These could have been fireworks, used by the Mongols to sow confusion, in which case the Mongols were the first people to use gunpowder in Europe. Whether it was the Mongol smokescreen or their fireworks didn't really matter. The ponderous European infantry and heavy cavalry stood no chance against fast-moving mounted archers.

At Mohi on 11 April, the King of Hungary, Bela IV, was also supported by both Teutonic and Templar Knights, which added heavy cavalry to the existing elite cavalry and mounted archers of the Hungarian forces. They were annihilated by a different Mongol army. The Mongol losses were light, and the Christian forces were all but destroyed. Bela fled the battlefield in terror and only just managed to escape with his life.

The near simultaneous nature of these shattering battles put Europe in a tailspin. The cream of Europe's troops had been slaughtered; realistically, France, Spain and Britain would fair no better. The Mongols had won. When Pope Gregory IX heard the news of these defeats at the hands of Satan's own minions, he collapsed and died. The gates of Europe had been flung wide open; the continent could only hold its breath and pray, and then ... well ... nothing.

Ironically, the man who saved Europe was the same one who had wanted to conquer it. Ogedai, the great Khan, died at the time of the invasion, which necessitated the return of the Mongols to Karakorum to crown their next warlord. So they travelled back, over 3,000 miles, to home.

This completely unexpected lack of action after such decisive victories led to interesting explanations. Some believed they had converted to Christianity and went off to fight the Muslims (they were to have many future battles against Muslims, but not because they were Christian). My favourite version of events comes from Poland, where the story goes that the Mongols had suffered such devastating casualties, they dared not go any further. This is complete rubbish, but the Poles would not be the first (nor the last) country to put a positive spin on the truth.

The Turin Shroud: Fake or Fact?

Medieval European Christians all knew that the remains of holy people had magical properties; the holier the person, the more powerful the magic. The dust that settled on these holy relics was collected and sold as if the dust itself had absorbed some of the relic's holiness. However, there was a problem with Jesus, who had ascended to Heaven, so left no body from which to absorb the holy aura. And yet, two monasteries managed to overcome this deficiency. It was common knowledge that Jesus was a Jew, so they both claimed to be in possession of Jesus's ... ahem ...

foreskin, which, there's no denying, would have been left on earth (although Jesus would not have claimed to have had two of them).

Since there was no body, the next best thing would be the shroud that Jesus had been buried in. This would be a special relic, indeed. Enter the Shroud of Turin.

The artefact is a puzzling one, mainly because nobody can satisfactorily explain how the cloth came to be imprinted with the faint image of a man. Some have said it could be a kind of medieval photograph. If so, this would make it an extraordinary find. What gives credibility to this theory is that what is feint and unclear in normal light looks very striking in a photographic negative – as if the shroud is waiting for the invention of photography.

Whatever the explanation, it's a colossal leap to say with certainty that this is the shroud of Jesus Christ. Radio carbon dating, done in the 1980s, shows it to be medieval, but critics have said that the scientists took samples from the wrong part of the shroud. There are indications that the fabric is woven in a first century AD style, and that it contains pollen from the Middle East, all of which has been disputed, but all of this could mean only that it was faked in the city known for making religious fakes.

The difference between what you want to be true and what you can prove are often two different things. In this case, the first is legend and the latter is history and/or science. If the shroud is a fake, it's an amazing fake – the work of genius by an unknown charlatan; if it's authentic, it will need much more in the way of evidence to support the claim.

It's telling that the Roman Catholic Church (which owns it) has never either endorsed it as the real deal, or decried it as fake. Even the papacy is exercising caution about this controversial religious artefact.

What Is an Assassin?

The term *hashashin* is the Arabic for 'assassin', and it's a corruption of the Arabic that has given us the word in English. The term is derogatory, meaning 'rabble' or, more colloquially, 'yobs'. It was never used by the sect known as the 'Assassins', which called itself the *Nizari Ismailis*. They were despised, partly because of their assassinations and partly because, as Ismailis, they were already a separate sect of Islam, regarded as heretics by the main Sunni and Shi'a sects.

Formed in the late eleventh century, the original assassins were called the *Hashashins,* and the enemy princes, warlords and generals of both Muslim and Christian cultures were their potential targets. The knives they used were coated in deadly poison, and the assassinations were often very public. Any secret religious society that carries out high-profile murders is likely to have some tall tales swirling around it. The stories were contemporary to the organisation in the twelfth and thirteenth and centuries, but most of the source material was written by people outside of (and often the targets of) the *Nizari Ismailis*. It is a coincidence that their name sounds like 'hashish', but it is that association that brings me to my favourite story about them.

According to a popular tale (one repeated by Marco Polo), in order to recruit new members, young initiates were taken to a castle where they were kept in the outer gatehouse and fed hash cakes. Once sound asleep, the men were transferred into the main castle where they awoke to find themselves surrounded by lush gardens, beautiful girls and plentiful food and drink. After a few days of indulgence, they were slipped more hash cakes and, once in a stupor, were returned to the outer gatehouse. When they awoke this time, they were informed by the *Hashishins* that they had experienced paradise, and if they wanted to go back, they would have to follow orders and die martyrs to the cause.

It's an ingenious way of explaining the fanaticism and single-mindedness of these hitmen. It also explained their seemingly joyous response to being captured and immediately dispatched by the bodyguards of their victims. Of course, the contemporary reader knows that it takes far less in the way of elaborate trickery to brainwash young men into carrying out terrible acts of violence in the name of God.

The *Hashishin*, led originally by Hasan-i-Sabbah (who became known as the 'Old Man of the Mountains', a title which future leaders also used), embedded themselves in a string of castles in remote desert regions, mainly in modern-day Syria, Iraq and western Iran. These strongholds allowed the group to spread terror from safe bases, and were essentially impregnable as no army could realistically besiege an arid area. But the *Hashishin* weren't the only ones in the assassination business in the Middle East at the time. Both the crusaders and the Muslim princes conducted their own targeted murders, so the *Hashishin's* exact number of successful hits will probably never be known. Because the sect was so secretive, and because almost all of our source material has come from its enemies, it is hard to dissect fact from fiction.

This aura of mystery and terror was exactly what the *Hashishin* cultivated. They maintained no large armies, nor did they conquer huge territories, but they were important players in the region for centuries. No person in power, from Acre to Astrakhan, was safe ... that is, until the Mongols arrived. The *Hashishin* made a huge error by sending one of their assassins to kill the Mongol great khan. They failed, and the full might of the Mongol empire to descend on them. By means of sheer bloody-mindedness, the Mongols did everyone a favour by capturing and destroying the *Hashishin* strongholds in Syria. They marched the survivors out into the desert, where most were massacred or died of thirst.

The Ismaili sect of Islam is very much alive today, but the violent *Nizari Ismailis* no longer exist.

The Largest Hoard of Coins Ever Found

In 1908, when Brussels was building a railway through its winding city streets, workers discovered something amazing. Underneath a recently demolished tavern, they found a container full of medieval coins – more than 140,000 – the largest coin hoard ever unearthed.

The hoard appears to have been hidden in 1267, and one of the most interesting facts about it was that the coins were not all local. While approximately 64,000 coins were continental European, more than 81,000 were English, minted during the era of Henry III. So many English coins indicated a major exchange. While Brussels was famous for its artisans and trade, the Flanders region was also famous for its mercenaries, so the coins could have been intended as payment for troops in one of Henry's many conflicts.

Whatever the reason for the accumulation of such a substantial amount, it can be assumed that the money was tucked away for safekeeping. The sheer quantity of coins means that whoever hid them had every intention of returning, and the fact that they weren't uncovered again until 1908 indicates that the hoarder died before being able to tell someone else about this buried treasure. His bad fortune worked to history's advantage.

When the coins went to auction, they were bought by Albert Baldwin, an antiques' auctioneer from London, for about £9,000 (around £2.7 million in today's money); however, the hoard, as a collection, would now be worth considerably more. Albert melted down some of the lower grade coins to pay staff, a few dozen more were stolen, and a few hundred of the rarer coins were sold again at auction, but the collection is largely intact and remains with the Baldwin family.

The Last Caliph Destroyed Islam's Libraries by Doing Nothing

The Islamic caliphate was the ruling political and religious dynasty that traced its heritage back to the family of the Prophet, and by 1258 had been in existence for more than 600 years. It's true that by the mid-thirteenth century its power had waned to the point where many areas of the Middle East were no longer ruled by Arab dynasties, but by Turkic families. However, from its epicentre at Baghdad, the caliphate had been a beacon, not only of power, but of science, knowledge and culture, for centuries.

This was all about to change forever, because in 1258 the Mongols arrived and sent out messengers with a simple statement: capitulate immediately or face the consequences. Al-Musta'sim was the caliph at the time, and he knew exactly what this meant. The Mongols' reputation had preceded them, and he understood that while capitulation was humiliating, provided he paid tribute, he could continue in his role; it would be business as usual under new management. Having weighed it all up, al-Musta'sim decided to reject the Mongol offer. Worse, he chose not to raise an army, order his people to flee, or bolster Baghdad's (formidable) defences; he simply sat in his capital and did nothing, hoping, presumably, that everything would be okay.

When the Mongols arrived, they set about laying siege to the city with their usual gusto and efficiency. Al-Musta'sim didn't negotiate with the Mongols and didn't send messengers to other Muslim princes asking for help. Instead, he just sat there, sending occasional threats to the Mongols, which of course goaded them further.

The sacking of Baghdad is one of the greatest atrocities in history. It is estimated that close to a million people were slaughtered. The stench of death was so great that for the only time in Mongol history they themselves found it too much to bear and had to camp outside the city. In the countryside so many peasants were killed that there was no one left to repair and maintain the extensive irrigation system. Iraq had been green and lush; today it is mainly arid. 750 years after the Mongol invasion, Iraq is still suffering the consequences.

Having done with the population, the Mongols turned to the destruction of the libraries. One eyewitness said that so many books were thrown into the river the Tigris ran black with ink. The Middle East had lost its most populous city, and centuries of learning were gone forever. The Golden Age of Islamic learning ended with the Mongol attack on Baghdad.

According to Mongol tradition, no royal blood may be spilt on the dirt, so the Mongols rolled al-Musta'sim in a rug and rode their cavalry over him. The honour accorded him in death was probably lost on him.

Mysterious Children

Sometime in the late twelfth century, Ralph of Coggeshall and William of Newburgh wrote that two green children arrived in the village of Woolpit during the summer. Ralph was the abbot of a Cistercian monastery at Coggeshall; William was a canon at an Augustinian priory in Yorkshire. The story goes as follows.

One day at harvest time, the villagers of Woolpit discovered two children, a brother and sister, beside one of the wolf pits that gave the village its name. Their skin was green, they spoke an unknown language, and their clothing was unfamiliar. Ralph reports that the children were taken to the home of Richard de Calne, where the pair refused all food for several days (according to both Ralph and William) until they came across some raw beans, which they consumed eagerly. The children gradually adapted to normal food and, over time, lost their green colour. However, the boy, who appeared to be the younger of the two, became sickly and died shortly after he and his sister were baptised.

After learning to speak English, the children – Ralph says just the surviving girl – explained that they came from a land where the sun never shone and the light was like twilight.

The story is certainly odd and also baffling. A number of people have tried to explain events by pointing out that some types of illness turn the skin a pallid green and can reduce appetite. As is often the case with medieval texts, they are frustratingly vague on detail, and all that any modern historian or doctor can do is add conjecture to the little that is known. So, exactly who these children were or where they came from will remain a mystery.

(Aliens ... got to be aliens ...)

The Maid of the North

Alexander III of Scotland was a man in a hurry. He became king as a minor and couldn't wait to become sole ruler. Then he couldn't wait to rid Scotland of the scourge of Scandinavian incursions (which were still going on in the thirteenth century). This led him to agree a treaty with Norway, which was sealed when his little granddaughter was dispatched to that country, where it was agreed she would eventually marry into the Norwegian royal family. However, despite Alexander's hurry to have a male heir, this was a goal which eluded him and was to be his undoing.

Alexander's first wife, Margaret, was the daughter of Henry III, King of England, but she died when a practical joke went badly wrong. She tried to push a courtier into the river but fell in herself and drowned in the strong current.

Margaret had borne Alexander children, but over the years they all perished. As time was running out to produce the desired male heir, her death was probably fortuitous for the succession. The middle-aged king needed a new wife, which he promptly acquired in the form of Yolande of Dreuxand, whom he married in the winter of 1284. However, in March of 1285 he was so eager to get to the queen on her birthday that he rushed out into the night and a proper Scottish storm. The next day he was found dead; his horse had taken a fall, and he had died in the storm. The result was a dynastic disaster for Scotland. The king was dead, the queen had been in the country for only a few months, and the only heir was a child: Alexander's granddaughter Margaret, then in Norway.

It didn't take long for the wolves to circle. John Balliol made a claim to the throne, and the Bruces, a powerful family, backed Margaret. It was civil war. The group of guardians appointed to rule for Margaret (known as the Maid of the North because she was growing up in Norway … long story) until she returned and was old enough to rule did their best to keep the peace, but tensions were running high.

However, Scotland found a potential saviour in Edward Longshanks, King of England. He was seen as a great diplomat as well as a great warrior. He had been involved in a number of continental disputes, both as antagonist and as conciliator, and he was viewed as a wise ruler – one who could work through the different grievances and come up with an independent solution. Why not ask him for help?

Edward's solution, readily agreed by the Scottish nobles, was that his firstborn son (who was about the same age as Margaret) would marry her, and together they would be the rightful rulers of both nations, uniting the two crowns of Britain. It was a simple and elegant solution that made Scotland a partner, not a subject, to the English throne. Edward had pulled off a diplomatic triumph.

So Margaret, now aged just seven, set off from Norway in 1290. True, there would be a long period of stewardship under the guardians, but in the long term, both nations would benefit from this union. However, the North Sea, even in summer, is rough, and the little girl fell ill on the journey. At the Orkney Islands, things got worse, and she died.

The fate of two nations had rested on Margaret, and her sad demise meant centuries of further warfare between England and Scotland. It was one of the great missed opportunities of British history.

Unlucky Ottomans

The Ottoman Empire lasted for more than 600 years and had many impressive rulers, but two of its early rulers were truly unlucky.

In 1389 the young Ottoman Empire, not yet 100 years old, was being led by the ambitious and successful Murad I, who was about to fight against the collective princes of Serbia in what would become known as the Battle of Kosovo. The fighting was brutal, but things were going well for the Ottomans. During the battle, however, one of the Serbian generals switched sides and demanded an audience with Murad.

The sultan would have been only too happy to welcome such an ally so, flanked by his elite bodyguards, he agreed to meet the Serb, who lunged at Murad and drove a dagger into his stomach. He had just enough time to wrench the blade up through the sultan's abdomen before being hacked to pieces by the royal bodyguards. This makes Murad the only Ottoman sultan to die not so much 'in' battle, but 'at' the site of a battle.

Despite his untimely death, Murad passed on a great legacy to his son. The Battle of Kososvo was an Ottoman victory and further solidified Ottoman rule in the Baltic as well as further east in Anatolia.

Murad's son, Bayezid, was also a successful warrior and became known as '*Yildirum*', lightning, for his speed in battle. He destroyed what was left of the Serbian resistance whilst swallowing up the few remaining Byzantium lands, except for the fortress city of Constantinople. As it was all but surrounded by Ottoman lands, the fall of Constantinople now seemed inevitable.

However, in 1402 the Ottomans faced a new threat, this time from the east, when they met Emir Timur (Tamerlane) at Ankara, then a tiny town, now the capital city of Turkey. Cast in the same style as Attila the Hun or Genghis Khan, Timur was the last great nomadic warlord, only he had an army which included armour-plated war elephants equipped with flamethrowers, a terrifying sight for any army, let alone medieval Turkish cavalrymen. The fighting was fierce, but the Ottomans lost, and Sultan Bayezid was captured and put in a cage by Timur. The son of Murad became the only Ottoman sultan to be captured in battle, and he died in captivity.

After this, there was a civil war, but the Ottomans got considerably luckier later in the fifteenth century, when Mehmet II (a descendent of Bayezid) finally conquered Constantinople in 1453.

Vampire Burials Are a Genuine Historic Phenomenon

It's rare to talk about mythological creatures in a history book, but the human fear of the blood-sucking undead has been around a lot longer than *Twilight*, *True Blood* or even Bram (short for Abraham) Stoker's *Dracula*.

This fear has manifested itself in a number of weird burial rituals in Europe and colonial America. In central Europe the occasional grave has a slab of stone placed over the coffin to stop it being opened from the inside. In northern Italy (and again, in central Europe), a few skeletons have been found with large bricks or stones wedged in the jaws so that any new teeth would be snapped by the hard object in the mouth. There are Spanish graves which exhibit the skull and crossbones to warn passers-by that the occupant may be a vampire.

Transylvania (in Romania), where the vampire legend originated, and Bulgaria both have dozens of medieval and renaissance era skeletons with iron spikes jammed through the heart or throat. This impaling of the dead has also been found in colonial American graves.

Clearly, the people buried in such graves had caused enough concern in life to be condemned in death. Some of the dead were high-born, which would explain the extravagant nature of the burials, as paupers would never have been given such an elaborate send off. The exact source of the vampire legend is unclear (and Vlad the Impaler is just one part of the tale) and is likely to be a mix of superstition and peasant ignorance. Whereas today vampires are often portrayed as deadly but sexy and darkly desirable, our ancestors had no wish to have any encounters with them, and the burials reflect those fears.

The Other Exceedingly Bloody 'Scottish Play'

In the year 1396, war was brewing in the Highlands, so the Chattan Confederation and the Clan Kay came up with a bizarre idea for resolving differences. Rather than the usual pitched battle, an alternative solution was proposed and accepted by both sides.

Exactly which clans are associated with these names is a bit of a mystery, but it's a good guess that this was an early clash between the Mackintoshes and the Camerons – a feud that would last about 350 years. However, in this instance the two sides agreed to build an arena and carry out what must be the bloodiest piece of theatre in stage history.

It was specifically decided that thirty men from each group would do battle in front of the North Inch Dominican Friary. The last man (or men) standing would be declared the winner(s). The summer house of the friary was turned into a grand stand for the King of Scotland (who was then Robert III), who attended along with hundreds of spectators.

On the day of battle, Clan Chattan was one man down, so Henry Smith, a local armourer (who was apparently 'bandy-legged' and not much to look at), agreed to join in so that it would be seen as a fair and even fight. The ensuing skirmish was accompanied by cheers from the crowd and bagpipe music (making it an almost chocolate-box version of Scotland).

The combat was furious and, surprisingly, Henry Smith proved to be one of the fiercest fighters for Clan Chattan. Clan Kay was defeated, and all but one of its number had been killed. Their last man, realising all was lost, jumped in the nearby river Tay and swam away. Eleven from Clan Chattan, surrounded by the dead and dying, remained on the stage, victorious.

So, just your average day in Perthshire then.

Vettor Pisani: a Legend in Venice but Forgotten Everywhere Else

Vettor Pisani was a hugely talented fourteenth century Venetian admiral, involved in the key war between Venice and Genoa that lasted from 1378 to 1380. The two city states had been at each other's throats for centuries and would continue to be for a few generations to come, but it was this war that finally broke the Genoese in their ongoing fight against the Venetians.

In this particular clash between the two republics, Genoa had allies in the form of Padua and Hungary. The idea was to surround and throttle Venice from all sides. Pisani was by then an already highly regarded admiral who had earlier engaged in raids on Hungarian outposts on the Croatian coast. He had carried out some sharp engagements with Genoese warships and merchant ships in the area, too.

Disaster struck at the Battle of Palo when Pisani, sensing a trap by the Genoese Admiral Doria, refused to engage. After furious debate between the leaders of the Venetian fleet, Michele Stano accused Pisani of cowardice, and against his better judgement Pisani led the Venetian galleys out into battle. His instincts were right, and while Doria was fatally injured (and replaced by his brother) it was a major defeat for Venice, which paved the way for the Genoese fleet to sail towards the open waters of Venice. Pisani was blamed for the defeat, returned home in shame and was thrown in prison, much to the disgust of the commoners of Venice.

Now the armies of Padua, Hungary and Genoa united against a battered and increasingly isolated Venice. The fighting was concentrated on a Venetian satellite town called Chioggia. The Genoese captured it in the summer of 1379, and Venice, just a few miles along the coast, looked extremely vulnerable. At this point the Venetian Doge sent the Genoese a blank piece of paper for peace terms, demonstrating that any price was acceptable to keep their independence. Doria, sensing victory was at hand, refused to sign and pushed forwards.

Venice was desperate and turned to its two best-known adventurers, Zeno and Pisani. After a few short months in prison, Pisani had been released to jubilation amongst the Venetian crowds, and now these two men added stout resistance to the Genoese advance. As the campaign dragged on, Venice was slowly starving to death. Despite this, Pisani and Zeno raided, counter-attacked and generally boosted morale.

The long siege had disadvantages for the Genoese as well, and when it became clear that the initiative had been lost, the alliance started to strain. Winter turned to spring and spring, to early summer. Finally, in June of 1380, Venice counter-attacked with all its remaining force and won back Chioggia. The Genoese retreated some distance and eventually made peace in 1381. Pisani never saw this, as after the victory of Chioggia he continued to raid Hungarian coastal sites and attack Genoese shipping. Exhausted by his years of exertions, he died aged fifty-six on one of his ships.

The war was important as it led to the decline of Genoa as a trading super power and, therefore, enabled the rise of Venice to a position of importance that would last for another 200 years. Several Italian naval vessels have been named after Vettor Pisani in his honour.

Arquebus? Arquebus! What the Hell Is an Arquebus?

One of the issues with learned tomes and erudite history books is that there is often no explanation of very specific and obsolete terms. The word 'arquebus' crops up frequently in the late medieval era and is obviously some sort of weapon, but here's an explanation.

An *arquebusier* is the user of an arquebus, and an arquebus was a very early musket. It was little more than a metal tube on a simple wooden stand (for balance), which fired like a cannon and, at close range, could pierce armour. It was very loud and belched smoke and flames. It took forever to reload (okay, an exaggeration, but we are talking minutes, not seconds). It was great at breaking up infantry or cavalry charges, but it was inaccurate and could only be fired in good weather (otherwise, the wicks and gunpowder would be ruined by rain).

The arquebus used in the fifteenth and early sixteenth centuries, but the design evolved from what had once been little more than a small cannon on a stick to a more recognisable firearm. The early ones were more of a novelty than anything else. There is one recorded death from such a weapon at the Battle of Agincourt, but it's the bows and arrows that are remembered from that clash.

Seeing that they were painfully slow to reload and were terrible at a distance, it's astonishing that gunpowder weapons took off at all, but they had two major advantages: cost and secondary effects. The cost of training a man to use a longbow was a huge investment of time. Training someone to light a wick and place it on a tube ... not so much. The other advantage was that they were loud and scary, with their flashes of light, which meant that enemy soldiers sometimes ran away. In general, humans don't like killing, so to have a weapon that frightened away the enemy was, in itself, an effective and humane defence. But make no mistake: get close enough and these primitive weapons could and did kill.

A century or so later, these firearms had improved significantly and were now called muskets. The people who fired them were musketeers. Hmm ... D'Artagnan and the 'three arquebusiers' ... doesn't quite have the same ring, does it?

Barbarossa: a Name that Oozes History

Barbarossa was the name of the greatest medieval German emperor and also that of the last great winter assault by the Third Reich in December of 1944. It literally means 'red beard'. However, it is the pirate brothers called Barbarossa I want to address in this article.

These two brothers understood the importance of a name. The elder brother was called Baba Aruj, which to Europeans sounded like Barbarossa (and helpfully, he did have a red beard), so this very Turkish pirate ended up with a very German-sounding nickname. He and his brother Hayreddin spent the start of the 16th century plundering North Africa and the western Mediterranean coastal regions. In 1512 Aruj got a second nickname, 'silver arm', after his left arm was amputated and he was fitted with a silver prosthetic arm and hand (I promise I am not making this up).

Over time, the brothers acquired a significant naval force and were now more interested in conquering territories than in merely plundering for treasure. They particularly focused on fighting Spain, the greatest naval power of the time, and in 1516 captured Algeria from the Spanish. The brothers were smart enough to pay homage and allegiance to the Ottoman Empire. Even if they were the ones who were managing these newly acquired lands, tribute to this powerful empire meant one less navy was chasing them. The sultan could claim to rule huge stretches of the North

African coast at no cost to himself or his empire, and the brothers received official recognition from the Ottomans. Everyone was happy ... except for the Spanish, of course.

By 1518 Barbarossa was in Morocco. He was defending his newly conquered city of Tlemcen when he was attacked by over 10,000 Spanish soldiers, supported by Bedouins. He died in the battle, and his brother Hayreddin inherited his lands, his navy and, most importantly, the Barbarossa name.

The new Barbarossa became an Ottoman admiral, who harassed Spanish forts for decades and captured Tunis (again expanding the Ottoman territories). He was so feared and respected that in 1540 the Holy Roman Emperor Charles V offered him anything he wanted if he agreed to switch sides. Barbarossa declined the offer.

Later he fought with France against Spain and the Italian states and won that campaign too. In 1545 he retired to Constantinople to write his memoirs, and died a year later having had one of the most illustrious and successful naval careers in history.

The Ultimate Cougar (or How a Teenage King's Head Was Turned by a Thirty-Five-Year-Old Woman)

When Henry II of France was a teenager, he was not then the heir to the throne, nor had he spent much time in France. His father, Francis I, had been captured at the Battle of Pavia and was released only on the condition that Henry and his brother were sent to Spain as hostages. Henry spent the next four years in Spain where, at the age of fourteen, he married Catherine de' Medici (of a similar age). However, the following year he began a scandalous affair with Diane de Poitiers, who was twenty years his senior. To be fair, she had become accustomed to these sort of age gaps, as at the age of fifteen she was married to Louis de Brézé, Seigneur d'Anet, who was thirty-nine years older than her.

While Diane was the seducer, Henry understood the implications of the situation, and to avoid suspicion made frequent visits to his wife's bedroom to cover his tracks. In another act of consideration (and probably preservation, too), Diane helped to nurse Catherine back to health when she contracted scarlet fever. These were most unusual relationships.

During a jousting tournament, both Catherine and Diane were present as Henry showed off his martial prowess. According to tradition, a knight would seek a lady's favour, and she would reciprocate by tying her ribbon or handkerchief to his lance (this is not a euphemism). It was only right that a married nobleman received the favour from his wife, but shockingly Henry chose Diane over Catherine.

Diane became the talk of the continent, and for a minor noblewoman in the early sixteenth century there are a surprising number of paintings of her, including one where she's naked. Diane de Poitiers remained Henry's lifelong companion (even though he was still married to Catherine), and for the next twenty-five years she was the most powerful influence in his life and, in fact, the most powerful woman in France.

But all good things must come to an end. In 1559 Henry was, once again, jousting in a tournament, and, once again, Diane had tied her favour to his lance, but this time Henry was mortally wounded. He was said to have called out repeatedly for Diane, but she was never summoned, nor was she invited to the funeral.

Immediately afterwards, Catherine banished Diane from the royal court. Catherine was still the legitimate wife of the king, and now the mother of the new King of France. Diane had been outmanoeuvred and her time with Henry counted for nothing after his death. It is said that as Diane left the court for the last time, Catherine asked her to return all the jewellery that Henry had given her, a final humiliation. Diane, however, was far from destitute and had, over the years, accrued a fortune. She spent her remaining years in her chateau in Anet, Eure-et-Loir, where she lived a quiet life, far from the royal court. She died aged sixty-six.

The Dancing Plague

When people talk about disease in the Middle Ages, the things that spring to mind are the plague and the pox (which today we call smallpox). While these were major killers, all kinds of illnesses were lurking in the sewers and water supplies of urban medieval Europe. However, not all of them are as well known as those mentioned, so there follows two stories (in this article and the next one) to illustrate the lesser known.

The dancing plague, also known as St Vitus's Dance and choreomania, was a truly weird medieval phenomenon from central Europe. It involved spontaneous and continuous dancing by crowds of people until they collapsed through exhaustion – or worse, died. Bizarre as it sounds, choreomania was regularly reported by eyewitnesses and was of genuine concern to the authorities. It also seems to have been contagious. For example, in June of 1374, one of the widest outbreaks began in Aachen, Germany, before spreading to other places such as Cologne, Flanders, Utrecht and, later, Italy.

There were still outbreaks more than a century later. In Strasbourg in July 1518, a woman named Frau Troffea began dancing in the street. Within four days thirty-three others had joined her, and within a month there were 400, many of whom suffered heart attacks and died.

At the time some people believed that the dancing was a curse brought about by St Vitus, who was, according to Christian legend, a saint from Sicily, so they responded by praying and making pilgrimages to places dedicated to Vitus. The recovery of some victims further bolstered the perceived connection between the illness and the saint.

Because no autopsies were carried out and because medical science at the time could hardly be described as advanced, only guesses can be made as to the causes. It might have been some kind of skin infection or muscular inflammation leading to spasms, but who knows?

The Mystery of the 'Sweating Sickness'

From 1485 to 1551 a highly contagious and virulent disease attacked England and Western Europe. Accounts of this illness were written at the very start of a more scientific approach to medicine, however it was around centuries before germ theory, which means that we will probably never know exactly what it was.

The disease began suddenly, with a sense of apprehension, followed by cold and violent shivers and a headache, with severe pains in the neck, shoulders and limbs. This malady was accompanied by a feeling of overwhelming exhaustion. I am aware that this all sounds rather like a hangover or a bad cold, but it gets far worse. After the cold and shivering stage, which might last anywhere from thirty minutes to three hours, the hot and sweating stage followed. The characteristic sweat broke out suddenly, without any obvious cause, and was accompanied by headache, delirium, rapid pulse and intense thirst. Palpitation and pain in the heart were also frequent symptoms. In the final stages, there was either general exhaustion and collapse or an irresistible urge to sleep. One attack did not offer immunity, and some people suffered several bouts before dying.

There were at least four pandemics, and although the mortality rate was not as high as that for the Black Death, it was still in the tens of thousands. The illness changed the course of history when Arthur, Prince of Wales, the elder brother of Henry VIII, contracted it and died in 1502, while his widow, Catherine of Aragon, recovered. How different would British history have been if Arthur had lived to sire a male heir with Catherine?

The cause of the sickness was never discovered, and why it faded away is also unknown, but after 1578, it was never seen again in England.

The Battle of Sekigahara: the Japanese 'Battle of Hastings'

Those who regard social history as far more important than military history are right. The evolution of farming, civilisation and culture affect far more people than most battles. The trouble is, and with all due respect to the noble breed of social historians, social history is dull ... worthy, but mind-numbingly dull. Social historians can be bothered to work out things like the change in life expectancy after the introduction of industrialisation. On the other hand, the roar of the battlefield is usually more interesting to the casual observer. Occasionally, however, there is a battle that also changes society, and that is why the Battle of Hastings is so important to England. The year 1066 ended 250 years of regular Viking invasions, brought the downfall Anglo-Saxon Britain, and introduced feudalism; big changes, we can all agree.

It's the same sort of story for the year 1600 and the Battle of Sekigahara in Japan, when the eastern and western regions clashed in an epic civil war – a phenomenon that occurred frequently over the centuries in Japan. The problem was the regional warlords, who were not interested in peaceful relations with their neighbours.

Contrary to popular belief, the emperor did not rule Japan but fulfilled more of a religious and spiritual role. In short, the emperors ruled theoretically, but in reality they sat around being gods incarnate while the country tore itself to pieces, with samurai, ronin and ninjas slaughtering each other. The Battle of Sekigahara was between the Toyotomi clan and the Tokugawa clan. Tokugawa Ieyasu had once been a general to the Toyotomi but now fancied his chances as a supreme ruler.

This battle, by European standards, was huge: each side fielded more than 80,000 soldiers (by comparison, the Battle of Hastings had about 7,000 each). Tokugawa had a slight numerical inferiority, but he had secured the area and should have carried the day; in order to ensure his victory, he bribed two enemy generals, Kikkawa Hiroie and Kobayakawa Hideaki, to support him. As the Toyotomi forces spread out and threatened to attack Tokugawa on three sides, the bribery proved to have been a vital move, and Kikkawa's deliberate dithering managed to foil the Toyotomi plan.

However, it is Kobayakawa who is remembered in this epic battle. He sat with his troops and waited on a hill; he knew that by joining either side, he could tip the battle, but he waited for maximum advantage. Tokugawa was incensed that his erstwhile ally wasn't living up to his side of the bargain, so he ordered his artillery to open fire on Kobayakawa. This was a very daring move as it could well have convinced Kobayakawa to side with the Toyotomis, once and for all. However, this 'aggressive reminder' provoked the desired response, and Kobayakawa stirred himself from his hilltop position to join Tokugawa on the battlefield. Thus, victory was ensured.

The battle was important for a number of reasons: First of all, Tokugawa introduced the concept of a *shogun,* a king of Japan who could run things while the emperor sat in his palace being divine. Secondly, it finally brought much-needed stability to the political situation in Japan. The Tokugawa Shogunate enabled long-term peace and lasted into the mid-nineteenth century. It was also responsible for cutting off Japan from the rest of the world.

Further, Tokugawa moved the capital from Kyoto to his own stronghold of Edo, which we now call Tokyo. The usurper had won, but he brought peace and effective governance with him. Consequently, Tokugawa Ieyasu is seen as one the most important people in Japanese history.

Why Was the Longbow Such an Effective Weapon?

While not uniquely British, in the medieval era only British armies used the longbow in any number. I use the term 'British' deliberately. The bow seems to have originated in Wales, and during a rebellion Henry V (then Prince of Wales) was on the receiving end of an arrow in the face, fired from a longbow. The resulting scar explains why his portraits are only ever painted side-on from the other side. Henry saw the point (I'm sorry, I just had to) and used longbows with great effect years later at the legendary Battle of Agincourt. However, during the Hundred Years War the archers in the English king's army would invariably be a mixture of English and Welsh.

It is well known that these bows had great range and could pierce most armour, including that made from steel plate, which was then the pinnacle of medieval technology. But that isn't why they won. After all, the crossbow was similarly lethal (so lethal that the Vatican tried to ban its use against fellow Christians and decreed that it was fit only for animals and Saracens, but the ban was never seriously observed) and much preferred on the continent.

So, let's examine the two main reasons for the longbow's success.

First of all, a longbowman could fire twenty arrows in a minute, whereas a crossbowman would be lucky to fire two. This meant that 100 British archers could do the work of 1,000 Genoese mercenary crossbowmen. That made them a cheaper option not just in terms of cost per man, but also in terms of fewer mouths to feed. It's remarkable how many times that significantly smaller English armies were able to beat much larger and better equipped French armies. No one doubts the bravery or military prowess of the French, but these count for nothing if you can't get to the enemy because of mud and arrows.

Secondly, while the nobles were the highest born people in the land and had traditionally constituted the best fighting forces in any country, the average archer was a peasant, and as there were plenty of those, the nobles were always going to be horribly outnumbered. It didn't matter that the knights were stronger, taller and better trained, armed and clad. In any contest, a heavily armed knight was always going to win against numerous grubby peasants armed only with knives, but if the knight couldn't get to the peasant mob due to the blizzard of arrows raining down on him, then all the noble advantages in the world were going to count for nothing.

As suggested above, the longbow had a further advantage simply because there were so many of them. This particular bow was made from a single piece of wood, and it could be crafted easily and quickly. Compared to the days needed to make a crossbow, a medieval longbow could be produced in just a few hours .... so it was cheaper than a crossbow, peasants were plentiful and cheaper than mercenaries, and the arrows could be fired quickly. Put all these together and the only conclusion is that hand-to-hand chivalric combat was killed off by illiterate peasants.

However, the use of mercenaries was not entirely eliminated because of the one not insignificant disadvantage of the longbow: it took a long time not only to train a man to use one, but to develop the immense physical strength required to pull the bow. (Indeed, several kings of England banned football, partly because football in those days was little more than an excuse to riot, but mainly because they didn't want the adult male population to be distracted from longbow training.) Over the years, the whole body was affected. Battlefield archaeologists can always spot the skeletons of longbow archers because their spines have been altered by all the years of tensing and pulling the bow string.

When you consider that Edward III ordered up two million arrows for one campaign, you can understand what the French knights were up against.

The 'Devil's Bible' or the Codex Gigas

This *Codex Gigas* is the largest medieval manuscript in the world. Its dimensions are huge: 92 cm tall, 50 cm wide and 22 cm thick, and it weighs 74.8 kg. It takes two men to lift it. It was completed in Bohemia in the thirteenth century, but after the area was attacked by the Swedes during the Thirty Years War it now resides in the National Library in Stockholm. The whole book has been digitised on their website (www.kb.se/codex-gigas), and if you take a look, you can see why it's sometimes called the 'Devil's Bible'. The horrific image is a 50 cm high drawing of the Devil, and there's a tale that goes with it.

A monk who broke his vows was walled up in his cell and told to complete a book full of all human knowledge in just one night. So he made a pact with the Devil and created the codex.

Great story; obviously not true. However, on closer inspection the prominent depiction of the Devil is facing a picture of Heaven, so overall it's a 'good vs evil' image and, therefore, not some kind of satanic book.

What is impressive is that the whole book was written and illustrated by just one man, and not (as was usual for the age) the work of a team of monks. It is estimated that it would have taken five years of constant work or, more likely, twenty-five years of regular writing to produce. The result is the work of one monk's whole adult life in one enormous volume. The rest of the book is mainly the Bible in Latin, but there are also incantations, instructions for the conduct of exorcisms, and even historical records and calendars.

Nowadays such a huge collection of writing and random musings are what appears on a Facebook page.

The Story of the Palestinian Who Became English

St George is the Patron Saint of England, but how did a Roman soldier, born in Palestine, who never went to England, get that honour?

The story of the real St George is the simple tale of a Roman officer in the early fourth century AD who refused to renounce his Christian faith and was executed for it ... and that's it. Sorry, no dragons.

However, in the medieval era saints became associated with certain roles: Mary was the mother of all women; St Honoré became the patron saint of bakers, and as St George was a soldier, he became the patron saint of knights, soldiers and men of war.

For a religion supposedly about peace, Christianity has been calling on military-based miracles for centuries. It started with the pagan Emperor Constantine, who had visions of 'the cross' before his pivotal battle at the Milvian Bridge. That was in the fourth century AD, so by the era of the crusades there had been more than 600 years of calling on God/Jesus/saints to help out in times of violence.

George became the protector of knights in battle and is reported to have appeared by the sides of crusaders at the Siege of Antioch during the First Crusade. The description of his presence at the battle is as matter-of-fact as that of any of the nobles who featured in the siege. It seemed logical to the medieval mind that of course the warrior saint would be helping this Christian pilgrimage to reclaim the Holy Land.

However, we have to go to the fourteenth century to see the specific connection with England, when in 1337 Edward III, King of England, claimed the throne of France, which triggered the dynastic feuding that would later be dubbed the Hundred Years War. In 1346 the French, with lots of Genoese crossbowmen, and the English, with lots more Welsh archers, faced each other at Crécy.

By the end of the day, the French nobility had been massacred. They barely reached the English frontlines for the volleys of longbow arrows (Edward used the first cannons in Europe on that day, too). If victory was sent by Heaven, than the warrior saint had deserted the French. This logic evolved into 'if the French had been abandoned, then the English had been shown special favour'. So St George had clearly blessed the English, and therefore it was on a bloody, corpse-strewn battlefield in France that George became 'English'.

However, the English do not have a monopoly on this saint. George is also the Patron Saint of Portugal, Russia and, of course, Georgia, the country that's named after him. The real George (if that was even his name) never visited any of these places either.

Similarly, St Patrick, often dubbed the most famous Irishman in the world, wasn't Irish. He had earlier been enslaved by Irish pirates, so he was either English or Welsh. And St Andrew never went to Scotland. Only St David, the Patron Saint of Wales, came from the country he became patron of.

The Real Game of Thrones

Game of Thrones is a popular book and TV series, which claims to have many historical influences. One particularly grisly moment in series three (there's a spoiler here if you haven't seen the series or read the books) has a less well known but genuine historical antecedent.

The 'Red Wedding' was TV gold, and if you haven't seen people's reactions as they watched it (on YouTube), that's entertainment in itself. The primary event of the Red Wedding is a massacre when two rival factions are meant to be healing their wounds through marriage. The wedding, however, is a trap to lure in one group and wipe them out. Using the element of surprise combined with horrific brutality, the plot succeeds. All of this seems to be based on the so-called Black Dinner, during which there was a spectacular massacre in fifteenth-century Scotland.

The Stewart Dynasty of Scotland (and later England) had very bad luck. When James I of Scotland was murdered in 1437, his seven-year-old son, James II, became the heir apparent. There was then an unseemly scrabble as to which aristocratic family would 'protect' young James.

In 1440 a dinner was arranged to resolve the matter once and for all. William Crichton, the Lord Chancellor, and Alexander Livingston invited the powerful Clan Douglas to the banquet, but halfway through the meal a black bull's head was brought out (an old Scottish symbol of death). This was the signal for the resident guards to turn on the Douglas Clan and drag them out into the courtyard, where they were given a mock trial and beheaded.

The incident finished the Douglas Clan as major players in Scottish politics for more than a decade. Twelve years later, the Douglas Clan again lost their leader when the newly crowned James II demanded William Douglas swear allegiance to him (rather than the oath he'd sworn to the English king). When William declined, James murdered him with his own dagger.

James II was killed by one of his own siege guns at Roxburgh Castle in 1460, and despite the setbacks the Douglas Clan gained status and dominance over many of the other clans in the next few decades.

So yes, this was all pretty much like *Game of Thrones.*

Was There a 'Renaissance'?

The gut response to this question is 'of course there was; don't be ridiculous'. But as always with defined eras, they tend to unravel when subjected to close scrutiny.

The first problem is that scholars cannot agree when the Renaissance happened. The fall of Constantinople is usually regarded as the trigger, because this resulted in the flow of eastern scholars and texts to Western Europe. It was the spark that ignited a rediscovery of ancient learning. There can be no doubt that when Constantinople fell to the Ottomans in 1453, many Byzantines fled west; when it comes to defining all things 'Renaissance', however, it's difficult to understand why an ancient poet like Plutarch, dead long before the fall, is included. Donatello, who is also considered to be a Renaissance figure, was an old man by 1453, and his greatest works had already been produced.

The connection between Constantinople and this movement of literature, science and art is an uneasy one.

The next issue is, how widespread was the Renaissance? The *Mona Lisa* and the Sistine Chapel are both wondrous and represent huge leaps forward from medieval art. But (and it's an important 'but') how many people saw them at the time? These were created for the fabulously wealthy, and the peasants of Italy or France would not have had better lives because of these great works of art.

True, the statue of *David* in Florence was intended for public consumption, but nobody claims that one sculpture triggered a complete change in the structure of society. For the vast majority of Europe's population in the fifteenth century, life plodded on, full of plague, back-breaking work and the occasional rampaging army. Art and poetry were nowhere on the daily agenda.

The final point raises the question of how much changed from, say, 1450 to 1550. Europe still had monarchs, endless wars, the papacy and, now, the Inquisition. Books were for the rich (even after the printing press had been invented), and the vast majority of the population was an illiterate, god-fearing peasantry. Gunpowder weapons may have developed, but they had existed since before 1453 and improvements were due as much to the evolution and refinement of an idea as to some magical era of change.

The biggest change to Europe in this era was the Reformation: the permanent dissolution of the Pope's monopoly of Christian doctrine. However, that was initiated by a German priest who was disgusted with the corruption of the papacy, rather than a man who was inspired by the writings of Plutarch and the astronomical discoveries of Copernicus. In other words, it's likely the Reformation would have happened with or without the artistic and scientific movements in Italy.

Like the Hundred Years War, the Renaissance is a term created generations later to summarise an era. Nobody at the time thought they were in an era called the Renaissance. Other terms like medieval, gothic, or (even worse) the Dark Ages are all lazy (and sometimes deliberately insulting) anachronisms.

The Battle of the Spurs, or How Henry VIII Won an Expected Victory

In the year 1513, Jacques de La Palice, the Grand Master of France, was on his way to the Pas-de-Calais to fight a large coalition army made up of King Henry VIII's English forces and the Holy Roman Emperor Maximillian's German forces.

The coalition was besieging eastern French towns, so La Palice headed the elite French heavy cavalry to allow him to move quickly to break the sieges as well as to push back the invasion forces. La Palice may have had the cream of French chivalry on his side, but he had numbers of only around 7,000, while the allies had an army of around 30,000. In other words, the French were outnumbered more than four to one.

Even worse for the French, they lost the element of surprise and were ambushed. As expected, the larger army won, having lost only a few men, while La Palice lost around half his force.

La Palice managed to escape, and nine years later turned up as the chief negotiator for a peace treaty with the new Holy Roman Emperor, Charles V. The negotiations failed, the war continued, and in 1525 La Palice was captured at the Battle of Pavia, another crushing French defeat. La Palice was later executed. The reasons to relate this are twofold.

First of all, the account shows Henry VIII in an unusual light. At the time he was still married to wife number one, he was a vigorous warrior as well as a king, and he was capable of winning victories against France. Henry was able to operate in the Pas-de-Calais area with ease because Calais was still an English territory. This battle was part of the Italian wars, when Germany, Spain, England and Venice fought against France and her allies to protect the papacy from unwanted French influence. It was also these wars that were to have two lasting effects on Henry's reign: first, his flagship the *Mary Rose* sank during this conflict; and second, the Pope was so pleased with Henry's actions (and his later personal letters rebuffing Protestantism) that Henry was given the title 'Defender of the Faith' (ironically, Henry kept the title after the split from the Roman Catholic Church, and today the British monarch is the Defender of the Faith even though it's a different faith from the original). It is in this context that Henry is seen as the young Catholic warrior king – not quite the image he has today – and it would be fair to say that this is probably the way Henry would want to be remembered, rather than as the fat guy with serious marital issues.

The second reason to write about this is to make a more general point. If you like your military history, stop reading about Stalingrad, Waterloo or Thermopylae. Less than 1 per cent of battles get mass coverage. The reality is that there are thousands of battles, campaigns, sometimes even wars, that have been forgotten (some of them have been highlighted in this book). Many prove the point that the better prepared, larger army wins more often than not; it's the exceptions that get the headlines, like the Battle of Agincourt. But it's disrespectful to all the men who died in these forgotten conflicts that we concentrate only on the well-trodden history of the most famous.

Was Lucrezia Borgia All That Bad?

Lucrezia was the only daughter of Pope Alexander VI, Rodrigo Lanzol de Borgia, who was not big on celibacy, but to be fair, he had all of his children before becoming Pope. Lucrezia was married three times, and as part of the Borgia family her name is inextricably linked to its debauchery and treachery.

At the age of thirteen she was married off to Giovanni Sforza. The marriage was intended to extend the Borgia power base into Sforza territory, but when allegiances changed and Pope Alexander no longer needed the Sforzas, so he sent assassins to get rid of the problem. Lucrezia found out about the plot and warned her husband, who fled. When the assassination failed, Alexander asked Giovanni to divorce his daughter, but Giovanni resisted and accused Lucrezia of incest with her brothers and her father. Alexander playfully retaliated with the suggestion that he (Alexander) should annul the marriage on the grounds of impotence. Alexander won and Giovanni was humiliated by having to sign a document to verify his impotence.

The charges of incest that have clung to Lucrezia for 500 years come from a bitter man who used the accusation as a political tool. However, she did appear to be pregnant during the proceedings, so either the baby was her husband's and he was a fully functioning male, or (more likely) she had a lover. Either way, she retired to a convent, and the next time she appeared there was no child with her. If there was one, it would probably have been adopted.

In 1498, aged eighteen, she married Alfonso d'Aragon, who was subsequently murdered after he made an enemy of Cesare Borgia. Again, there is no reason to think that Lucrezia had blood on her hands, but there was gossip that she had poisoned her husband. In fact, almost any aristocrat in Renaissance Italy was at risk of assassination; it was an occupational hazard. In any case, Lucrezia was looking for her third husband at the age of just twenty.

In 1502 she married the Duke of Ferrera. They had a number of children, and after all the other Borgias had died she appeared to have a relatively happy marriage. Following complications from childbirth, she died in 1519 at the age of thirty-nine.

Putting aside the gossip and considering the facts, Lucrezia was an average aristocratic woman. Her reputation as an incestuous serial poisoner does her a great injustice.

John Dee: Scientist, Astrologer ... Magician?

Some people have such bizarre lives that they get hijacked by conspiracy theorists or pseudo New Age historians. John Dee is just such a man.

Born in 1527 in London, this Elizabethan scholar, like many scientists of the time, not only studied orthodox science, but also what would now be considered pseudo-science. Sir Isaac Newton is one of the 'greats' of science, but 150 years after Dee, Newton spent more time studying alchemy than gravity.

To put John Dee in context, many of the great scientists before the modern era found themselves in the weird dead-ends of superstitious study. This does not make any of them powerful wizards, and Dee was no more a magician than the better-known Leonardo da Vinci or Nicolaus Copernicus.

Dee gained respect and prestige through the scientific study of navigation; he trained many of England's most courageous navigators during the Elizabethan Age. He was so highly regarded that he mingled with the most powerful English nobles and even tutored the young Queen Elizabeth I. However, it was his creation of the Enochian language, an alleged divine language spoken by angels, which has led to the exaggeration of John Dee's mystical connections by contemporary occult writers.

Enochian has an alphabet of twenty-two hieroglyphic symbols, not readily equitable to any other known alphabet. It's said to be proof of Dee's ability to use real magic and that no human could create from scratch such a complex and complete language. Unfortunately, on closer inspection, the language is not perfect, nor is it as complex as something like Latin. Subsequently, many people have created languages with their own alphabet, grammar and vocabulary, for example, Tolkien's Elvish or Star Trek's Klingon.

Dee himself was a devout Christian, and it's highly unlikely he wanted to dabble in anything dark and un-godlike. The language could just be an example of a smart man creating something because he had too much time on his hands. As his influence in Elizabeth's court waned, it became something of an obsession; perhaps it was just an old man casting around to gain recognition once again. What it certainly was not was emphatic proof of Dee's ability to commune with spirits. Saying that, an internet search will take you to connections between Dee and demons and, of course, Atlantis ...

The Greatest Admiral You've Never Heard Of

Unless you're Korean, Yi Sun-Sin is a man you are unlikely to have heard of, but he has a great story. Throughout the ages, the Koreans have suffered waves of invasions from China, the Mongols and the Japanese.

After passing his military examinations in 1576, Yi became an officer and, later, a general in the army. During this time the Jurchen people from Manchuria regularly invaded Korea. Yi's successes in battle meant that by 1583 he had crushed the invaders and captured their chief. The Jurchen incursions ended and Yi was the man of the hour. His acclaim was so great that he was imprisoned by a rival general so as not to garner too much power and admiration. The undefeated general was a prisoner in his own country.

His incarceration was relatively brief, but it was an appalling way to treat a national hero. After a few years of lying low, Yi saw that the political landscape in Korea was changing. This allowed him to climb his way up the military ranks once again, and by 1591, rather than being a general in charge of an army, he was an admiral in charge of the navy.

His promotion came just in time, because between 1592 and 1598 the Japanese repeatedly attempted to invade Korea as a springboard into China. Yi understood that because the Japanese had more in the way of resources, Korea was in great danger.

The Koreans built stouter ships than the Japanese. Their design meant they had more cannons and could sustain more damage than the Japanese, but even so Yi was often outnumbered. Knowing he had less of everything, Yi ensured that his navy was fighting fit, that its logistics were up to scratch and that his ships were in a good state of repair (even after a naval victory, damage would have been inflicted on the fleet).

His tactics worked like a dream. Over the next six years, he fought a total of twenty-three naval battles against the invading Japanese. Each one may not have been a crushing victory, but he terrorised the Japanese vessels.

An example of this was the key battle of Myeongnyang in the autumn of 1597. In this engagement Yi had thirteen ships against 133 (the numbers are contested). This battle followed a major naval defeat for the Koreans, so it was seen as a last stand.

Yi anchored his 'turtle' ships in the Myeongnyang Strait. Initially the current brought the Japanese in, and the heavier Korean ships soaked up the damage as they pounded and sank numerous oncoming Japanese vessels. Then the current changed and led the Japanese vessels away from the battle. Their sheer number soon became a hindrance as they collided into each other, which allowed

Yi and the Koreans to pour on the cannon fire. Thirty-one Japanese vessels were severely damaged or sunk, with no losses for the Koreans.

Yi was so effective that the Japanese had to use a double agent to discredit him. Amazingly, this worked, and once again he was imprisoned and tortured. The (useless) King Seonjo of Korea wanted to have him executed, but calmer heads prevailed. Yi was released (again) and allowed to return to his post, where this remarkable man resumed his duties as if nothing had happened.

In the winter of 1598, Yi was winning against the Japanese at the Battle of Noryang when he was struck under the armpit by a bullet. He knew he was dying but did not want to let something as minor as his own death jeopardise another victory. At his request, Yi's nephew wore his armour, and the battle was won. The Japanese invasion faltered and Korea was saved. When the news came out that Yi had died, the entire navy wailed in grief and shrines were erected in his honour. It is unsurprising that Yi Sun-Sin is a national hero in Korea to this day.

William the Silent Didn't Die Quietly

William I, Prince of Orange, known as William the Silent, was a wealthy nobleman serving the Habsburgs as the governor of the Spanish Netherlands. He was, however, no puppet. Unhappy with the centralisation of political power away from the local estates and the Spanish persecution of Dutch Protestants, William joined the Dutch uprising and turned against his former masters. To the Habsburgs this was the highest form of treason, and William knew he was a wanted man.

William turned out to be the most capable of rebels, not only in terms of politics and diplomacy, but also in war. He steered the Dutch to several successes in the fight against the Spanish, and it was this rebellion that led to the so-called Eighty Years War.

William is an example of an important man who has been largely forgotten, and a reminder of how little history makes it into the general consciousness: he's not even that well remembered in the Netherlands. But it isn't his silence in history that gave him his nickname. This came from the fact that he was a serious and thoughtful individual. Compared with the rowdy and loquacious monarchs of Europe, William was the quiet ruler of the age.

William's successful rise as a rebel leader led Philip II of Spain to declare him a 'pest on the whole of Christianity and the enemy of the human race' and put a price on his head of 25,000 crowns – enough to make anyone fabulously wealthy. There was a spiritual precedent to this, as around this time the Pope signed a decree stating that killing the Protestant Queen Elizabeth of England would get the same favour with God as going on crusade against the infidels.

In 1581 Balthasar Gerardts vowed to carry out the will of Catholic Philip and played a very long game indeed. Balthasar joined the Dutch Army, hoping that as an armed guard he would have a legitimate opportunity to get close to William; after two years of fighting for a cause he didn't believe in, However, he gave up on the plan. He went to the Duke of Parma to see if the duke could get him near William, but Parma wasn't interested.

So after years of trial and error, in 1584 Balthasar bought two wheel-lock pistols, the height of firearms technology at the time. Then he simply asked for an audience with William and shot him twice in the chest. William died almost immediately, although his last words were reportedly,

My God, have pity on my soul; my God, have pity on this poor people.

Balthasar tried to escape, but the gunshots were so loud that William's household was immediately alerted and he was quickly captured. Once in custody, Balthasar was shown no mercy, and even for the times his punishment was seen as cruel and unusual. The Dutch magistrates decreed that his right hand should be burned off with a red-hot iron, that his flesh should be torn from his bones in six different places, that he should be quartered and disembowelled alive, that his heart should be torn from his chest and flung in his face, and finally, that his head should be cut off.

William was the first head of state ever to be assassinated with a gun, so the event marks historic change. Up until this point, assassins would leap forward with a dagger, as in the case of Edward I, who managed to kill his assailant with a wooden stool, or Ottoman Sultan Murad I who had no stool, only bodyguards. After the 1580s, the technology of killing changed fundamentally. Since William was felled by those gunshots, we have seen many political leaders suffer the same fate.

The Accidental Start of a Dynasty

In 1589, with the death of the childless Henry III, his cousin Henry IV became the first French Bourbon monarch. This was the start of a long-running and important dynasty that was to last through the French Revolution and beyond.

Henry was also the first Protestant King of France, but this proved to be so controversial that he converted to Catholicism ... which managed to please no one. The Catholics saw him as a usurper, and the Protestants saw him as a traitor (as a Huguenot, he had already survived vicious sectarian violence). He obviously had a sense of humour about this highly fraught situation, because he was quoted as saying (about why he converted to Catholicism),

Paris is worth a Mass.

However, despite his sense of humour, he was in constant mortal danger. Henry was the monarch that survived at least a dozen assassination attempts (uncovered or attempted). His private life may have been one of persistent threats, but in reality his reign brought a period of relative stability and an end to the religious wars that had raged through France for decades.

Henry turned out to be a natural diplomat: he helped to end a war of succession in Germany, and brokered a treaty with the Ottoman Empire which gave France a number of advantageous trade concessions in the eastern empire.

Overall he was a remarkably tolerant king, much less bellicose than other French Monarchs and open to all forms of Christian worship. Unfortunately, his luck ran out in 1610. He was stuck in traffic (even kings had that problem), which was backed up due, in part, to his wife's coronation. While the royal procession remained stationary, a Catholic fanatic, François Ravaillac, managed to jump into the carriage and murder the king.

After his death, Henry became known as 'Good King Henry', despite the fact that he was the founder of the Bourbon Dynasty, which is probably best remembered for its Louis (that's Louis plural). It was his grandson who was the famous Louis XIV, the Sun King, but that's another story.

Hoist by His Own Petard

'Hoist by his own petard' is a phrase originally used (and only once) in Shakespeare's *Hamlet*. It is a phrase we have all heard, and most of us even know what it means: your plans have been defeated by your own actions; you have nobody to blame but yourself.

But what exactly is a 'petard', and how could it end up hurting you? I thought it was some sort of pike that you could easily get entangled in. I was wrong. A petard is an explosive device used in sieges. It is basically a bomb at the end of a rod (or rods) that is propped up against a wall and then detonated to create a breach.

This would mean that with the invention of gunpowder, an attacking force now had a new way into the fortification it was besieging and, predictably enough, they were used by most of the armies of Europe during the era of gunpowder.

The phrase refers to the concussive blast that comes from the petard exploding. If the operator was directly behind it as he ran away from the lit fuse, the blast could hurl him into the air, hence, 'hoist (or hoisted) by his own petard'. The correct procedure was to run from it perpendicularly – that way the blast couldn't catch you.

Now you can enthral everyone with this little-known pearl of knowledge.

The Greatest Swordsman in History

The greatest swordsman in history was a ronin (a masterless samurai) called Miyamoto Musashi. Born around 1584, he had his first duel at the age of just thirteen and won. He had his second when he was sixteen. While neither opponent was a sword master, it was a precocious start to a career that would stretch for decades. Among other battles, he fought in the pivotal Japanese Battle of Sekigahara in 1600 ... on the losing side, which wasn't his fault.

Musashi wasn't a typical Japanese warrior. For one thing, he had some kind of skin condition (probably eczema), which made him ugly, and, shockingly for a samurai or ronin, he was scruffy, not to mention he was quite often late for his duels, something else that was regarded as disgraceful in feudal Japan. What was even more controversial was that he quite often used a *bokken*, a wooden practice sword, in duels (sometimes against opponents using the *katana*, a steel sword). Make no mistake, the *bokken* could still knock you unconscious, or possibly even kill you, but it was less lethal than a *katana*. To lose a duel against a man wielding a training weapon was a disgrace: a fate worse than death for a samurai.

Two clashes in particular made his reputation. Around the age of twenty-one, Musashi went to Kyoto to challenge the head of the Yoshioka School (a training camp for some of the best swordsmen) to a duel. Musashi arrived late and he won with a *bokken*, concussing the master of the school and humiliating him in front of his pupils. The master's brother sought revenge and a second duel ensued, which Musashi also won. By now Musashi had caused a lot of trouble and stirred up a great deal of bad feeling in Kyoto, but the school's swordsmen got him to agree to a meeting near the Ichijo-ji Temple, where they planned to ambush him and force him into a third duel. However, on this occasion Musashi arrived early, saw the host of swordsmen waiting for him, and counter-intuitively surprised them when he attacked on his own. Exactly how many men were waiting is unknown, but numbers as high as eighty have been suggested. While that is surely an exaggeration, one man beating even a dozen trained samurai would be an amazing feat. Musashi recounted how he had to draw his secondary sword to protect himself as he carried out his onslaught singlehandedly. He was seriously outnumbered but finally fought the swordsmen to a standstill, having killed many from the finest school in Kyoto.

Musashi would have been automatically considered the greatest swordsmen of his generation had it not been for the lethally efficient Sasaki Kojiro, who was everything Musashi wasn't: noble, refined and clinical. Kojiro was a master of the *nodachi*, which was a two-handed samurai sword, much longer than a *katana*. It was inevitable that the two would meet in a duel, which took place in 1612 on the beach of Funajima Island. Musashi was late (as usual), had no formal head scarf so had used a dish cloth to tie back his hair, and forgot his *bokken* so instead improvised with a whittled-down oar. The duel was settled by a simultaneous strike from the two masters. Kojiro's blade was close enough to cut the dish cloth from Musashi's head, but at the same time, Musashi brained Kojiro with the oar.

It turned out Musashi knew that Kojiro was so well drilled in all the weapons in Japan that he would never deliberately position himself within striking range of Musashi. Musashi had calculated to stand a hair's breadth within his opponent's reach with the *nodachi*, while Kojiro had misjudged the length of Musashi's DIY *bokken* and paid for the error with his life.

These are just two of Musashi's most famous encounters, but he travelled for years around Japan, fighting duels and honing his skills against the best swordsmen the samurai class of Japan had to offer. It is therefore hard not to think of him as the greatest swordsmen who ever lived (although it's a little ironic that his preferred weapon of choice wasn't a sword).

In 1615, after perfecting his swordsmanship, he became a construction supervisor, overseeing the building of Akashi Castle, among others. Later he became known as a philosopher, writer, artist and sculptor. Musashi is a legend in Japan and should be better known around the world.

Chocolate Has a Strange History

Chocolate is derived from Theobroma cacao seeds, better known as cocoa beans, which are indigenous to South America. The very earliest evidence of chocolate being processed for human consumption comes from drinking cups that have been dated to around 1750 BC. These were found in Olmec sites, Central America's earliest great civilisation, predating the Maya and Aztecs by about two millennia. This means the history of chocolate is nearly 4,000 years old.

Chocolate has been consumed mainly as a drink for most of history. The Aztec version was drunk in its purest form, so it was quite bitter, but chillies were added to make it spicy. They called their drink *xocolatl*, or *chocolatl,* to be a little more phonetic about it. The word means 'bitter water' and is a clear indicator that the original recipe was not some kind of dessert.

There is evidence to suggest that cocoa became integral to all of the societies of Mesoamerica. The Maya used the drink in some religious ceremonies, and the Aztecs accepted cocoa beans as tribute. They even used it as currency at times, making it far more than just a treat. Chocolate has been found to contain antioxidants and caffeine in small amounts and has been shown to lower blood pressure, so chocolate, in its pure form, does you good.

Chocolate as a bitter drink was not an immediate hit in Europe. While Columbus did bring some back to Spain (in one of his later voyages), it took a few decades for the Spanish court to acquire a taste for *chocolatl*. Cocoa beans were only regularly available after Cortés conquered the Aztecs by means of stunning brutality and cold-blooded murder. The fall of the Aztec Empire is thought to have involved the death of around 250,000 people. Are cocoa beans worth such a price?

It was about this time that either sugar or honey was added to sweeten and enhance the rich flavour. The recipe for cocoa was a jealously guarded secret and its consumption became a status symbol associated with the Spanish court, which got a taste for the drink in the early sixteenth century. It was regarded not only as a novel delicacy, but as a sign of their dominions across the ocean.

It was also during this period that England was carrying out government-backed piracy against Spanish shipping in the Atlantic. These so-called 'privateers' were after gold, silver and precious gems, so they didn't know what to do with the sacks of cocoa beans in the cargo. Finding the beans to be inedible and of an unknown origin, the privateers usually cast them overboard, not realising they had found something that was, in some ways, more valuable than the precious metals they had plundered.

By the seventeenth century the secret of chocolate had clearly leaked out, and cocoa was becoming a popular drink around Europe. However, as demand grew, so did the need to produce both the beans and the sugar to sweeten them. Crops of sugar cane and cocoa beans require back-breaking work, and so the need for slaves also increased.

Yes, one of the drivers for the brutal and inhuman black slave trade was Europe's appetite not only for chocolate, but for sugar too. Again the question arises, was the love of cocoa worth the price?

By the eighteenth and nineteenth centuries, chocolate was widely available as a sweet drink or, now, as a solid confectionary. It had taken a couple of centuries, but chocolate consumption in Europe had evolved into something we recognise today. The original drink was all but forgotten. (Side note: Cadbury World near Birmingham used to have an area on the history of chocolate that included a chance to taste the original Aztec recipe. I tried it and liked it, but it was so different to what most people were expecting that they stopped offering it.)

The great irony in all of this is that as its popularity rose, the areas in the Americas where it was cultivated prospered (which was also true for the other two popular exports from America: tobacco and potatoes. Imagine a world without these three things). Using slave labour, many European empires began growing it in other tropical countries, and today West Africa produces almost two-thirds of the world's cocoa, with the Ivory Coast producing 43 per cent of the world's cocoa beans.

So, from a bitter drink, to currency, to a catalyst for mass slavery, the history of chocolate is long, complex and unexpectedly bloody. That's worth remembering the next time you get a craving.

Could These Be the Coolest Women Ever?

Unless you're Japanese and love your feudal history, *Onna-Bugeisha* is a phrase you will probably not have heard before. The term was used for female warriors of the noble class in feudal Japan. The term 'samurai' is strictly masculine, but the *Onna-Bugeisha* were women who received similar training in martial arts and strategy, so they are essentially female samurai, and along with their male counterparts they were known to participate in combat. The traditional role of a Japanese noblewoman was that of a homemaker and mother, and as historical texts offer relatively few accounts of these female warriors it was assumed they were a tiny minority.

However, new evidence shows a different story. For example, remains from the site of the Battle of Senbon Matsubaru in 1580 were DNA-tested, and thirty-five out of 105 bodies were female. The remains were all heads, showing either death in battle or ritual dismemberment after the fight. This would imply that the sight of warrior women on the battlefield in feudal Japan was commonplace, compared with almost all Asian, Middle Eastern and European cultures. Their weapon of choice was usually the *naginata*, a spear with a curved, sword-like blade that was versatile yet relatively light.

While there are legendary stories of earlier female warriors, the first solid evidence of these female fighters comes from a civil war in Japan in the 1180s, when the widowed Tomoe Gozen fought as an *Onna-Bugeisha*. This means there were female warriors for centuries in feudal Japan. As the samurai are considered some of the best-trained and most lethal warriors in history, this has to make the *Onna-Bugeisha* the most fearsome women – ever.

THE EARLY MODERN TO THE VICTORIANS

The Sack of Baltimore

On reading the title you might think this has something to do with American history, but it doesn't. In southern Ireland there is a small village called Baltimore. It had little to contribute to history until the summer of 1631, when it was attacked – but by whom?

Was it the French planning an invasion of England via the Emerald Isle? Or perhaps it was some kind of pro-Catholic uprising, leading to a vicious English assault? Or the Spanish getting up to their old tricks? These are all reasonable guesses, but they're all way off the mark, and this is where fact becomes a lot more bizarre than fiction.

You might be surprised to learn that the perpetrators were about as exotic as they come in the seventeenth century. They were Barbary pirates from North Africa, led by a Dutch captain and Muslim convert-turned-pirate Jan Janszoon van Haarlem, also known as Murad Reis the Younger.

The attack was quick and unexpected. The villagers (mainly English settlers, but some native Irish, too) were taken captive and forced into slavery. Because there were different types of slavery, some prisoners were destined to live out their days as galley slaves (a brutal and short life) while many of the younger women would spend long years in the seclusion of the sultan's harem or labouring within the walls of the sultan's palace. Sadly, it is thought that only three of the settlers ever saw Ireland again.

This wasn't the only raid by Muslim pirates on the British Isles. During the English Civil War, the island of Lundy (the largest island in the Bristol Channel) was captured and, for a few years, was technically part of the Ottoman Empire. On this occasion there was no mass enslavement as the island rarely had inhabitants.

What Exactly Is a 'Harem'?

The word 'harem' instantly fills the mind with bevvies of beautiful women, veiled and dressed in silks, languishing on sofas, eating exotic fruits from golden trays. Most of this is Western fantasy, so what really happened in the harem ... apart from ... y'know?

Harem is a Turkish word taken from the Arabic *ḥaram*, which means forbidden. The Ottoman harem is probably the best-known example, though it was certainly not the only one. At the height of the Ottoman Empire, the sultans lived in Topkapi Palace, and its harem was the private living quarters of the sultan and his family, which included the sultan's mother, wives, daughters, other female relatives, and concubines. It was home to dozens, sometimes hundreds, of women, most of whom were there to work as servants and many of whom were little more than slaves.

The harem quarters were separate from the rest of the palace and were guarded by black eunuchs (who were there not only to protect the residents, but to ensure that all of the children were the sultan's). None of the women in the Ottoman harem were 'Turkish', nor were they born Muslim. Islam forbids the enslavement of other Muslims, so young Christian (often Greek) girls from around the empire were brought (sometimes kidnapped) to spend the rest of their lives in this golden prison. Once inside, women rarely got out again.

Apart from the eunuch overseers, the only males allowed in the harem were the sultan and his sons, up to the age of sixteen. The older boys were usually schooled and kept separate from the rest of the harem. There are cases where a future sultan's potential rivals were kept in so-called gilded cages, essentially awaiting execution when the new sultan ascended the throne.

Let's digress, for a moment, to consider the implications of every sultan's mother being European. It meant that, after a few generations, the sultans simply didn't look very 'Turkish'. Some sultans had blue eyes, and there are records of some dying their beards in order to look more like ethnic Turks. By the time the Ottoman state had reached its pinnacle in the 1500s, Sultan Suleiman the Magnificent (sometimes referred to as the 'Grand Turk') was about as Turkish as the King of England.

But for all that, the harem was a family home; it was also a hierarchy of power, mimicking in many ways the hierarchy of power in the outside world. If the sultan was in charge of his empire, it was his mother who ruled supreme in the harem, and woe betide anyone who crossed her. The wives came next in the hierarchy, their status directly connected to the order in which they were married.

In keeping with Islamic tradition, the sultan could have four wives, but he could also have countless concubines – women who were there purely for his pleasure – and this is where the competition became cut-throat. The concubines were instructed in harem etiquette and learned how to amuse and entertain the sultan in various ways, perhaps by playing musical instruments or reciting poetry. Most certainly they would be instructed about his tastes in the bedroom, but a new arrival might not see the sultan for years – if ever.

Every concubine was anxious to catch the sultan's eye, hoping to become a 'gözde', a favourite. At best, she might become a wife or, if not a wife, perhaps she might bear a son. Although it was almost always the son of a wife who inherited the throne, even giving birth to a son gave a concubine increased power and status. So the harem was full of scheming women who were desperate to improve their lot in whatever way they could. If there was luxury and glamour, there was also intrigue and murder.

More than anything, every mother wanted to ensure that it was her son who gained the throne, and most were prepared to lie, cheat, manipulate and even kill to achieve this end. In this mini-world of power politics, more than one mother saw her son – or sons – murdered in cold blood so that another might see her son ascend to the throne. For generations, new sultans observed the tradition of strangling their brothers and half-brothers (no royal blood was spilled!) in order to avoid rival claims and to ensure the line of succession was pure. This changed when it was finally recognised for the barbaric act that it was.

I think we can conclude that the dark side of harem life showed women to be just as ruthless as men in the pursuit of power, position and wealth.

Why Do Men Wear Ties?

Nobody likes wearing ties, so why do men wear them, and where did they come from? Scarves go back millennia, but the idea of a thin cloth necktie dates back to the scarves of the Croatian mercenaries who fought in the Thirty Years War in Europe (1618–48). The neckties became popular in Paris, where the name Croat is the term for 'cravat', the item which is the basis of today's tie.

The originals were popular for a long time and evolved into elaborate lace cravats. However, like all fashions, they began to fade. Sometime in the late eighteenth century, however, cravats began to reappear in Western Europe. This can be attributed to a group of young men called the Macaronis (as mentioned in the song 'Yankee Doodle Dandy'), young Englishmen who returned from Europe, bringing with them new ideas about fashion (and learning) from Italy. The French contemporaries of the Macaronis were called the Incroyables. These two groups were directly responsible for the reintroduction of the tie, a symbol of new thinking and a new generation finding its feet.

After the industrial revolution, men who were not involved in manual labour wanted neckwear that was easy to put on, comfortable and would last an entire workday. A necktie's design was long, thin and easy to knot, so they did not come undone. By the mid-nineteenth century, the tie had become a status symbol; it meant you didn't work with your hands, you worked in an office and were a 'white collar' worker.

While bowler hats (the Derby) and other fashion items of the late industrial era faded, the tie remained an essential item of business dress for men and remained so until the first dot-com boom of the late 1990s. The informal nature of that workplace meant ties were no longer a must in the office, but they are still worn for important meetings and more formal occasions.

So the next time you mutter under your breath that you have to wear a tie, blame Croatian mercenaries.

Someone Regarded as Legendary but Isn't

D'Artagnan, or to give him his full name, Charles Ogier de Batz de Castelmore, Comte d'Artagnan, was pretty much the man you'd hope for. He was the captain of Louis XIV's elite Musketeer guard, and in this instance the legend isn't far from the reality of the man's true character. He lived during the time of Cardinal Richelieu, he was a brave and accomplished warrior, and he fought in many battles. However, the plots of the Musketeer books and films bear little resemblance to events in his life.

After the Musketeers were disbanded in 1646, D'Artagnan fell under the influence of Richelieu's protégé, Cardinal Mazarin, who was then the chief administrator for the King of France. D'Artagnan became a spy and the leader of small bands of men who carried out daring raids, secret missions and all the good stuff that builds legends.

When some of their more nefarious activities were uncovered, both Mazarin and D'Artagnan were exiled, showing how closely connected the two were. However, when the Musketeers reformed in 1658 (there are echoes of this in the stories), he was, once again, made an officer. Legends don't die but men do, and in 1673 D'Artagnan was killed at the siege of Maastricht when he was hit in the throat by a musket ball at the age of sixty-two (a ripe old age for a man who was rarely out of harm's way).

So I've managed to bring to life and kill D'Artagnan in the space of a page. Sorry about that.

The Battle of Portland: the Decisive Victory that Both Sides Won

It was 1653 and Cromwell ruled England (and the Commonwealth). After the civil war, England continued to press towards becoming a maritime superpower and was increasing its dominance of trade routes. However, England's ambitions threatened the Dutch, the maritime power that had most to lose from this plan, and the result was the First Anglo-Dutch War (there were four of them, the last ending in the 1780s; more on this later).

As might be expected, there were numerous sea battles all over the Atlantic and the North Sea. The Dutch were, at this time, the larger naval power, and in 1652 they began to dominate the English Channel. This meant that as well as invasion, Cromwell faced the strangulation of England's communications with its overseas territories. So the English fleet, under General at Sea (or Admiral) Robert Blake, confronted the experienced Dutch Admiral Maarten Tromp with roughly identically sized fleets in the English Channel at Portland.

Unusually in maritime history, the battle lasted three days. The English planned to disperse the Dutch fleet, but as the battle wore on the English failed each day to break up the Dutch formation. By the evening of the third day, Tromp knew that his fleet had, at best, half an hour's ammunition left for fighting on the fourth day, so Tromp and his fleet sailed away. Blake had cleared the English Channel of enemy vessels and, shortly after that, captured five Dutch warships and around thirty Dutch merchant ships.

Tromp claimed victory because he was undefeated, and his lines had held against successive English attacks. Blake also claimed victory because he had cleared the area of enemy vessels and came home with a large number of Dutch ships. Both are valid points of view.

That said, it was a major English victory, and the Dutch never again (during this war) threatened the English coastline as they had done at Portland. This major naval win resulted in an English victory in the war, even though the Dutch didn't see it that way. The result was clear and spoke for itself.

The Prussian Who Was a Political Genius and a Benevolent Dictator

Frederick William of Prussia's rule (from 1640 to 1688) coincided with the bloody end of the savage Thirty Years War, a Europe-wide convulsion of Catholic-versus-Protestant violence, after which neither side could walk away with their heads held high. It was such a savage war that, to this day, it is considered to be the single most destructive conflict to have occurred in Germany (and that includes the destruction from the Second World War). The Thirty Years War drew in Scandinavia, France, the Low Countries and even Switzerland, and you don't often read about wars in Switzerland.

The war meant that the fledgling Prussian state had been in turmoil for a generation, and it is to Frederick William's eternal credit that, despite being a staunch Calvinist, he promoted peaceful coexistence between his Protestant and Catholic subjects, rather than instigating bloody pogroms.

However, in the seventeenth century Prussia was a tiny realm compared to other European powers, and Frederick William was a minnow surrounded by sharks. So while he carefully rebuilt the local army, he had no option but to allow his lands to be held as a vassal state by the more powerful Swedish crown. However, Frederick William was a canny politician and recognised that, as Sweden's

Above: 1. Chinese 'knife money' was created during the Zhou Dynasty. They came in various shapes and were cast, rather than struck like today's money. (Courtesy of Jerry "Woody")

Right: 2. The Swastika has been used for millennia by many different civilisations, and only once for evil. (Courtesy of Steve Browne and John Verkleir)

Above: 3. Deir el-Medina: the results of the first recorded strike action. (Courtesy of the Institute of the Ancient World)

Below: 4. Looking at cinnamon in its raw form you can see how people might have thought it was part of a bird's nest. (Courtesy of Anna Lennon-McCartney)

Above: 5. The famous Nazca lines were not runways for aliens. (Courtesy of funkz)

Right: 6. The Ainu people of Japan. (Courtesy of A Collection of Old Photos)

Above: 7. Hagia Sophia in Istanbul, arguably the most important building ever built. (Courtesy of Farhan Chawla)

Left: 8. The Minaret of Jesus on the Great Mosque in Damascus. (Courtesy of Varun Shiv Kapur)

9. Illuminated page from *Beowulf* in Old English. (Courtesy of the British Library Illuminated Manuscripts)

10. Much of our information from the Anglo-Saxon era comes from the *Anglo-Saxon Chronicle*. (Courtesy of the British Library Illuminated Manuscripts)

Above: 11. The Habsburg dynasty had many variations of their crest and they can be found all over Europe. (Courtesy of Joe Ross)

Below: 12. *Kamikaze*, meaning 'divine wind', is most often associated with the Japanese in the Second World War, but the term is medieval in origin. (Courtesy of the National Museum of the US Navy)

Above: 13. Malbork Castle in Poland, the largest castle in the world, built by the Teutonic Knights. (Courtesy of Arian Zwegers)

Right: 14. A woodcut dramatization of Vettor Pisani being arrested. (Courtesy of seriykotik)

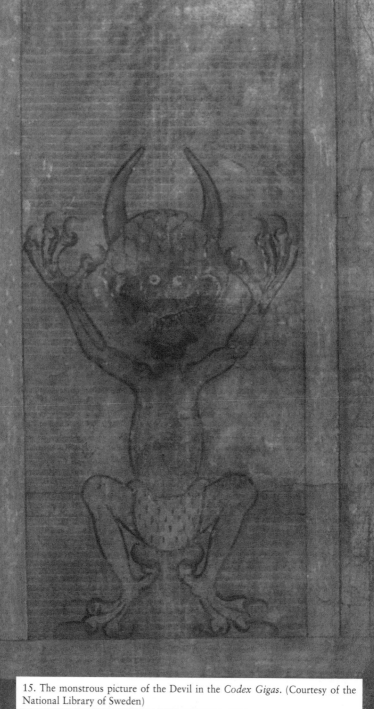

15. The monstrous picture of the Devil in the *Codex Gigas*. (Courtesy of the National Library of Sweden)

THE EMPEROR DRANK CHOCOLATE.

Above: 16. Chocolate in its raw and liquid form was bitter, but still a favourite of the ruling classes. (Courtesy of Patrick Gray)

Right: 17. Did you know that D'Artagnan was a real person and a real musketeer? (Courtesy of jodi0327)

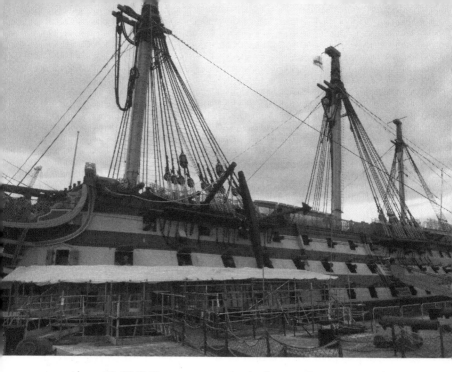

Above: 18. HMS *Victory*, an example of a first-rate ship. (Courtesy of Elliott Brown)

Below: 19. Founded in 1694, the Bank of England was given exclusive possession of the government's money and fixed our interest rates. (Courtesy of DncnH)

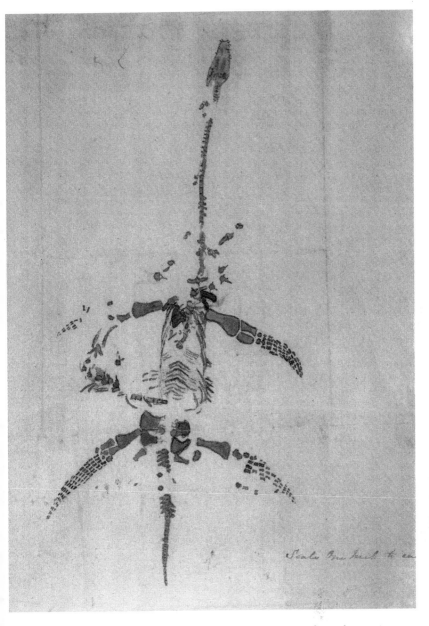

20. Mary Anning now gets credit for her finds (such as this magnificent *Plesiosaur*), but that wasn't always the case. (Courtesy of the Wellcome Library)

21. Most of the Houses of Parliament aren't as old as you think they are. (Courtesy of Olivier Bruchez)

22. After falling victim to Stalin's purges both before and after the Second World War, today Cossacks are recognised as a special ethnic group. (Courtesy of the Library of Congress)

23. The twelve-inch guns on HMS *Dreadnought*, the battleship that heralded a new (but short-lived) era in naval warfare and gave its name to the new Dreadnought class. (Courtesy of the Library of Congress)

24. HMS *Colossus*, a Dreadnought-class battleship of the British Navy. (Courtesy of the Library of Congress)

Above: 25. Although not as large as Schwerer Gustav, this gun from the German Krupp armaments factory was so large it had to be moved on rails. (Courtesy of the Library of Congress, Bain Collection)

Below: 26. Sergeant Stubby with a young girl in a parade. (Courtesy of the Library of Congress)

27. A winged version of the German V-2 rocket that devastated London. The proposed V-3 would have been even more destructive. (Courtesy of the National Museum of the US Navy)

Above: 28. A B-52
Stratofortress releasing its
bomb load in the 1960s.
(Courtesy of the US Air
Force)

Left: 29. General George
Marshall, the economic
mastermind behind
the Marshall Plan in
post-war Europe, lost
a war he should have
won against the Chinese
communists under Mao
Zedong. (Courtesy of the
Library of Congress)

authority was starting to wane, he had the opportunity to slowly unpick his lands from their grip; later in his reign he was able to back up his political prowess with a small but well-disciplined army that managed to inflict defeats on the formidable Swedes. Unfortunately, because of Prussia's lowly status, these gains were given back to Sweden at the behest of France.

While the end game for Prussia in the twentieth century was one of extreme militarism and war crimes, there was no way Frederick William could have foreseen that. What we saw during his reign was a leader who, although he had inherited a crisis and was surrounded by larger, more aggressive powers, transformed his state into a peaceful and well-run realm.

Croissants Aren't French

In 1683 Vienna was under siege by the Ottomans for a second time. 150 years earlier, Suleiman the Magnificent had nearly captured the Austrian city with a massive Ottoman force. This time, however, the Ottoman Grand Vizier, Kara Mustafa Pasha, came even closer to capturing the Habsburg capital. The Ottomans had arrived with a massive army of 150,000 and set up their camp, which was said by contemporaries to be larger than the city itself. It was as if the Ottomans had decided to establish a rival city next to Vienna.

The siege was bitterly contested. The Grand Vizier ordered tunnels to be dug under the city walls, which were pounded by cannons, and the resulting breeches allowed many sorties by thousands of troops. While the damage to the city was huge and both attackers and defenders fought bravely, the siege ground on. Weeks turned into months, and by September the Viennese forces were clinging on by their fingernails, outnumbered and outgunned. It is estimated that tens of thousands died as a result of disease, hunger and combat. Vienna needed reinforcements and it needed them soon.

As if in answer to their prayers, a relief army, led by armoured Polish cavalry, came sweeping into the Turkish encampment on 11 September 1683, catching the Ottomans completely by surprise. The Ottomans were routed, and they never again came as far west as Vienna. Indeed, this siege unlocked Eastern Europe for a Habsburg attack that eventually rolled the Ottoman forces out of Hungary and pushed them back to the east. The Grand Vizier, Kara Mustafa Pasha, returned to the Ottoman Sultan Mehmed IV to tell him the bad news and was beheaded for his failure.

The Viennese had now twice survived a serious onslaught from the Ottoman Empire and survived, so how to celebrate? A local baker made a pastry in the shape of a crescent moon (an Ottoman symbol). When the pastry was later taken up by the French, their word 'croissant' became the term used by everyone. The croissant, then, is a delicious reminder of an Austrian/Polish victory over the Ottoman Empire.

What's a First-Rate Ship Anyway?

The terms 'first-rate' and 'ship of the line' are related. From the 1600s to around 1850 naval combat changed little. Enemy fleets would line up like train lines, parallel to each other and side to side, to allow the broadside guns to blast away at each other. As battles weren't always fought on calm, summer days, this involved highly complex manoeuvring and close communication between ships, as well as considerable seamanship. Because these ships were fighting in a line, they became known as 'ships of the line'. There were exceptions to this type of battle formation (Trafalgar being the most famous), but in general the skills of a captain had more to do with getting into a straight line and less to do with anything that happened in the subsequent battle.

This type of combat encouraged shipbuilders to make the ships ever larger, with reinforced walls and more and more cannons. With so many variations in size, manoeuvrability and firepower, it became necessary to categorise ships, with the largest vessels classified as 'first-rate'.

In this instance 'first-rate' meant 'largest with the most cannons', but that invariably made them some of the slowest ships in a fleet. Many eighteenth and nineteenth-century naval engagements were little more than slugging matches, where the biggest bruisers (the first-rate ships) could shred smaller warships.

With the invention of the steam engine and the propeller screw in the mid-nineteenth century, this type of combat was no longer necessary, and more in the way of tactics came back to naval engagements. It is interesting to note that the then innovative 'ironclad' warship was the ancestor of the twentieth-century battleship, whose very designation is once again a contraction of the phrase 'ship of the line of battle'.

Jonathan Wild: Thief Taker General

Jonathan Wild was a criminal mastermind. Born in London during the time of Charles II, Wild came into his own in 1713 when he became, on the surface of things, a kind of chief investigator of crimes – what we might now call a police inspector. However, Wild's official identity cloaked a genius scam.

Under the self-created title and cover of 'Thief Taker General', he ran a gang of thieves, kept the stolen goods, and waited for the crime to be announced in the newspapers. When the crime became public, Wild would claim that his 'thief taking agents' had 'found' the stolen goods and would return them to the owners for a reward (to cover the expenses he had incurred, he said). He was, in essence, selling people's property back to them. In some cases, if the stolen items or circumstances allowed for blackmail, he did not wait for the theft to be announced but used a third party to do a little blackmailing. As well as 'recovering' stolen goods, he offered the police assistance in finding the thieves. The thieves that Wild would help to 'discover' were rivals or members of his own gang he had no further use for. Wild controlled the underworld, made a fortune, and appeared completely legitimate. You have to admire his audacity, if not his morals.

For a time, Wild virtually monopolised crime in London. In public, by contrast, he presented a heroic face. In 1718, he gave himself a thoroughly earned promotion and the title 'Thief Taker General of Great Britain and Ireland', but Wild was not just a thief. There was a deeply sinister side to all this, and his testimonies sent over sixty thieves to the gallows. Wild made even more money by offering to help find criminals for an extra fee (which in reality was more cash for the same job). By 1720, Wild's fame was such that the Privy Council (the king's inner circle of advisers) consulted with him on methods of controlling crime. His predictable recommendation was that the rewards for evidence against thieves should be raised. He, of course, profited further from the now larger rewards.

By 1725 the mood in London was changing, and Wild's luck was running out. On 15 February, Wild was arrested for helping one of his men in a jailbreak. He was sent to Newgate Prison, where he tried to continue to run his business. No longer a pillar of the community, Wild's schemes unravelled, and his days of criminal activity came to an end as gang members testified against him. There was no way out, and on 24 May 1725 he was hanged.

What Is One of the Single Greatest Achievements of Scholarship?

Samuel Johnson was a well-regarded writer who came from humble origins. Recognised for his intelligence from an early age, he won a place at Pembroke College, Oxford, but only attended for just over a year due to financial difficulties. There followed years of earning a crust writing magazine articles and a few biographies to pay the bills while he spent nine years creating his masterpiece. It was a book with no plot and no characters, and yet it was as important as anything Shakespeare wrote.

Printed in 1755, *A Dictionary of the English Language* is considered to be the greatest dictionary ever and is the basis for all subsequent dictionaries ever written. However, it was not the first dictionary; it wasn't even close to being the first. That honour belongs to the first list of words and meanings from a bilingual Sumerian–Akkadian wordlist found in Syria, dating from around 2300 BC. In other words, Johnson was beaten by the Akkadians by over 4,000 years.

Johnson's dictionary wasn't even the first English dictionary. That honour belongs to Richard Mulcaster's version from 1582, which described the meaning of 8,000 English words. But Mulcaster hadn't thought to put them in alphabetical order, making it a curiosity rather than a useful tool.

The reality was that while the concept of a dictionary had been around for a long time, Johnson, a towering intellectual of the day, was asked to get behind the idea of a well-researched and usefully laid-out dictionary. He did it as a paid commission, not to fulfil a lifelong dream.

It instantly became the standard dictionary in the UK and even in Europe. It was immediately recognised as a remarkable achievement, especially considering it was the work of just one man. The first edition had 42,773 words listed and explained. Just as helpfully, it enabled the standardisation of spelling and reduced regional variations in meanings.

After the works of Shakespeare, Johnson's dictionary is probably the single greatest contribution to the English language.

The Worst Natural Famine in History

In 1768 in Bengal, a minor shortfall in crops was nothing out of the ordinary, but this was followed by more severe conditions, and by September of 1769 there was a serious drought. At the time the country was under the control of the British East India Company, and alarming reports of famine in the rural areas were ignored by the company's officers.

By early 1770 starvation was widespread, and by mid-1770 deaths from starvation were occurring on a large scale. Subsequent rainfall later in that year resulted in a good harvest and the famine abated. However, other shortfalls occurred in the following years, and the death toll continued to rise. About 10 million people, approximately one-third of the population of the affected area, are estimated to have died in the famine.

As a result of death and migration, large areas of agricultural land were abandoned, returned to jungle, and were virtually impassable for decades afterwards. From 1772 onwards, gangs of bandits and thugs became an established feature of the Bengal countryside and were only brought under control by punitive actions in the 1780s.

While food shortages were a regular occurrence throughout India's history, the severity of the famine in this particular case was due to the policies of the British East India Company. As a commercial organisation, the company's purpose was to maximise its profits through trade and taxation. When areas came under company control, the land tax was raised, sometimes as much as fivefold over previous levels. In the first years of its rule in Bengal, the British East India Company's total land tax income doubled – and most of this revenue flowed out of the country.

As the famine approached its height in April 1770, the company announced that the land tax for the following year was to be increased by a further 10 per cent. So, in order to pay the increased taxes, many farmers switched from low-value cereal crops (which feed people) to high-value opium. You can't eat opium. The company also outlawed the so-called 'hoarding' of rice. This prevented traders from accumulating the reserves that in times of drought would have fed starving populations.

While the great famine in China in the 1950s was even worse (records here are conjecture, but it could have been more than 50 million deaths), that was almost entirely man-made. The Bengal famine (1769–73) was a natural disaster which could have been mitigated by effective governance. Instead, 10 million died when a bad situation was made worse by the incompetence and greed of a British company.

Casanova Was More than a Lover

Casanova (1725–98) was a man whose very name is synonymous with seduction and prowess with women. He was a Venetian who, you may be surprised to learn, had a career carved out in the church. He started as a clerk under the supervision of a rich benefactor, Senator Malipiero, who moved in the best circles and taught young Casanova how to behave in society. When Casanova was caught trying his luck with Malipiero's intended object of seduction, the senator drove both of them from his house. This kind of promiscuous behaviour meant that his career in the church was over, but the undaunted Casanova went on to lose his virginity with two sisters – a promising start to the legend. From his early conquests, Casanova moved into the upper classes of Italy, where he charmed his way into the confidences of the men and the bedchambers of the women.

He toured Europe extensively as a musician and playwright and became a Freemason. His behaviour abroad was seen as so scandalous that the Venetian Inquisition took an interest in him, and he was imprisoned after his return. An accomplice smuggled a metal spike inside a Bible (yes, that old trick may have originated with Casanova), and he was able to escape through a hole in his roof, leaving his jailers a quote from the Psalms, 'I shall not die, but live, and declare the works of the Lord,' a typical theatrical flourish.

He returned to Paris where, to top off everything, he became a spy, and a successful one, during the Seven Years War between Britain and France. He accrued enough cash to set up a factory, but was too much of an adventurer to run a business and ended up deep in debt. To avoid the repercussions, he fled, and wound up in England in 1763, where he managed to bluff his way into meeting King George III. Of course he found a number of English women to seduce and have fun with, but after a few years he was broke and sick with venereal disease (an occupational hazard for a serial seducer before the era of antibiotics).

His last years were spent in Venice and Bohemia, where he carried out numerous literary projects (more plays and translations), but what sealed his reputation were his memoirs. These, of course, are exaggerated, but even his contemporaries recognised him as a clever, charming and remarkable man. Not many people can claim to have been a writer, musician, convict, businessman, spy and prolific lover. Casanova was a busy man.

The American War of Independence and the Battle of the Island of Jersey

No matter how hard some try to portray the events of 1776 as American colonials versus British redcoats, the facts refuse to fit. Putting it simply, the colonials had no hope of winning without the help of France, and they got a lot of help. In fact, had Britain had the alliances it often had with other major European powers (as they did, for instance, in the Seven Years War, just a few decades earlier, or in the Napoleonic Wars, a few decades later), France wouldn't have had the luxury of focussing all her efforts on stirring up trouble and supplying the American rebels. Putting it bluntly, the French won the American Revolution but were to pay the price when that revolutionary zeal was exported back home.

The close association between France and America can be shown when, in 1781, France felt it necessary to attempt to invade the English-held Channel Islands; although closer to France, the islands had been under English control for centuries. In the late eighteenth century, they were an epicentre for privateers, who harassed and plundered French ships heading for the American colonies. If they could neutralise Jersey (the largest of the Channel Islands), their ships (and the supplies they contained) would no longer be under threat.

It was a reasonable idea and the logistics were, in theory, well within the capabilities of the French army and navy. The execution of the plan was, however, shambolic. It's never advisable to attempt an invasion with fewer forces than the garrison waiting (in this case, about 1,000 versus 2,000), but that's exactly what happened.

Because the local British guards abandoned their posts to go drinking, the initial landing in Jersey was unopposed. Before they were detected, the French were able to get most of their forces to the edges of the Jersey capital, St Helier, where British forces, finally alerted, massed on the opposite side of the main market square. The French refused the British offer to surrender and fighting broke out.

Although called the Battle of Jersey, the actual shooting lasted only fifteen minutes. Once the smoke had cleared, a total of thirty men from both sides had died. The French were outnumbered and had no wish to incur further fatalities, so the remainder of their force surrendered. Eyewitnesses say only about a third of the British troops saw any action. Had there not been fatalities, the whole incident might be considered a farce.

While this invasion plan was an attempt to help the American rebels by securing a French base in Jersey, the island remained British, while, ironically, America did not.

Alcohol and Soldiers Are Never a Good Mix

The following is yet another example of a story that could be true, but historians need more than a warm fuzzy feeling before they can declare something to be fact. Let's look at the story and then examine the circumstantial evidence around it.

In the year 1788, the Austro-Hungarian Empire was, once again, at war with the Ottoman Empire. The army of Austria, approximately 100,000 strong, set up camp around the town of Karánsebes. The vanguard, a contingent of Hussars (cavalry), crossed a nearby river to scout for the Turks. There was no sign of the enemy, but they ran into a group of Romanies who offered to sell them schnapps. A price was agreed, the deal was done, and the schnapps was opened.

Soon afterwards, some infantry from the main body of the force crossed the river and saw a party going on. The infantry demanded some of the booze, but the drunken Hussars refused and set up makeshift fortifications to protect their schnapps.

Angry words were exchanged, which led to shots being exchanged. Chaos erupted as the Austrian units assumed that it must be the Turks attacking. As the fleeing Hussars ran through the camp, a commander thought it was an Ottoman cavalry charge and ordered artillery fire. The entire camp awoke to the sounds of battle, and the Austrian troops fired at every shadow, thinking the Ottomans were everywhere. In reality they were shooting fellow Austrian soldiers. The incident escalated to the point where the whole army retreated from the imaginary enemy, and Emperor Joseph II was pushed off his horse into a small creek.

Two days later, the Ottoman army arrived. They were bemused to discover 10,000 dead and wounded Austrian soldiers and, without hesitation, swiftly took Karánsebes.

The first historic reference to this battle is in the mid-nineteenth century, nearly sixty years after the event, so the reference could merely be repeating what was, in fact, a fanciful story. Emperor Joseph II's letters and diaries make no mention of the incident, and no specific officers can be identified as being there, but then again, who would want to admit to being part of this debacle? Interestingly, the Ottomans did capture the town rather easily in 1788. Maybe the whole story was created to explain why Austria failed to fend off the advancing Ottomans, or could there be some truth to the tale, which then became exaggerated with each subsequent retelling?

Fact or fiction? You decide.

The Immovable Interest Rate

Britain did not invent banking. Many of the concepts were copied from Holland, but with a growing empire England rapidly became the master of what today is recognised as modern banking. The Bank of England was founded in 1694 and was given exclusive possession of the government's money. It was also the only body authorised by the government to issue banknotes. One of the first things the bank did in the year of its founding was to set the first national interest rate, and it was set at 6 per cent.

Today we are familiar with changing interest rates, but they didn't start moving around on any kind of regular basis until the late nineteenth century. In 1719 the Bank of England moved the interest rate from 4 per cent to 5 per cent (so far, so dull), but it didn't move again until 1822, which means that this rate of interest lasted 103 years, the longest fixed-rate term in British banking history.

This is even more astonishing when you consider all that happened during this period; while there were a number of smaller conflicts during these 103 years, three wars were really big deals. There was the Seven Years War (1754–63, with the main conflict in the seven-year period 1756–63), which shunted Britain to the top of the heap in terms of empires by taking Canada from the French and making it part of Britain. Canada is an enormous country that would, over time, improve Britain's position financially and politically. However, these huge changes in Britain's fortunes were apparently not important enough for a change in interest rates.

Then, fifteen years later, there was the American War of Independence (1775–83), fought between Great Britain and its thirteen North American colonies. In reality, the colonies cost money to run, and the locals really didn't like paying tax, so it wouldn't be unreasonable to think that a declaration of independence by the colonies could be seen as a welcome opportunity for Britain to save money – and that the situation might prompt the Bank of England to change the rate of interest. But no.

The business of slavery (and it was a commercial enterprise) came to an end in this era of an immovable interest rate. It was clearly the morally right thing to do, and Britain led the world in this regard, but doing the right thing cost money to implement and, for a time, meant some companies were less profitable. Putting morality to one side, a major shift in trade patterns usually leads to interest rate adjustments, but on this occasion not so much.

Finally, there were the years of war with France, from the 1790s to 1815 (for much more on this, see my book *The Napoleonic Wars in 100 Facts*). This was a hugely turbulent and costly period, which involved sending fleets to places like the Caribbean and Egypt. Soldiers were landed in America, Argentina and Spain; France threatened invasion and, at one point, had a trade war with Britain, which – for a brief time – led to a big slump in the London stock market. But again, none of these prompted any interest rate adjustments. It was almost as if changes in interest rates had been forgotten – and then someone was dusting off some old ledgers and thought, 'Oh, I remember those. Let's give them a try again.'

In 1822 the 5 per cent interest rate, which had stood firm for over a century, went back down to 4 per cent.

The War Where Nobody Died

Wars are usually accompanied by sad lists of casualties; however, the Kettle War is remarkable because there were no casualties and only the smallest amount of collateral damage was suffered.

The Low Countries were an area of Western Europe, split along dynastic and religious lines and backed by the very largest European powers. This meant that a very small portion of Europe was being contested, over and over again, by armies far larger than the local population would suggest possible.

In the 1780s, the Holy Roman Emperor Joseph II took advantage of the Fourth Anglo-Dutch War to demand the return of territory in Flanders. (Britain had a lot of wars with the Dutch, which have been completely forgotten by the general population. Today we think of the Netherlands as our friendly neighbour and ally, but in the 1600s and 1700s, we were more often at war with them than we were with France.)

The Holy Roman Empire was supported by Britain, the Netherlands's enemy in the recent war. Meanwhile, France supported the Dutch. Joseph, while an Enlightenment ruler, was a relatively impatient man, and on this occasion acted as a bully by threatening war. He calculated that the Netherlands would not dare to react and, for good measure, sent three ships to the area. The so-called 'flagship' (it was a merchant ship, rather than a warship) was called *Le Louis*.

However, the Dutch were a tenacious bunch and a seafaring nation of considerable calibre, so on 9 October 1784 the Dutch ship *Dolfijn* was sent out to intercept the incoming enemy vessels. The Dutch ship fired one shot, which hit a kettle. This panicked the merchant crewmen and *Le Louis* immediately surrendered. While the diplomatic 'war' lasted months, this was the only shot fired in anger. The only damage done was to the crew's lunch.

The Most Expensive Dress Disaster in History

It is a largely forgotten fact that Marie Antoinette, Queen of France, whose son was heir to the French throne, wasn't French.

Marie Antoinette was the daughter of the illustrious Austrian royal family. Her father was Francis I, the Holy Roman Emperor, and her mother was the formidable Maria Theresa; between them, they founded the Habsburg-Lorraine Dynasty. Marie Antoinette (her full name was Maria Antonia Josepha Johanna) was brought up expecting to be married to a prince in one of the royal families of Europe. A woman of her status would be found a husband that suited her family's political purposes. This meant that in April of 1770, she was married by proxy (not unusual for the time) to the Dauphin of France at the Augustinian Church in Vienna, with her brother filling in for Louis. In May she was sent to France to start her new life.

On the outskirts of Paris, she stopped to prepare for her first meeting with her new husband. According to the fashion of the times, she was dressed in an elaborate wig and a sumptuous gown to ensure that she looked the part as she arrived in the city. Decadence and extravagant excess were the hallmarks of the French court (in comparison to the other royal houses of Europe at the time), and she would do what the occasion demanded. It's not recorded what she thought of all this, but she had been brought up to do her duty and to do it well.

Marie Antoinette was due to marry Louis (technically, marry again, but at least this time the bride and groom were in the same room – and the same country) a few days after her arrival, but as she would only have been in Paris for a short time before the big day, the ostentatious wedding dress had to be made ahead of time – and her measurements guessed at. (Okay, no internet at the time, but you would think that her measurements could have been despatched to Paris for an occasion as important as her wedding.)

However, as flamboyant as it was, the couturiers had guessed wrong, and the dress was too small. No matter what they did, she couldn't fit into it, and there was no other suitably amazing gown to take its place. So, the only thing left to do was cut into the dress and fit it around her. The gaps were covered with strips of silk in an attempt to camouflage the catastrophe. Contemporary accounts do not comment on any imperfections, reporting only that the gown was dripping with silver thread, diamonds and, as might be expected, every other opulent adornment available.

As grand as she must have looked walking down the aisle, a close inspection would have revealed a wedding gown that was nothing more than an ill-fitting patchwork, making it, perhaps, the most expensive folly in fashion history.

The dress, like many French royal excesses, was either destroyed or sold off during the revolution.

Angry Americans

People like a neat story and an easy narrative. Therefore, Shays' Rebellion, which occurred almost immediately after the American Revolution, has been largely forgotten. After all, the fact that America's Founding Fathers faced insurrection rather undermines the widely held belief that everyone supported the revolutionary idea of a 'United States of America'. America is currently the most powerful country on the planet, but that was certainly not the case in the years following independence from its British imperial overlord.

By 1786 (just a few years after independence was achieved), the former colonies were suffering from a severe economic depression, and many of those who had supported and fought for freedom believed they deserved more than tough times. In the later months of that year, protesters in the state of Massachusetts (some led by Daniel Shays, hence the name of the rebellion) began shutting down county courts to stop the judicial hearings for tax and debt collection. It was pesky taxes causing trouble in the American colonies ... again! When the state government started to arrest some of the leaders, the protests turned violent.

A government militia raised by Benjamin Lincoln defeated a Shaysite rebel attempt to seize the federal Springfield Armory (that would be 'Armoury' if the British still had a say in things) in late January of 1787. The situation had gone beyond an exchange of angry words to a shooting war; four men were killed and twenty were wounded. On February 4 1787, the main Shaysite force was scattered after an unexpected attack on their camp at Petersham, Massachusetts. Sporadic resistance continued until June 1787, when the single most significant incident of the hostilities took place in Sheffield. In late February, thirty rebels were wounded (one mortally) in a skirmish with government troops.

The actions weren't large enough to be considered 'civil war', but there was a certain irony in the fact that the new state authorities, once the rebels against British taxation, were now putting down an uprising of their own over citizens' protests about taxes. Quick responses by the state militia quelled this rebellion before it grew, but it shows that life was not immediately better for the colonies after the War of Independence.

The Mad Danish King

Democracy has an advantage when it comes to mental illness: if the leader acts strangely, there is a system in place for getting rid of him. Not so with kings, and unfortunately not so for Christian VII of Denmark.

His is an unhappy story, which starts with an abusive childhood. In the mid-1700s, it was believed you could beat sense into a child, and Detlev Reventlow, the king's chamberlain, delivered 'stern discipline' when he regularly thrashed and abused the young prince. Christian's father (Frederick V) had been ill for some time and died aged forty-two, so the frail Christian became king at the tender age of seventeen. Almost immediately he married his British/Hanoverian cousin Caroline Matilda, a sister of George III, who was of the even more tender age of fifteen. Christian took an immediate disliking to her and made the curious statement that it is 'unfashionable to love one's wife'.

Given his cruel upbringing, it is little wonder that Christian's behaviour became increasingly bizarre. Following the example of his late father, Christian lived the thoroughly debauched life of a hedonist, drinking to excess and bedding a long line of, ahem, 'working girls' and 'rent boys'.

Unsurprisingly, Caroline Matilda felt neglected; she put on weight and started wearing male riding costumes. It was commonly said at the time that she was 'the better man of the two'. She was unable to do anything to curb her husband's excesses and died in 1775 at the age of just twenty-three.

For all the poor choices he made, Christian did, make one good one when he hired the German Johann Friedrich Struensee as his personal physician. Because Christian was inept as a ruler, Struensee became, in all but name, the country's regent – an exceptional one, who carried out a string of highly effective reforms. So by complete serendipity, Denmark was in good hands, at least for a time. Unfortunately the good doctor's good judgment did not extend to Caroline Matilda, with whom he had an affair (well, the king wasn't interested in her), which led to Struensee's arrest and execution. There is a lesson in this for anyone who is an effective and efficient regent on behalf of an insane and completely debauched king.

Meanwhile, Christian descended into longer and stranger bouts of madness. He sometimes gabbled and talked gibberish, at other times he was found banging his head against a wall, and on other occasions he would explode with rage or mad laughter, for no apparent reason. Think of the Joker with a crown and you're getting there in terms of his increasingly crazy behaviour.

Like his contemporary and cousin George III, the king's authority was eventually taken over by a formal regent. The first was his stepmother, who loathed him, but she was later replaced by Christian's son Frederick. King Christian was never put under house arrest or confined; instead, he was kept from the public eye, which was probably best for everybody. During the Napoleonic Wars, and with the French pushing further north, he was moved to Rendsborg in Schleswig for his own safety. When the French invaded Denmark with their Spanish allies, it was said that Christian died (in 1808) due to the shock of seeing Spanish troops enter the city.

Tsar Paul I Was Like a Cheap Sandwich

You know the situation: you buy a sandwich, which you hope will be filling, only to discover that you've purchased two thick pieces of bread with only the tiniest sliver of ham in the middle. Welcome to the world of Tsar Paul I, the thin sliver of ham between two giants of Russian history.

Paul was the only surviving son of Russia's Catherine the Great. His mother was a titan in early modern European history, but she was so busy being 'great' (and having lovers), she didn't spend much time with Paul. Her neglected son was raised by a series of incompetent nurses. How incompetent? When he was a baby, he fell out of his cot and was only discovered the next morning, lying on the cold floor – and this was the heir to the great throne of Russia! Later in childhood he caught typhus but survived.

Things didn't get better for Paul as he grew up. While his mother insisted he attend court functions, he was largely ignored. He married young and his first wife died in childbirth; however, he got into his mother's good books when he married for a second time and his wife bore a son whom they called Alexander. Catherine could relax now that she knew the Romanov Dynasty was secure. Not wanting to leave anything to chance, Catherine put Alexander and, later, his brother Constantine under her own protection and seems to have toyed with the idea of cutting Paul out of the succession altogether. A mother's unconditional love for her child didn't exist between Catherine and her surviving son.

However, when Catherine died in 1796 Paul got his dynastic revenge and quickly ensured he was the next tsar. While attempting a more peaceful approach to relations with Russia's neighbours, Paul also devoted a lot of energy to destroying the power of his mother's favourites. This proved to be a bad move, as Napoleon was on the rise and Russia's nobility were not about to take orders from the tsar who undermined them – a man his own mother didn't love.

Paul lasted five years before an attempt was made to force him to abdicate. When he declined, he was stabbed and then strangled (just to be sure). By contrast, his son Alexander I ruled for nearly twenty-five years. He was responsible for resisting Napoleon and ruling Russia with an iron fist. Russian history has largely forgotten Paul, wedged as he was between his mother and his son, two of Russian's most successful monarchs.

The Origins of a Well-Known Tongue Twister

Not many women of humble origins in the nineteenth century became important in history and science. Mary Anning is one of the few.

Mary was one of ten children, but only she and her brother Joseph survived to adulthood. However, Mary had the good luck to be born in Lyme Regis in Dorset, which, millions of years earlier, had been at the bottom of a shallow tropical sea. In 1811 at the age of twelve, Mary and her brother dug up a four-foot ichthyosaur skull, and a few months later Mary found the rest of the skeleton. Like many locals, the family sold fossil finds to supplement their meagre incomes. They had no interest in science; as far as they were concerned, they were merely selling their finds to those who would pay them.

Anning continued to make important finds, and her reputation grew. On 10 December 1823, she found the first complete plesiosaurus, and in 1828 the first British example of the flying reptiles known as pterosaurs, called a 'flying dragon' when it was displayed in the British Museum. By 1826, at the age of twenty-seven, Anning had managed to save enough money to purchase a home with a glass store-front window for her shop, Anning's Fossil Depot. The business had become important enough that the move was covered in the local paper.

Mary was becoming so skilled at the new science of palaeontology that she outshone many of the professors in the field, but as a poor and lowly woman she would never get the credit of the richer, male experts who consulted her about their fossil finds and later published works on them. Indeed, many of these specialists depended on her shop for the finds they wanted to study, and she was regularly asked for her advice and observations. In 1835 a wealthy friend, William Buckland, persuaded the British Association for the Advancement of Science and the British government to award her an annuity, known as a civil list pension, in return for her many contributions to the science of geology. The £25 annual pension gave her some welcome financial security.

Although most today would not recognise her name as that of a significant contributor to the study of palaeontology, it is Mary and her fossil business that are forever immortalised in the tongue twister 'she sells seashells on the seashore'.

Forgotten Spanish Wars

History is full of events and dates that, unless they are connected to your background and education, remain unknown. What you were taught, what you know, even the events that pique your interest, depend to a large extent on where you were born. So, in that context, let's look at Spain, a country that was technically neutral in both world wars, partly because just prior to the Second World War it had been torn apart in its own civil war, and partly because it had suffered bitter fighting throughout the previous century. Those nineteenth-century wars are collectively known as the Carlist Wars.

The trigger (as is so often the case) was a disputed succession. When the Spanish King Ferdinand VII died in 1833, his fourth wife, Maria Cristina, became the Queen Regent on behalf of their infant daughter Isabella II. This would have been fine had Ferdinand's brother Carlos not made a grab for the throne as Carlos V. His supporters (known as Carlists – hence the name of the wars) wanted a return to an autocratic monarchy, but the queen and her government were (ironically) supported by the party of the liberals and wanted a more democratic Spanish government. They were known as the Cristinos, and with the Cristinos and the Carlists at loggerheads over the future of Spain, fighting, inevitably, broke out.

While some historians consider that there were three wars, others count only two, each of which was centred on a major engagement. The First Carlist War (1833–40) spanned most of the country at one time or another, although the main conflict centred on the Carlist homelands of the Basque Country and Aragon, Catalonia and Valencia in the north of Spain.

It's worth remembering that Spain had been in steady decline since its glory days in the sixteenth and seventeenth centuries. It had been a French ally in the Napoleonic Wars but was later attacked by Napoleon, which resulted in bitter fighting across the Iberian Peninsula. While this was going on in Europe, many of Spain's South American possessions were lost, and in 1821 Mexico broke away from its Spanish motherland. By 1833, Spain was broke.

The Carlists made the mistake of looking backwards, believing they could achieve victory, once again, by means of manpower and steel. The Cristinos asked for assistance from the two most powerful countries in Europe – Britain and France – and, quite predictably, won. (Yes, that's right. Before the Crimean War and less than a generation after the Napoleonic Wars, France and Britain were fighting on the same side in Spain, in a series of battles that have now been completely forgotten by everyone except the very mustiest of Spanish historians.) The victory was a crushing blow for the Carlists and their Basque separatist affiliates too. The peace treaty that followed had the charming name 'The Embrace of Bergara'.

The Second Carlist War (1846–49) was nothing like the size of the first one and was really little more than a minor Catalonian rebellion, with a maximum number of 10,000 militia involved. The rebels tried to install Carlos V's son (another Carlos, known as Carlos VI) on the throne, but failed and, while there were casualties, it should probably be seen as an insurrection rather than as a full-blown war. Again the Cristino liberals won.

Spain clearly loved its autocratic rulers, because from 1872–76 there was a Third Carlist War. In 1868, Queen Isabella II had been overthrown by a conspiracy carried out by her own liberal generals. The Cortes (Spanish parliament) replaced her with Amadeo, the Duke of Aosta. There was an uneasy peace, which fell apart when the Spanish elections of 1872 resulted in government violence against Carlist candidates. The Carlists, true to their name, were now backing yet another Carlos (a grandson of the original Carlos), who decided that only force of arms could win him the throne. Once again Spain erupted into violence.

The Carlist strongholds were still in the north, mainly in the Basque and Catalonia regions. For a time, the Carlists were even able to set up their own state, in somewhat the same way that the Confederacy set up its own shadow government during the American Civil War. After yet more years of fighting (when, again, the Carlists still failed to seek outside help), the liberals, unsurprisingly, won their third victory. (Undaunted, Carlos VII later tried to make a claim to the defunct French throne in the 1880s.)

Apparently the Spanish had not yet had enough of fighting, because they went on to have a more famous war in the 1930s, the Spanish Civil War (1936–39). Some considered this to be the final Carlist War as, once again, Basque factions and Royalists groups fought for dominance. In reality, the Spanish Civil War was more complex than that: there were multiple sides, all with different agendas, all fighting each other for these three years in Spain.

For several reasons the Spanish Civil War was a crossroads in history. Many nations became involved, perhaps most notoriously the Soviet Union and Germany, and it can be legitimately claimed that they used this war as a giant laboratory for testing the tactics and equipment that would prove to be the near future of warfare. It also marked the closure of two long conflicts. Firstly, the Carlist uprisings, which had been going on for a century, were finally crushed, once and for all, under the fascist boots of General Franco. Secondly, the wars were a bizarre footnote to a much longer series of conflicts. Among other things, the Carlists saw the wars as their attempt to turn back the rising tide of secularism, particularly against the atheist Soviets and communists. They appealed to the Pope, who issued a papal bull (written papal authority) to raise funds by means of what was essentially a crusader tax, thereby making the Spanish Civil War, technically, the last crusade in history.

The Mysterious Story of Crystal Skulls

Sometimes it's fun to delve into pseudo-history, mainly to expose the stories for the frauds that they are. If you remember Arthur C. Clarke's TV show from the late 1970s or have flicked through a *Fortean Times*, you'll be familiar with the idea that Pre-Colombian Meso-American civilisations (usually Aztec or Mayan) crafted beautiful skulls from perfect pieces of quartz (as seen in the Indiana Jones film *The Kingdom of the Crystal Skull* ... which should not be regarded as a serious documentary about 1950s archaeology). There are a number of these quartz skulls of varying quality in museums around the world, and the skulls are said to show the near supernatural skill of the craftsmen, who were, we believe, in possession only of stone tools.

Could the skulls be evidence of human psychic powers?

Could they be proof of telekinesis?

Are they evidence of technological assistance from another world?

No ... they are all nineteenth-century fakes. They are an example of how readily we humans want to believe in the mysterious, and certainly the late nineteenth century was just bursting with the need to explain the seemingly inexplicable in terms of the paranormal or occult. Why not explain unusual finds by looking at the exotic and obscure from the Mexico? Tests conducted on the quartz show it can only be found in Madagascar and Brazil, so the skulls can't be Mexican, and the carving has been shown by the British Museum to have been carried out by nineteenth-century jewellery drills.

Those are the facts, but they don't stop people believing what they want to believe or declaring that the major museums of the world are involved in some kind of sinister cover up. These items are undeniably beautiful, but the only history they belong to is the history of fakes.

Don't Mention 'the Scottish Play' in New York

Shakespeare's play *Macbeth* has a tradition of being unlucky, and those involved in its production refer to it only as 'the Scottish Play', lest they incur some sort of vague supernatural retribution. It's not entirely clear why the play got this reputation, but it was the trigger for a riot in New York City.

In 1849, two productions of *Macbeth* were playing to audiences at the same time. One starred Edwin Forrest, a great American theatre actor; the other starred the renowned English actor William Charles Macready. Macready and Forrest had each toured the other's country twice with their productions before arriving in New York. Both had received good reviews, so surely the city was big enough to accommodate two simultaneous productions, wasn't it?

During Macready's second visit to America, Forrest followed him around the country to appear in the same plays as a challenge to determine who was the better actor. Most newspapers supported Forrest, the home-grown star. Forrest had local working-class (and gang) sympathies. He was seen as the tougher, more muscular version of Macbeth, while in the American press the British Macready was painted as the usual cliché: clever but effete, which the cream of New York preferred. Opinions divided on the basis of wealth and class, with the 'haves' and the 'have nots' on opposite sides of the argument. It was a potentially explosive situation.

On 7 May 1849, three nights before the riot, Forrest's supporters bought hundreds of tickets for the top level of the Astor Opera House, where Macready was playing. They brought his performances to a grinding halt by shouting, 'Shame! Shame!' and throwing rotten eggs, shoes and even ripped-up seats at the stage. This was a mini-riot in itself, but it was just the opening act. The performers persisted in the face of everything the protesters could, literally, throw at them. After this disastrous experience, Macready announced his intention to leave for Britain on the next boat, but he was persuaded by some American patrons to stay and perform again.

The city's police chief and its new mayor were well aware of the situation and the potential for violence. Believing they had insufficient manpower to quell a serious riot, the militia were brought in. On the night of 10 May, rioting broke out around the Astor theatre and between twenty-two and thirty-one people were killed, with a further forty-eight injured. It wasn't all one way, either. Fifty to seventy policemen were injured, as were 141 militia. The rioting died out, but there was blood on the streets.

The Astor Opera House did not survive the incident: it became known as the 'Massacre Opera House' at 'DisAster Place' and shut a year later.

The New Palace of Westminster

The Palace of Westminster, better known as the Houses of Parliament, probably isn't as old as most people think. Consider, for a moment, that clock towers aren't medieval, and yet the most famous part of the Palace of Westminster is Elizabeth Tower, known to the world as Big Ben.

The site itself is historically ancient; the first royal Palace of Westminster was built there in the eleventh century and was the primary residence of the kings of England until a fire destroyed it in 1512. The complex was rebuilt, but then in 1834 there was an even greater fire that again wiped out most of the site (Turner painted that fire). Westminster Hall (the very hall where Charles I was put on trial) still stands, but almost everything else that we consider to be the 'Houses of Parliament' is, in reality, Victorian(ish).

After the 1834 fire, King William IV offered the almost completed Buckingham Palace to Parliament, hoping to dispose of a residence he disliked. However, the building was considered unsuitable for parliamentary use, and instead the original site at Westminster was chosen for a rebuild.

So why does it look Gothic and not very Victorian? The simple answer is that the Victorians loved to build monuments in a neoclassical style. Doric columns and triangular facades were how the West, especially the Americans, built things at the time. And in a way, that was the issue. It was felt that if the new parliament building was built in neoclassical style, it would look … well, too French or too American … and we couldn't have that, could we?

The design of the new Palace of Westminster was to be decided by a competition, and it was Sir Charles Barr's design that won. The Houses of Parliament and the ancillary buildings were largely finished by 1860.

The palace has recently been in the news because it's crumbling, and the potential cost to repair and restore it is estimated at an eye-watering £6 billion. The Victorians are often cited as being able to build things that last for centuries: sewers, bridges and train stations. It's just a little ironic that the cradle of democracy, which was such a high profile construction project, is falling to pieces after just 150 years.

The Engineer Who Came up with a Killer Invention

Joseph Whitworth was an English engineer and mathematician. He spent most of his life working on ornamental lathes and standardising various mechanical processes (please wake up; I'm getting to the good bit).

He also worked out that one of the reasons contemporary muskets were so inaccurate was because the bullet didn't spin much unless the barrel was 'rifled' (had grooves inside the barrel); the more the bullet spins, the more it stays on its original trajectory and, therefore, the more accurate the shot. Taking this to its logical conclusion, he invented a hexagonal bullet that fired down a special barrel to create the maximum amount of spin.

The traditional English musket, the Brown Bess, was accurate to 100 yards. The Whitworth rifle was revolutionary because now you could hit a target up to 1,000 yards away.

His weapon was meant for the British forces, but while nobody doubted its accuracy, it was seen as too expensive, not least because it required a brand new machine to produce millions of hexagonal bullets. So its service in the British military was limited;

however, it was extensively used by Confederate sharpshooters in the American Civil War. Confederate snipers were well-known for their lethal ability to hit targets from long distances. While this was no doubt thanks in past to their skill, it was also because they had Whitworth rifles. The Confederacy never manufactured hexagonal bullets, but got around this problem by having soft slugs that followed the rifling of the barrel and, in essence, became hexagonal as they travelled down the barrel of the gun. This was an ingenious solution.

The Whitworth rifle achieved further fame when Union General John Sedgwick, on seeing his men cower in trenches 800 yards from the Confederate frontline (at the forgotten Battle of Spotsylvania Courthouse), became known for his famous last words, when he got up and declared, 'They couldn't hit an elephant at this distance,' and was promptly shot in the face, dead before he hit the ground. Sedgwick was the highest-ranking Union death in the American Civil War.

The German Chemist Who Got into Big Trouble with His Wife

Quite unfairly, Christian Friedrich Schönbein has been forgotten by history, but he shouldn't be, as not only did he make two important contributions to chemistry, he was also that kind of batty professor we often see so amusingly portrayed in films. To add to the image, he was jolly and plump, something of a mad inventor.

In the late 1830s, Schönbein recognised a distinct smell during certain chemical reactions and gave this smell the name of 'ozein' (Greek, meaning 'to smell'). It turned out that he had discovered ozone (which is O_3, as opposed to the normal O_2 in the air), and he published his findings in 1840.

So far, so good, but the problem for Schönbein was that he had no laboratory in which to work, so he was always getting into trouble with his wife when he tried to conduct experiments in the kitchen while she was cooking. One day in 1845, when his wife was away, he decided to test a mixture of acids. He knew what he was doing and he'd be careful; what could go wrong? In the middle of his experiment, he spilled a mixture of nitric and sulfuric acids. After using his wife's cotton apron to wipe it up, he hung the apron over the stove to dry; after drying, however, the apron spontaneously ignited and burned so quickly that it seemed to disappear. The accident meant that he'd disposed of any evidence that he'd been fiddling in her kitchen, but how would he explain the disappearance of her apron?

The unintended consequence of Schönbein's test was that the acids had broken down the cellulose in the apron to create nitrocellulose. He immediately understood the discovery's potential, and it didn't take long for the military to attempt to weaponise it. Because nitrocellulose factories had a habit of exploding or burning down, it took more than forty years to produce a militarily practical material. Schönbein's accidental discovery of 'guncotton' (today, often gelatinised into cordite) is the substance used to propel all modern munitions from bullets to artillery.

Sadly, it isn't recorded how he explained to his wife the disappearance of her apron, or indeed if he ever bought her a new one.

The Great Wall of India, or the Inland Customs Line

It's a myth that the Great Wall of China was built by just one emperor and that it's millennia old, but it is the most famous wall in the world (with Hadrian's coming in at number two), having been built, for the most part, a few centuries ago. What is not well known, however, is the 'Great Wall' of India, which is not made of stone, brick or wood.

India's great wall was built for possibly the most mundane of reasons: tax collection. By the 1840s, the East India Company (EIC), in terms of both power and wealth, had a stranglehold on most of India. The EIC was fundamentally a commercial enterprise, concerned with making a profit, and it was realised that a lot of Indian traders were avoiding the tax the company had levied on salt and sugar.

The solution was a novel one: plant a giant thorny hedge across most of India. Some of it was dried thorn bush and fencing, but most of it was living bush. It was a genuinely formidable barrier, some three to four metres high and around two metres thick. The thorn bush had huge spikes that would lacerate anyone foolish enough to try and push through it and was guarded by Jemadars (up to 14,000 at its peak) to stop smugglers. The barrier stretched for over 2,500 miles. This was a genuine Great Wall of India.

Except that it wasn't as formidable as it seemed. A bush can be cut back; four metres is high, but you could still throw something over it. Storms, fires and even insects destroyed parts of it, and gaps were only discovered days later. And it was unpopular because it impeded movement across India by people other than salt and sugar traders.

Not to mention it cost a fortune. Both guards and repairs incurred expenses that made some question the value of the whole enterprise, and whether they were, in fact, collecting enough in taxes to cover the cost of maintaining the wall. By the 1850s, the EIC had been wound down, and it was now the turn of the British government to consider the effectiveness of the bizarre structure they had inherited. The (wise) decision was taken to abandon this audacious (foolish) plan, and the wall was dismantled. It formally ended as a taxation frontier in 1879.

The American Invasion of Korea (Not the One in the 1950s, the One in 1871)

In the nineteenth century a number of Asian nations sealed themselves off from the outside world – most famously Japan and China, but Korea did too. America had decided it was time to 'unlock' these Asian states and trade with them. The plan had worked well in Japan, with the diplomatic mission led by Commodore Perry in the 1850s, but the idea was put on hold during the American Civil War. It wasn't until 1871 that a small fleet of American ships returned to the Pacific and travelled to the coastline of Korea. The American diplomatic vessel (which was a merchant ship, not a warship) came in towards the shore and was fired upon by Korean shore batteries.

Ten days later, the Americans landed with 650 marines and sailors. They made contact with the local Korean officials, but the Koreans wanted to avoid any discussion about their opening fire on a diplomatic mission. They did not want to lose face over the error, but the Americans mistook this for arrogance and decided to teach the Koreans a lesson. It was a classic case of cultural misunderstanding.

The US Marines assaulted and captured Ganghwa Island's forts and the batteries that had (probably) fired on the diplomatic mission. The series of clashes were one-sided: Korea had not moved with the times and was using virtually medieval technology and tactics against well-trained and well-equipped American troops. By the end of the day, the Americans had captured all the forts, with the loss of just three men, while the Koreans had suffered 243 casualties.

The Koreans had the last laugh, though. Not only did they not apologise, but they refused to speak to any member of the US government and didn't reopen diplomatic negotiations for eleven years, during which time they maintained their isolationist policy (only thawing a little to Japanese trade). The American expedition was, in a way, like the British Suez crisis in the 1950s: it was a military success, but a political failure.

Is an Ordinary Train One of the Most Devastating Weapons in History?

If you're hit by a train, it's going to hurt, but it may come as a surprise to learn that trains played key roles in four bloody wars.

In the Crimean War they tipped the balance in terms of logistics because they were able to transport much-needed provisions from the ships in port to the British frontline troops. The conditions on the ground were a nightmare, and thousands died of largely preventable causes such as frostbite. However, towards the end of the campaign, the construction of a small railway allowed the much faster movement of supplies, which made the lives of the frontline troops immeasurably more bearable. So, in this instance, the railway saved British lives, although the ammunition it carried would have led to more Russian dead.

The Crimean War took place in the 1850s, but it took less than a decade after that to appreciate how effectively trains could add to the carnage of war. Because railroads were the fastest and most efficient way to move large numbers of troops over the USA's massive interior, many of its civil war battles were fought near railway lines. The Battle of Bull Run was fought near a railway terminus, which allowed both sides to quickly bring in reserves. No railway, no battle.

In addition to burning thousands of acres of crops, Union General Grant deliberately destroyed railway lines, not merely out of wanton destruction, but rather to stop the Confederate forces from quickly retaking territory. The American Civil War was the first instance of trains playing a decisive role, mainly because they allowed the generals to quickly move large numbers of troops to the places where they were needed most. Putting it another way, without trains, the battles and the loss of life would have been smaller.

From America we must move continents and a couple of generations to Germany in 1914. The German Schlieffen Plan to overwhelm Russia and France was predicated on the mass movement of troops by locomotive. It nearly worked, and suddenly troop movements weren't counted in the thousands or tens of thousands, but in the millions, as whole armies were transported across countries and borders. Without the railways, the level of carnage in the First World War would have been greatly reduced.

Also, taking a leaf out of the lessons learnt in the Crimea, the trench-based soldiers would have been unable to remain in their positions without the regular supplies that were sent in by hundreds of trains. Quite simply, the trains added to the stalemate and fossilisation of the frontlines. And it wasn't just troops and supplies that could be easily moved on the railroads: massive train-mounted cannons, the largest artillery the world had ever seen, were used by all sides. Their shells were the size of small cars and had to be hoisted into position, so it could be said that the trains themselves had become weapons.

Then we come to the Second World War and the most shameful use of trains. Due to improvements in the internal combustion engine, trains were now less important but still used, especially for troop transportation. No longer as necessary for the provisioning of the frontlines, they were still vital for industry, and were therefore targets for bombing, which meant death to the civilians who lived near the lines and stations.

However, there was worse: the most efficient way of moving large numbers of people around was still trains, and so the Nazis built new railways so that trains could take millions of innocent Jews and other civilians to the death camps. At Auschwitz the train lines went straight to the main gate and into the compound for maximum efficiency. The Holocaust (also known more correctly as the 'Shoah'; more on this later) was a deeply disturbing part of history and one to which I cannot possibly do justice here, so let's just conclude by saying that trains had gone from being tools used for logistic support to tools used for genocide.

Railways continued to be of strategic interest in the Korean War, but by then their importance was waning. However, their impact on a century of warfare (from the 1850s to the 1950s) was horrifying, and the deaths directly linked to the use of trains as a weapon of war can be estimated in the millions.

Sir Joseph William Bazalgette: a Great Man with a Dirty Job

HIV/AIDS, bubonic plague, smallpox: their very names can spread fear and panic. However, the diseases that come from dirty water kill more humans than anything else. Cholera may not have the same fear factor as the Black Death, but it's killed more people. It is an undeniable fact that the closer humans live together, the more likely the water supply is to become tainted with human waste, which increases the chance of disease and death. Malaria, which comes from mosquitoes breeding in stagnant water, has killed more humans than anything else – ever – in the whole of history.

Joseph William Bazalgette was the chief engineer of London's Metropolitan Board of Works, whose major achievement was the creation of a sewer network for central London. This feat came in response to the Great Stink of 1858 and was instrumental in relieving the city of cholera epidemics. At the time, the River Thames was little more than an open sewer, devoid of any fish or other aquatic life and an obvious health hazard for Londoners, so a proper sewage system meant that the River Thames could finally be cleaned up.

Bazalgette's solution was to construct eighty-two miles of underground main sewers to intercept sewage outflows, and 1,100 miles of street sewers to intercept the raw sewage which, up until then, flowed freely through the streets of London. The new system was completed and opened in 1865.

This was Victorian engineering at its best not only in terms of what it could achieve, but also in terms of its magnificent constructions. Something as mundane as pumping stations (at places like Crossness) are things of beauty in their own right. However, Bazalgette's true genius was in his vision for the future: he didn't build the sewage system just to cope with a nineteenth-century-sized London, he estimated the city's population growth and, 150 years later, it all continues to work and is still not at capacity, even though London is five times the size it was at Bazalgette's time.

The exceptional level of planning for the future and the willingness to spend huge sums of money on something useful and practical was the epitome of Victorian construction. Britain had the largest empire the world has ever seen, but it did not have the world's largest palaces. The peak of British Imperial power was not personified by ostentatious royal estates, but by structures like the Clifton Suspension Bridge or Paddington Railway Station – or Bazalgette's sewers.

Sir Joseph William Bazalgette, for saving countless lives and for ensuring London continues to be sewage-free, we salute you!

Are You a Bohemian?

A 'Bohemian' now tends to mean someone who is free-spirited, open-minded and lives in a kind of liberal nirvana. But did you know that Bohemia was a real country? It was established in central Europe in the ninth century AD and lasted until the twentieth century. The Bohemian region now makes up the western two-thirds of the Czech Republic.

As countries go, its history is similar to many minor kingdoms/principalities/duchies of central Europe. It faced the perennial problems of powerful neighbours, with the rise of the Austrian Empire to its east and interference by the Holy Roman Empire to its north and west. It had its own monarchy and army, and a thriving economy based on trade, but it was never powerful enough to tip the balance in European wars and gets very little mention in history books.

One of the rare high points of Bohmeia's impact on European history was, in reality, a defeat. A blind king of Bohemia was at the Battle of Crécy (on the French side) in 1346. His name was Jan Lucemburský, which literally means 'John the Blind', and he was the founder of the Luxembourg dynasty, which was to last until 1918. Despite his disability, John was determined to join battle and ordered his steed to be tied to one of his knight's horses so that he could follow them into the fight. Unfortunately, John and his knights, along with the cream of the French heavy cavalry, perished when thousands of longbow archers poured arrows on the oncoming ranks of armoured cavalry. His ostrich-feathered helmet was found by the English after the battle, and it is this three-plumed ostrich feather arrangement that became the symbol for the Prince of Wales (and is still found on the 2 pence piece).

The kingdom became a possession of the Habsburgs, and therefore became Austrian in the sixteenth century. However, it's a quirk of language that links this medieval country with a nineteenth-century art movement. The term 'Bohemian' emerged in France when artists and writers began to concentrate in the lower-rent, lower-class, gypsy neighbourhoods of Paris. Because they had originally come from Bohemia, Bohémien was then a common term for the Romani people of France, but the phrase gradually encompassed the creative and artistic types who also lived in the neighbourhood. The Bohemian art movement has nothing to do with the attitudes or history of the Kingdom of Bohemia.

Was Jesus's Younger Brother Chinese?

Hong Xiuquan certainly thought so. Hong had been trying for years to pass the necessary exams to get into the Imperial Chinese bureaucracy. The exams were notoriously hard, and some people spent their whole lives trying to pass the tests. In 1836, after another failure, Hong fell ill, but after he'd recovered he read a Protestant pamphlet about Christianity. The fever had clearly addled his brain, because after reading the pamphlet he came up with the unusual conclusion that what had seemed to be an illness was, in truth, a message from God to tell him he was the younger brother of Jesus.

It's worth restating that Hong got all his Christian information from a leaflet, not the Bible, so to call him 'Christian' would be stretching things. However meagre the source of his inspiration, Hong believed it was his duty to bring the name of Jesus to the population of China and to rid the nation of the blight of Confucianism.

For inexplicable reasons, people started to listen to Hong, and a cult grew up around him. At this stage in his career he was genuinely trying to help the poor and the sick, deeds which were bound to make him popular, but popularity in China was a dangerous thing. It was a coincidence that his power increased as the Qing Dynasty's collapsed under aggressive Western imperialism, but he was the right man at the right time, and his charisma attracted the disenfranchised.

Hong declared himself the Heavenly King of the Heavenly Kingdom of Peace, and to be fair to the man, his self-appointed mission was, at first, similar to that of Jesus; as the years passed, However, this similarity faded away. Nevertheless, as his followers suppressed banditry and created stability where there had been none for a generation, more sections of the country began to fall under his sway.

Unsurprisingly, as his popularity increased, Hong came to the attention of the central Qing authorities, who could not tolerate what appeared to be a genuine threat to their rule, and in 1850 what had started as a grumbling, low-key rebellion turned into full-scale war. The resulting Taiping Rebellion was the second bloodiest conflict in world history, with an eye-watering casualty count of between 20 and 40 million (so that's give or take an unimaginable 20 million!) By comparison, the First World War had 10 million dead, and the Second World War saw 60 million fatalities.

The Taiping Rebellion was so-called because Taiping (Nanjing) was Hong's capital. The war was fought with incredible ferocity for fourteen years (1850–64), with Hong's forces extending as far as the gates of Shanghai. It was during Hong's attempt to capture this city that, after ten years of mainly rebel victories, the Qing finally managed to change the course of the war. However, the Qing were able to gain the upper hand only because they had the support of Western powers in possession of the latest military technology.

It still took four more years of hard fighting to push the rebels back to their capital. Nanjing fell in 1864, with Hong dying from accidental food poisoning a few days before the siege ended. His fifteen-year-old son was left in charge, but he was a guileless boy when his forces needed a charismatic leader. While this effectively ended the rule of Hong's pseudo-Christians, the numbers involved were vast, and there were still several rebel armies, numbering in the hundreds of thousands, who remained undefeated and wanted revenge. Although by now the endgame could be in no doubt, this extremely bloody civil war rumbled on for many years more.

Hong was cremated and his ashes were fired from a cannon, partly to ensure his tomb did not become a shrine to lingering rebellious ideas, and partly as spiritual punishment by not giving him a final resting place.

So, to conclude: Jesus's younger brother was Chinese. He started a war, died of food poisoning, and his remains were fired out of a cannon. Can't see that being added to the New Testament anytime soon.

William Marwood Was the Most Humane Hangman in History

Prior to William Marwood's tenure as a hangman for the British government, most criminals who were hanged would be strung up by the neck and the stool they were standing on kicked away. This meant that the victim was left to dangle, slowly asphyxiating. It was a grisly and drawn-out process. Some thought it fitted the crimes of the criminals; others thought it was unnecessarily cruel. Marwood was keen introduce a more ... humane way of executing people.

At the age of fifty-four, he persuaded the governor of Lincoln Castle Gaol to allow him to conduct an execution. This was no mean feat, as Marwood was not a rich lord, an officer of the law, or even a doctor. No, Marwood was a cobbler, but the efficient way in which he conducted the hanging, without a hitch, on 1 April 1872 directly led to his appointment as hangman by the Sheriffs of London and Middlesex in 1879. He was paid a retainer of £20 a year plus £10 per execution. This wasn't a huge sum even in those days, and it was, by no means, a full-time job, so it's probably safe to assume that Marwood continued to mend shoes most days of the week.

Marwood had the time and the inclination to develop what he called the 'long drop', a technique that ensured the prisoner's neck was broken the instant he dropped. This meant that he died of asphyxia while unconscious, and was considered to be a more merciful way to die than the 'short drop' method, which was particularly distressing for those required to witness executions at close quarters (not forgetting that the man being hanged didn't enjoy it much, either).

The long drop system (where the convicted prisoner stood over a trap door) originated with Marwood in the 1880s, so the portrayal of hangings being conducted this way from earlier periods like the American Civil War is historically inaccurate. Capital punishment is a grim business, but at least Marwood made it quick.

The History of ... Jeans

It's not often that an item of clothing is historically significant, but jeans, which have been around for about 150 years, have had a huge impact on many world cultures. Designed by Jacob Davis and Levi Strauss in 1873, they were originally intended for cowboys and others who needed hardwearing work clothes. In the 1950s they became popular with teenagers after James Dean wore them in his films *Giant* and *Rebel Without a Cause*.

Thick cotton cloth had been around for millennia, but a type called 'denim' (from *serge de Nîmes*) came from France and had been in America for some time before Jacob Davis, a tailor who frequently purchased cloth from Levi Strauss & Co., wrote to Strauss proposing a partnership to patent and sell denim clothing reinforced with rivets. Davis's original idea used copper rivets to reinforce points of stress, making them ideal for work clothes. In the film *Grapes of Wrath*, poor farmers wore denim overalls because they were inexpensive and functional; the same applied to the clothing worn by the gold prospectors in the late nineteenth century. Jeans were cheap and durable, so when James Dean wore them (and looked good in them), they were an easy way for teenagers to mimic their idol.

It's at this point that jeans (the word comes from Gênes, the French for Genoa, Italy, where the first denim trousers were made) suddenly turned from being a drab uniform of the working man to a fashionable item of clothing associated with glamour. They became an icon of the market economy, particularly in the USA, and eventually spread all over the world. Communist countries banned them as a symbol of capitalism, but jeans began to represent a new counter-culture in places like Leningrad. Interestingly, all Soviet attempts to create their own version of jeans failed, which further drove the desire for these forbidden American imports. A healthy black market developed, and jeans were smuggled into the Soviet bloc, where they changed hands for many times their original price.

So, jeans: from cowboys to communists, everyone loves them!

The History of the History of Jack the Ripper (Yes, You Read That Right)

In 1888 a person (or persons) went around murdering young women in the Whitechapel area of London. And that's about all the hard, checkable facts there are. Yes, the dismemberment of the women was unusual, but that doesn't mean that either a maniac or a surgeon carried out the crimes. The deaths of these poor women were brutal, and the fact that the culprit(s) was never caught led to endless speculation and a number of good stories, which is not the same thing as good history. On top of this, the crimes were committed when forensic science was just getting started and a more systematic approach to police work was being introduced, both of which were to become important in the early study of criminology as well as to the social history of Victorian London.

First, a bit of myth busting: whoever the murderer was, his name was not 'Jack the Ripper' – that came from a fake letter printed by a newspaper. There was also a famous 'from hell' letter, which arrived with a human kidney and is thought to have come from a copycat killing. We complain about the press today, but this was a time when editors would print just about anything to sell their newspapers. It could be that some of the letters taunting the police were made up by the newspapers themselves.

However, as the murderer(s) eluded capture, a wealth of stories started to emerge to explain the events of 1888. Contemporary images focused on the bumbling police and the victims themselves. The police were so desperate for clues they even photographed the victims' eyes, because there was an old wives' tale that said there would be an imprint of the murderer on the retina. This, of course, turned out to be nonsense. Police reports referred to interviews with a scruffy-looking man who had been seen in the area of the crimes, but nobody was ever charged. Later explanations largely ignored the few known facts and seemed almost to revel in their inventiveness.

The earliest alleged image of the murderer shows a wraith-like entity, with suggestions of a bestial quality, something not human at all. He became a bogey man to scare children, but by the first half of the twentieth century he's depicted as a more realistic 'everyman', someone's neighbour – with a dark secret.

After the Second World War, we see the rise of the 'gentleman ripper', and this was the start of the wild speculation that he could have been Queen Victoria's surgeon (an utterly sensational idea for which there was no evidence), or even a royal relative. Increasingly the murderer was portrayed as a well-dressed man in a top hat, a member of the upper classes, intent on murdering members of the lower orders. Jack was now a symbol of class war!

Nowadays everything is up for grabs, and there is something for all tastes, from sombre reassessments to sensational and shocking revelations (i.e. made up stuff). Hollywood, of course, has its own version of events, based on the graphic novel *From Hell*. In the movie of the same name, Johnny Depp plays a sympathetic police inspector who investigates the crimes and moves around a Victorian London possessed of 'working girls' with lovely complexions and perfect teeth.

Whatever your personal views, it says a lot about the human condition that, more than 125 years later, we still are fascinated by the story of a mysterious serial killer.

Tourism Needs a Reason

Very early on, enterprising businessmen understood that a local attraction brought inquisitive visitors, who enriched local coffers. The longest place name in Britain (Llanfairpwllgwy ngyllgogerychwyrndrobwllllantysiliogogogoch) is not ancient and was created in the 1860s to drum up business on the Welsh island of Anglesey. It worked remarkably well and is still bringing in the tourists today.

William George Crush was an agent for the Missouri–Kansas–Texas Railroad (popularly known as the Katy), and in 1896 he came up with an epic publicity stunt to drum up tourism in Texas: he would stage a train crash in a spectacular one-off event.

Today, everyone is equipped with camera phones, and with twenty-four-hour rolling news seeing accidents is common place, but prior to modern technology, catching an accident as it happened, either on film or in front of your eyes, was exceedingly rare. Who wouldn't want to see a train crash … from a safe distance?

So a special track in the temporary 'city' of Crush, Texas, was built, and circus tents were brought in to accommodate the 40,000 people who came to see two locomotives crash into each other. The publicity (and the economics) around the attraction was such that train fares throughout Texas were reduced to encourage people to come and witness this free event. The plan came together and, for one day only, Crush was the second most populous city in the state. While the event itself was free, food, lodging and everything else connected to it was not.

The spectacle was delayed as the crowd fought against the police, who wanted the spectators to be at a pre-arranged safe viewing point. It was a fine balance between wanting to be close so as not to miss a thing, while at the same time keeping a safe distance as two locomotives raced towards each other. Eventually, towards the end of the day, the trains set off. They were both travelling at around 45 miles per hour when they crashed, head on. However, the force of the collision was greater than anticipated and caused the steam boilers of both engines to explode. The photo from the moment of impact was taken by a man who lost an eye to a steel bolt. He was lucky, as three others died.

Because of the fatalities, Crush was fired from the Katy railroad. Somewhat cynically, he was reinstated days later after most of the resulting publicity had only been around the amazing images of the actual train wreck. This is yet another salient reminder that human beings are fascinated by shocking events.

What Is a Cossack?

You've heard mention of them, invariably to do with Russia and the tsar, and they seem to be militaristic horsemen? But who were they? Are they related to Mongols or Huns? And what happened to them?

The Cossacks first appear in history during the fourteenth century in the area that is now Ukraine and southern Russia. At the time, the whole region was under Mongol control. Cossacks are of Slavic origin, but their culture was heavily influenced by the horse raiders of the Mongol warlords, and while they were Christian, they didn't pay much attention to the whole 'love thy neighbour' concept.

For the most part, the Cossacks fell under Russian imperial control. However, they were a loose federation of warring groups and only came together to do the tsar's bidding – if it meant there was booty in it for them. You might say they became Imperial Russia's irregular cavalry forces.

They frequently clashed with the Muslim Tartars of Ukraine, who were to the Ottoman sultans exactly what the Cossacks were to the Russian tsars. While the Cossacks raided Ottoman lands, they also did a fair amount of raiding into Lithuania and Poland, too.

As their relationship with the Russian state evolved, the Cossacks became the tsars' secret police and a name to be feared in Russia. As well as successfully holding previously separate areas such as Siberia, the Moscow-based tsars depended on them to scout out new territory and act as the spearhead as they conquered far into the east.

It wasn't all plain sailing – there were revolts, raids and disagreements with central authority – but by and large the relationship between the Cossacks and the tsar was mutually beneficial. The irony was that this semi-autonomous group came to be a symbol of the tsar's autocratic rule. After the October Revolution of 1917, the core of the pro-tsarist White forces were Cossacks, but some groups fought on Lenin's side, too. It was always difficult to generalise about them as a group.

However, as they were autonomous, with a long history of working mainly for the old regime, there was a 'decossackization' (there's a word you don't see very often), which was, in essence, a vicious purge leading to the deaths of tens of thousands at the hands of the Red Army. Approximately half a million Cossacks were killed or deported from their homelands. This was followed by the great famine in the 1930s, which killed hundreds of thousands more. By the Second World War, the Cossacks in the Ukrainian region were a shadow of their former selves. While not all Cossacks joined the Nazis in the 1941 invasion of the Soviet Union, it is understandable that, after a generation of harsh treatment at the hands of the communists, many did.

The 'Betrayal of the Cossacks' saw the British hand over tens of thousands of Cossack families to Stalin at the end of the war. Stalin continued purges and massacres against them, and in the space of just forty years a culture and civilisation that had lasted for 600 years had been effectively destroyed.

To end on a happier note, in 2005 Vladimir Putin recognised them as a special ethnic group, and nowadays there are around 7 million Cossacks living in Russia.

THE TWENTIETH CENTURY

The Boxer Rebellion

Just scraping into the twentieth century, the Boxer Rebellion (1899–1901) occurred in the middle of what the Chinese call their 'century of humiliation', when, from around 1840 to 1949, China was plagued by weak central government and attacked by predatory foreign powers. The people Westerners called 'boxers' called themselves the 'Righteous Harmony Society', and were the poor people of China, many of whom had no weapons and used traditional martial arts in combat. Because Westerners had not previously encountered Kung Fu, the best analogy they could come up with was 'boxer'.

The Boxers were able to thrive due to the lack of law enforcement aligned with a deep suspicion of the missionary movement in China. (It was just a generation earlier that Christian missionary pamphlets had led to the Taiping Rebellion and the deaths of 20 million or more Chinese.

Their solution to what they saw (with justification) as the takeover of their country by foreigners was to attack missionaries, Chinese Christians, and pretty much any other symbol of Western power in China. It is estimated that by the end of the uprising the Boxers had killed about 100,000 people, only 1 per cent of whom were soldiers. So, while resisting foreign powers is justified, massacring people for their beliefs is not, and the Boxers were in no way the 'good guys'.

This unexpected and violent uprising caught the foreign imperial powers completely off-guard, which led to unprecedented cooperation. It is odd to think that in 1901, Germany, Italy, Britain, Austro-Hungary, Russia, France, Japan and America were all fighting efficiently together, and yet, just a few years later, they would all be at war with each other. This rare alliance was not lost on them at the time, and there are photos of a group of soldiers, each one representing a different empire.

Let's digress for a moment to comment on the American position in all of this. At the time and according to the fashion of the day, the USA seemed to be intent on building an empire of its own. In the space of ten years, it had a war in Cuba, it had captured the Philippines, and it was keen to advance its interests in China. When things didn't work out, rather than admitting that they had come too late to the game, the Americans just pretended they were always anti-empire – a position they have maintained ever since.

Meanwhile, back at the rebellion, things were heating up as the Boxers concentrated on major urban areas like Tianjin and Beijing, where the Western powers had their compounds. It was a race against time to get foreign troops to these inland areas before they were overrun and the foreign populations massacred. The

Chinese had the advantage of recently purchased Krupp weapons from Germany, and the multinational forces were regularly harassed and attacked as they made several attempts to move inland as fast as possible. While the Boxers had some of the best weapons in the world, they were not enough to overcome poor tactics and discipline, and the much smaller force of professional soldiers got through to the cities just in time.

The end result was further humiliation for China and an increase in Western presence in the country for another half-century. The cooperation in China proved fleeting for the foreign imperial powers; Japan and Russia were at each other's throats just a few years later; the First World War was only a decade away.

What Do You Get if You Mix a Scottish-Born Canadian Émigré with a North London Factory?

James Paris Lee (1831–1904) was a Scottish-born Canadian émigré who invented a bolt-action repeating rifle. He had been tinkering with the design for some time, but no one seemed interested until, in the late nineteenth century, the British were looking to update their Martini-Enfield rifles. As the name suggests, those rifles were made in a factory (the Royal Small Arms Factory) in Enfield, north London.

The result was the Lee Enfield .303 rifle, first produced in 1895. This was to become the standard infantry rifle of the British Army in three major wars, including both world wars. In the Boer War, it roughly matched the capabilities of the Boers' German Krupp rifles. This competition between Lee Enfield and Krupp continued in the First World War. The German rifle had the longer range, but the rifle itself was longer and, therefore, more cumbersome in the trenches.

There was one simple innovation that made the Lee Enfield an outstanding weapon: it had a bent bolt. With a non-bent bolt-action rifle, the user had to look away from the target in order to place another round in the chamber and then spend seconds re-aiming the rifle before firing. A bent bolt eliminated the messiness of reloading, and as a consequence the speed at which the rifle could be fired meant that there were times when the Germans thought they faced multiple machine-gun fire, when in reality it was just soldiers armed with Lee Enfields performing with brutal efficiency.

The rifle was still the standard sidearm in the Second World War, and as it was a proven weapon it continued in service in other subsequent conflicts. Even today it is possible to see, say, Afghani tribesmen with rifles, simply because they are more accurate over distance than an AK-47. While not the most mass-produced firearm in history (that would be the AK-47), about 17 million Lee Enfield rifles were made in the twentieth century.

The Dreadnought

Over the years the Royal Navy has commissioned eight vessels called *Dreadnought*, but it was the seventh version that caused a storm.

Built in 1906, HMS *Dreadnought* was commissioned as the result of a challenge by Admiral Sir John 'Jacky' Fisher, who ordered the design for a more efficient and faster weapons platform, a battleship, armed with twelve-inch guns and able to cruise at a speed of twenty-one knots. In other words, make it fast and deadly, and when the *Dreadnought* was launched, it caused shockwaves around the wold.

The *Dreadnought* was the first battleship of her era to have a uniform main battery, rather than having a few large guns complemented by a secondary battery of smaller guns. She was also the first capital ship to be powered by steam turbines, making her the fastest battleship (but certainly not the fastest vessel) in the world at the time. It was *Dreadnought*'s launch that helped spark a naval arms race as navies around the world, particularly the German Imperial Navy, rushed to match her in the build-up to the First World War. *Dreadnought* had set the bar in naval technology. Could anyone match her?

Dreadnought's entry into service in 1906 represented such a marked advance in the design of battleships that her name became associated with an entire generation of battleships, called the 'dreadnoughts', as well as with the class of ships named after her. The generation of ships that had come before her and had been made obsolete became known as 'pre-dreadnoughts'.

Interestingly, despite being the cause of such concern to the world's navies before the First World War, she did not participate in any of the war's key naval battles. The largest one was the Battle of Jutland in 1916, when the German navy attempted to break out of its blockade. At the time of the battle, *Dreadnought* was being refitted and was out of action, but she did achieve one military success during the war: she became the only battleship to sink a submarine when she rammed the German U-boat SM U-29 as it unexpectedly broke the surface after firing a torpedo at another dreadnought in 1915. *Dreadnought* cut the submarine in half, showing she could be deadly even without firing her guns (although the contact was unintentional).

Dreadnought underlines the speed of technological advances at the time – advances which caught up with her when she was reduced to reserve status in 1919 and sold for scrap two years later. Having shocked the world with her amazing technology and been in service for fewer than fifteen years, she was now obsolete.

The arms race started by *Dreadnought* in 1906 was an irrelevance by the Second World War, when aircraft attacks from land or carriers could easily sink these huge and relatively slow capital ships.

Jack Daniels Is One of the Most Famous Men in the World

And yet it's just his name that is well-known, and then only in association with intoxicating liquor. The name 'Jack Daniels' has evolved beyond the man to become a brand. Little is known about him, including his year of birth. Some think he was born in 1849, others claim that it was 1850, but we do know that he was the youngest of ten siblings and that his mother died of complications from Jack's birth.

Daniels founded his famous whiskey distillery in Lynchburg, Tennessee, as a young man (again, the date is contested) and he was, in short, a shrewd Southern businessman with a bit of a temper. He never married or had children, but he did have a large extended family. In 1907, Jack was beginning to feel his age, and entrusted his business to one of his nephews. The nephew was a good accountant and had been doing the numbers for the business for years.

In 1911 (now in his sixties), Jack, although semi-retired, was in his office and had forgotten, once again, the combination of his safe. Annoyed and frustrated, he allowed his temper to get the better of him, and he did what anyone might do: he kicked the safe. The safe was made out of reinforced steel and weighed more than a ton, so it was a one-sided contest which Jack didn't win. He managed to break one of his toes, and the toe became infected, which led to his death.

If there's a moral to this story, it probably has something to do with anger management.

The First-Ever Air Raid Didn't Happen in Europe

1911 and 1912 saw a short, sharp war between Italy and the Ottoman Empire in Libya. The Italians invaded with 100,000 troops against an Ottoman and Libyan force of 28,000. The Italians also brought the latest technology: airplanes and zeppelins.

The war was one-sided. The Italians had the numbers and the technology, and no matter how bravely the Libyans and Ottomans fought their cause was doomed. The invasion would eventually lead to an Italian takeover of Libya and a further weakening of the Ottoman state. However, it was not a key moment in the war, but a bright idea by an obscure pilot, that was to change warfare forever.

In November 1911, Lieutenant Giulio Gavotti wrote in a letter to his father,

> Today I have decided to throw bombs from the aeroplane. It is the first time that we will try this and if I succeed, I will be really pleased to be the first person to do it.

Gavotti did indeed hang out of his flimsy aircraft and fling a bomb at troops in a desert oasis below. It was an inauspicious start, but the point had been proven, and by the end of this war the Italians were regularly dropping bombs from the zeppelins as well. Just a few years later, in 1915, much larger

German zeppelins bombed London during the First World War. Paris was also attacked in January of 1916. These raids saw *tons* of explosives dropped on some of the largest, most famous cities in the world. Dozens died, but it was all, still, somewhat rudimentary. It would, of course, get far worse a generation later in the Second World War.

All of this death and destruction can be traced back to a forgotten Italian lieutenant in a forgotten colonial war.

The First World War Wasn't What You Think It Was

The First World War is such a big subject, with such a glut of reference material, it is possible to spend years researching even the narrowest of its topics. However, in order to simplify some of the complex stories, TV dramas and documentaries often perpetuate inaccuracies and incorrect assumptions. Here are some examples:

Soldiers spent 7 to 10 days (not months) in the trenches before being sent behind the frontlines for R & R.

More days were spent in the trenches *not* fighting than suffering under barrages and assaults.

In order to break the deadlock, those in charge invented the 'creeping (or rolling) barrage' and used air power, submarine warfare, gas attacks and tanks in innovative ways. Although remembered as the exact opposite, this was one of the most experimental wars in history.

The first day of the Somme was horrific for the British, but it relieved pressure on the front from the Verdun area, where the French forces were in danger of collapsing. After the carnage, the British had suffered about 400,000 casualties (combined dead and wounded), but the Germans had lost 500,000 (figures vary, but the German losses were greater). At the time of the battle, the German General von Fuchs said,

> Enemy superiority is so great that we are not in a position either to fix their forces in position or to prevent them from launching an offensive elsewhere. We just do not have the troops.

The Somme was neither pointless nor an Allied defeat.

Although the question is frequently raised regarding whether this was a 'world' war, it is a fact that it was genuinely global. Japan was on the Allied side fighting German Imperial possessions in the Pacific. There was fighting in many areas of the Middle East and not just at Gallipoli. This was the war that made Jerusalem a British Imperial possession after the British took it from the crumbling Ottoman Empire. There was also fighting in Africa, particularly in the east of the continent, and it was here that the Germans technically surrendered last.

Finally, it was a victory, *not* a stalemate, particularly for Britain, which gained large amounts of overseas territory and was, at the end of the war, at the peak of its empire. Compare that to the end of the Second World War, when Britain was on its knees financially, with ruined cities and an empire on the brink of collapse.

At the time of this book's publication, we are in the middle of anniversary fever, which, with so many aspects of this war to commemorate, will only intensify. (For more on this, have a look at my book *The Busy Person's Guide to British History*.)

An Unpronounceable Battle that Was Important in Both World Wars

Heligoland Bight is the part of the German coast that was fought over at the start of both world wars, but in rather different ways.

In August 1914, as war was breaking out across Europe, German destroyers and cruisers heavily patrolled the area. The British Royal Navy, eager to gain control of the seas, sent a large force of thirty-one warships to confront the German High Seas Fleet. Germany had long wanted to match the Royal Navy's might, and this was a chance to prove itself in an engagement that was the largest the British had fought since the Battle of Trafalgar in 1805. Unfortunately for the Kriegsmarine (the German navy), it turned out that they were no match. One British cruiser was badly damaged, but the Royal Navy sank one German destroyer, three light cruisers and two torpedo boats, as well as heavily damaging a number of other ships. It was an emphatic British victory, which resulted in the Kriegsmarine spending most of the rest of the war safely in dock (except for the Battle of Jutland).

The second Battle of Heligoland Bight was very different but also occurred early on in the war. This time it was December 1939, when three squadrons of Wellington bombers were sent by the RAF to destroy the support ships that were resupplying the dangerous U-boats hunting in British and Atlantic waters. Unlike the first encounter, this mission was not a success, and twelve of the twenty-four Wellingtons were shot down. The Germans lost a couple of fighter planes, but the target ships were never hit. Just as the first battle had been an emphatic victory for Britain, this was an emphatic victory for Germany.

However, the bombing raid resulted in two important changes. The RAF realised how vulnerable their bombers were in daylight and adapted their strategy to attack at night for most of the rest of the war. The Luftwaffe, however, came to the entirely different conclusion that their daylight fighters had huge superiority and that their naval bases were safe from British bombing. Both assumptions led to a lack of development in these two areas, which meant once the tide turned later in the war, the Germans had little time to compensate for their deficiencies.

So, two forgotten battles were both fought in the same area in two different wars, with two different results – and important consequences for both sides.

The Many Deaths of Rasputin

Grigori Rasputin is one of those rare historical figures who lives on, more as a myth than as a man. There's no denying his power as an adviser to Tsar Nicholas II's court, where he was associated with spiritual healing and the occult; the photos of him are genuinely eerie. A dispassionate view of him reveals a man who was like many other influential hangers-on in imperial courts over the centuries; however, it was his almost supernatural stamina that makes him a fascinating subject. The story of Rasputin's death is full of contradictory evidence, mixed with hearsay and exaggeration, so let's try to stick to the known facts.

There are many stories about people who were *nearly* assassinated, the point being that the assassin missed and the target lived. That was not the case in June of 1914. Rasputin was on his way home when a woman jumped him in the street and stabbed him in the stomach. He managed to fend off any further wounds by beating her away with a stick. Stomach wounds are notoriously fatal; Rasputin bled profusely and underwent weeks of surgery, medical treatment and recuperation. It's not often you hold your own guts and live to tell the tale, but Rasputin did.

There was a second assassination attempt eighteen months later. The facts are that in December of 1916, Rasputin was invited to the Yusupov Palace in St Petersburg (the Yusupovs were a hugely wealthy and influential family). Because he often met secretly with courtiers, Rasputin had no reason to be suspicious; however, unbeknown to him, an entire cabal of assassins was waiting for him in a soundproof room.

Rasputin arrived at what looked like the end of a dinner party, and he was offered poisoned cakes and drinks laced with cyanide. One version says he declined the offers; another, that he ate and drank but appeared to suffer no ill effects. Either way, Felix Yusupov grew bored with the proceedings, walked behind Rasputin and shot him twice in the back. The later autopsy revealed that both wounds had caused colossal internal damage and bleeding – something which should have been fatal.

Rasputin fell to the ground and most of the conspirators left. When Yusupov went back to the body, Rasputin lunged at him, and a vicious brawl ensued. Caked in his own blood, Rasputin escaped up the stairs. He was shot twice more, stabbed a few times and clubbed to the ground, just for good measure.

A policeman heard the shots and came by to investigate. Yusupov was honest about what had happened and asked the policeman to keep quiet about the murder of one of the most famous men in Russia. Unsurprisingly, the policeman ignored this request and went looking for assistance.

The race was now on to get rid of Rasputin's body, which was pretty damning evidence. He was rolled up in a curtain and thrown from a bridge into an ice-hole in the Malaya Nevka River. However, in their haste, Yusupov and his accomplices forgot to attach weights to Rasputin's corpse, and his body was found three days later.

The autopsy revealed that one of the final shots had hit him in the head, and even Rasputin's bear-like stamina couldn't survive that. It is now part of the legend that it took drowning in the river to ultimately finish him off, despite all that had gone before, but

Rasputin was dead before his body had been removed from the palace.

But the story doesn't end there. The final chapter of Rasputin's life ... erm ... death had yet to be written.

As a testament to his close connection to the Romanovs, Rasputin was laid to rest in a prestigious burial site in the grounds of the Alexander Palace. However, early 1917 saw the start of a revolution in Russia, and palaces, as symbols of a despised regime, were prime targets for destruction. Because Rasputin himself was seen as an embodiment of the old imperial system, it was never likely that he would be allowed to rest in peace for long.

When the revolutionaries arrived at the Alexander Palace, they found Rasputin's grave and dug him up. He hadn't been in the ground that long and, as Russian winters are notoriously bitter, decomposition was minimal, so the angry mob had a chance to gaze into the face of their enemy. It was decided to take him to the nearby forest and burn him.

A funeral pyre was built; the body was placed on top, and the bonfire was set alight. But as the flames rose higher and higher, Rasputin appeared to be getting up. He was alive and the communist revolutionaries had angered him! The terrified mob turned into a hysterical crowd that fled the scene. (Well, you would, wouldn't you?)

The reason for Rasputin's apparent resurrection was not black magic but something all undertakers know. If a person is to be cremated, certain tendons have to be cut. This is because as the body heats up, these tendons contract and can cause the body to move. The last thing anyone wants to hear is a body bumping around inside its coffin, apparently being burnt alive. Oblivious to this information, the crowd assumed it was more of Rasputin's black magic, but the reality was a little more mundane.

Sergeant Stubby

Stubby is an unusual name for a soldier ... unless the 'soldier' is a bull terrier and the most decorated dog in the First World War. He is also the only animal the US Army ever promoted to sergeant.

Stubby first appeared at Yale University while a group of soldiers were in the midst of training. He made friends with Corporal Robert Conroy, who smuggled Stubby under his coat when he was sent to France.

When Stubby was discovered, he charmed the commanding officer, who allowed him to stay, and he became the mascot for the 103rd Infantry. He served in the trenches of France for eighteen months and participated in four offensives and seventeen battles during the last year of the war. His enhanced canine senses allowed him to detect sound and smell before humans could, so Stubby was used to warn soldiers of incoming mustard gas and artillery attacks, saving the lives of countless men. Stubby was also able to locate and comfort wounded soldiers who had been separated from their units. He himself was wounded on several occasions.

On one occasion, he was solely responsible for capturing a German spy in the Argonne, a feat for which any soldier could expect a commendation.

Stubby's exploits became front-page news, and Sergeant Stubby (having been promoted for action in combat) became the most famous dog in America. After the war, he was smuggled back to the United States, where he became a celebrity and met US presidents.

Somewhat bizarrely, when he died in 1926, his body was stuffed and put on display at the Smithsonian Institution in Washington DC.

There Really Are Such Things as Submarine Aircraft Carriers

The first nation to think that combining an airplane with a submarine was a good idea was Germany in the First World War. The SM U-12, a U-boat, had one Friedrichshafen FF.29 reconnaissance plane attached to the outside. The U-boat didn't actually submerge, but the plane did carry a twenty-six-pound bomb, which would be dropped in a bombing raid closer to the target. The idea was that the two would travel together to the English coast, the plane would detach from the sub, fly to its target, drop its bomb and return to dock with the submarine. The plan went into effect over London on Christmas Day of 1914. It was an inauspicious start for an obscure and highly complex area of naval flight, but the point was proven, although the vessel had yet to submerge with an aircraft on board.

After the war, Italy, Germany, Japan, the US and UK all looked at the idea of combining seaplanes with submarines, to greater or lesser extents. The idea persists today using a submarine with nuclear weapons. If you could creep up to the shore of an enemy nation and launch an air attack, the mission would be over before the enemy could respond, with the additional bonus that once docked back on the submarine, the attacker would likely be able to slip away to fight another day.

All these countries had prototypes and some even made it into the Second World War, but the country that got really excited about the idea was Japan. Towards the end of the war the Japanese designed and built the I-400-class submarine. This giant ship was three times the size of a traditional Japanese submarine. Inside it were three Aichi M6A Seiran dive bombers. They would have to be partly assembled and disassembled before launch and recovery, but the fact was that the Japanese now had a secret floating airbase, capable of striking anywhere in the Pacific. The concept and design were exactly what your brain comes up with when you say 'submarine carrier'. However, the whole project was extremely complicated, expensive and time consuming. It turned out not to be the future of the Japanese Imperial Navy and made no real impact on the war.

After the Second World War, with aircraft ranges constantly improving and with missile technology constantly advancing, the idea of a submarine carrier was just too unworkable and almost too old-fashioned to pursue. The earlier problem of striking the enemy with impunity was solved with ballistic submarine and drone technology. Today, a nuclear submarine armed with a weapon like the Trident missile is far more deadly than a submarine large enough for three or four fighter planes. Although admittedly, drones and missiles are not as cool as the idea of a submarine emerging from the sea, opening a hangar door and letting loose fighter aircraft.

The Battle of Los Angeles: an Example of Mass Hysteria

The attack on Pearl Harbor was no joke. It was a ruthlessly efficient assault on what was thought to be the impregnable naval base of a rising global power. As the sun set on 7 December 1941, nearly 2,500 Americans were dead, with many capital ships sunk or heavily damaged. The attack shocked America to its core.

There had been no warning, not even a declaration of war. So after this, it is unsurprising that America both feared and hated the Japanese Empire. A few short months later, on 23 February 1942, a Japanese submarine surfaced and shelled Ellwood, California. Damage was minimal, but the shock and horror of the Japanese navy being able to attack mainland America caused general panic. Everyone was on edge.

The next night, something happened. Nobody is quite clear exactly what triggered events, but it was thought that a spotter on one of the anti-aircraft guns in Los Angeles mistook a weather balloon or a cloud formation for an incoming wave of Japanese bombers.

All hell broke loose. Air-raid sirens blared and every anti-aircraft gun in the city roared into action. Spotlights combed the sky for the attacking aircraft, people stampeded in the streets or drove, terrified, back to their homes. It was complete pandemonium.

More than 1,400 shells were fired at an empty sky. Five people died: three from car crashes and two from heart attacks. The incident is clearly an example of the paranoia created by the outbreak of war, but has been turned by some into evidence that the US Army was trying to repel an alien invasion. No, really. Quite frankly, given the level of incompetence, the US Army in Los Angeles couldn't have repelled the Italian air force, let alone alien spaceships.

This event was the inspiration for Steven Spielberg's only attempt at a comedy film and his only flop to date: *1941*.

A Bizarre Second World War Battle

Castle Itter is a small fortification in Austria used by the SS during the Second World War as a prison for high-profile detainees. It is also the site of one of the most curious battles of the war.

On 6 May 1945, the Third Reich was collapsing and peace was on the horizon. When the German commander in charge of the castle (he was also in charge of Dachau concentration camp) committed suicide and some of the Waffen SS soldiers fled, one of the prisoners, Zvonimir Čučković, a Yugoslav freedom fighter, escaped and went looking for some Allied troops to rescue the rest of the prisoners.

At the same time, Major Josef Gangl (an Austrian in the German army), who had collaborated with Austrian resistance in the closing days of the war, also intended to free the castle prisoners, but decided instead to surrender to the Americans. When Čučković found the American column and persuaded them to follow him, an unexpected alliance formed: Major Gangl and his Wehrmacht troops would fight alongside the Americans against the SS guards.

The Battle of Castle Itter was hardly pivotal, but the SS faced not only the Americans, but also Austrian partisans and French prisoners who joined in. It was a wonderful symbol of the unifying effect of the Allies compared to the polarising effect of the Nazis.

The battle may not have been big (a maximum of 100 men were involved), but it was vicious. The Americans' Sherman tank was destroyed, and Major Josef Gangl was killed by a sniper, but it was the only time the American army fought alongside the German army in the entire war.

The SS were defeated and surrendered, and the rest of the prisoners were released unharmed.

The Horrors of Sook Ching

There have been many dreadful massacres, but there's one that is largely unknown in the West and is, proportionately, one of the worst in history: the Sook Ching massacre.

During the Second World War, Singapore was part of Malaya and under British rule. Britain had done an excellent job of protecting this key port from naval attack, so it's hard to understand why it paid no attention to an attack from the land.

The Japanese arrived with fewer fighting men than the Brits. They were at the end of a fragile supply chain, and their troops were tired and worn down after traversing the jungle. All of this gave the British forces an advantage. The fighting was brief, and had the British, with their colonial forces, dug in their heels, it's likely that the Japanese assault would have failed. Churchill even advised the British commander, Lieutenant General Arthur Percival, of the situation, probably assuming that Percival would do his utmost to defeat the enemy and save the colony.

In a desultory attempt to defend the city, the causeway to Singapore was destroyed, but was rapidly repaired by the Japanese; on 15 February 1942, Percival's 80,000 troops surrendered to 35,000 Japanese. This is considered to be one of the most humiliating moments in British military history.

While most of the British soldiers were marched off to their doom in the various horrific Japanese labour camps, it is what happened to the indigenous population that is truly chilling. Commander Masayuki Oishi ordered the systematic extermination of perceived 'hostile elements' in the Chinese population of Singapore.

The 'Sook Ching' operation was later extended to include the Chinese in Malaya as well, although, since they were in the countryside, it was harder to round up ethnic Chinese locals. The subsequent massacres took place from 18 February to 4 March 1942, at various places in the region.

The Japanese have admitted to premeditated murder, but claim they killed 'only' 5,000, whereas Singaporeans estimate numbers as high as 100,000. If the latter is accurate, it means that in a colony of 800,000 people, one person in every eight was killed.

General Percival survived the war and returned to Britain; he was reviled by some for his failure in Malaya, while others respected him because he had been a POW and had been held for a time in Changi Prison.

After the war, seven Japanese officers were tried for the massacre; five were given life sentences, and two (including Oishi) were executed.

The Most Dangerous Substance Ever Discovered

New chemical compounds are regularly discovered and created. Some of those created are done so intentionally, and the results are largely as expected; others turn out to be complete shocks. In 1930 a new, very volatile compound was discovered in Germany by the scientists Ruff and Krug. It was so unstable that it was ignored until a few years later when interest in it was rekindled by Nazi scientists at the Kaiser Wilhelm Institute.

The compound was dubbed 'n-stoff' (substance N), and it had some remarkable properties. It boiled at room temperature and produced a toxic gas; if the gas ignited (which it did, *very* easily), it burned at over 2,400 degrees Celsius. If it decomposed, it turned into a hydrofloric and hydrochloric acid, usually in steam form. It was corrosive and explosive on contact with water. If it bonded with carbon, it formed an explosive that would detonate if touched. It turned out to be a better oxidising agent than … oxygen. What does all of this mean in layman's terms? It was so good at setting fire to things that it made substances not normally considered to be flammable very flammable – things like sand, or glass, or even asbestos.

Research and production of n-stoff was moved to Falkenhagen Industrial Complex, a bunker network in Brandenburg where other nasty chemicals like sarin gas were manufactured. The plan was to produce fifty tons a month and use it to melt defences, burn tanks, destroy armies and set fire to cities. The chemical name for this highly dangerous compound is chlorine triflouride, and it really was a mad scientist's weapon.

However, by the end of the war, only about thirty tons had been produced. The reason? The stuff was simply so unstable and so dangerous that there was no practical way to use it. One plan to put it into flamethrowers failed because it ate its way through all the components of the flamethrower that weren't steel and then set fire to everything else, just because it could.

The Falkenhagen Industrial Complex was captured by the Soviet Union, and exactly what happened during the next few years is unknown, but n-stoff disappeared from the pages of history ... until a very different organisation took an interest in it.

Oxidising agents are vital in rocket fuel, and it was chlorine triflouride's extremely effective oxidisation properties that interested NASA for its potential use as rocket fuel. That was until the early 1950s, when a tank ruptured and spilled 900 kilograms of the compound over a concrete floor. The substance caught fire (as it inevitably does; it was a miracle it didn't just explode) and proceeded to set fire to the concrete. The fire was so fierce it burned through thirty centimetres of solid concrete and then, as a finale, burned through ninety centimetres of gravel. Under any other circumstances, gravel wouldn't burn. It can be scorched, and it can melt under extremely high temperatures, but it takes a very special kind of chemical fire to make gravel burn.

If that wasn't bad enough, NASA faced another problem with chlorine triflouride: when it was mixed with any other propellant needed to turn it into rocket fuel, it instantly ignited – every single time. Chlorine triflouride doesn't play well with others.

Dr John Drury Clark (an expert in rocket fuels for NASA), once made this remark:

> The operator is confronted with the problem of coping with a metal-fluorine fire. For dealing with this situation, I have always recommended a good pair of running shoes.

Unsurprisingly, NASA ended tests on this vicious compound, and that was that ... until a peaceful application for the compound was found. It is now used (in teeny-tiny amounts) to clean superconductor chambers without having to dismantle them.

When Was the Last Person Executed at the Tower of London?

Many nobles have lost their heads either in the Tower of London or nearby on Tower Hill. You would assume that the last execution happened quite a while ago, and while there was certainly a long gap before the very last one, it happened as recently as the Second World War.

Josef Jakobs was a German citizen born in Luxembourg in 1898. After fighting for Germany in the trenches of the First World War, he married and became a dentist. None of this is likely to get you executed in the Tower. However, during the Second World War, Jakobs was recruited by the Abwehr, the German secret service, and became a spy. Exactly how much of what he did was part of the act and how much was genuine, we'll never know; however, we do know that he spent a few years in a Swiss prison for selling counterfeit gold and was later found to be helping Jews escape mainland Europe (for a fee). The latter may have been the sign of a decent man doing the right thing, or the perfect cover for a Nazi spy.

However, what happened next was undeniably a sign that he was a spy. In 1941, Jakobs was flown from the Netherlands and parachuted into Britain, where he was spotted descending by the local Home Guard. He was quickly discovered because he broke his ankle in the jump and fired his pistol in the air to summon help. He was caught still wearing his flying suit and carrying £500 in British currency, along with forged papers, a radio and, just for good measure, a German sausage. Jakobs wasn't exactly a master of stealth.

He was imprisoned in the Tower, which was then being used as a makeshift jail, often for Luftwaffe pilots. Under interrogation it became clear that, as well as being uncooperative, Jakobs was a fanatical Nazi. Other captive Abwehr agents were incarcerated for the duration of the war in exchange for information, but Jakobs gave the British authorities nothing. He was blatantly guilty and unrepentant – not the best defence.

He was court-martialled, found guilty, and because he had been captured as an enemy combatant (and not by civilian police) he was sentenced to death by firing squad. (Hanging was the usual means of execution for uncooperative German spies when they were discovered by the British civilian police.) Because of the broken ankle, he had to sit down for his firing squad, and was shot on the morning of 15 August 1941. His chair was damaged and is sometimes on display at the Tower. So the last execution at the Tower of London is within living memory.

A Lethal Historian

It is estimated that a million women served in the Red Army during the Second World War. Some of them were in supporting roles, but hundreds of thousands were trained combat troops, fighting on the frontlines in the air force, the infantry, and tank divisions. Amongst these was Lyudmila Pavlichenko, who is a reminder that 'Soviet' and 'Russian' are not interchangeable. While she fought tenaciously for the Soviet Union, she was Ukrainian and spent most of her combat tours fighting in and around the key Ukrainian cities of Odessa and Sevastopol.

Before the war, Lyudmila worked in a factory and was an amateur sharpshooter. When war broke out, she was assigned to the Red Army's 25th Rifle Division where she trained as a sniper. By the end of the war, she had 309 confirmed kills, making her the deadliest female sniper in history (nearly double the kills of Chris Kyle of 'American Sniper' fame).

Pavlichenko could be brutal as well as lethal: on one occasion she admonished a comrade for finishing off a wounded German soldier (an act of mercy), saying that the enemy deserved no sympathy. Snipers traditionally take out key personnel like officers or communications teams, rather than general infantry, but Lyudmila was so good that she also targeted enemy snipers and killed three dozen of them during the war.

Among her many decorations, she was *twice* awarded the Order of Lenin, the highest military decoration of the Soviet Army.

She was so important that she was sent on a tour of the Allied nations as a goodwill ambassador, and she was the first Soviet citizen to be received by a US President when Franklin Roosevelt welcomed her to the White House. She was later invited by Eleanor Roosevelt to tour America and to relate her experiences through an interpreter. While meeting with reporters in Washington DC, she was dumbfounded by the questions and comments put to her.

> One reporter even criticised the length of the skirt of my uniform, saying that in America women wear shorter skirts and besides my uniform made me look fat.

Needless to say, no man would have had to endure snide comments about his appearance in uniform.

Pavlichenko rose to the rank of major and retired from active service in 1953. Following the war, Pavlichenko became a military historian, making her probably the most dangerous historian that's ever lived. She died in Moscow in 1974. Apart from her war medals, her outstanding achievements were recognised and commemorated on two Soviet stamps. In 2015 a joint Russian and Ukrainian film called the *Battle of Sebastopol* was made about her wartime career.

The Story of the Nazi Super Cows

This may sound like an internet hoax, but it isn't. In January 2015, Devon farmer Dereck Gow had to put down seven of his rare breed Heck cows. The reason for this? The cows were so aggressive that they had tried, on multiple occasions, to attack him and his farm hands (this is a breed with large horns, so attacks by goring could lead to very serious injuries). Farmer Gow shouldn't have been surprised, because the Heck cow was the result of Nazi breeding experiments.

It is a well-known fact that Hitler and Himmler were obsessed with the Aryan history of Europe, and when they couldn't find it, they made it up. Archaeological finds were faked or the wrong information was assigned to innocent artefacts in order to support the idea of a pre-Christian nirvana in northern Europe.

Well-respected archaeologists of the day were co-opted to look for pagan Germanic ancestors. Some of the research and conclusions were legitimate, but when the facts didn't match the fantasy, the facts were discarded in favour of Aryan propaganda.

All of these were attempts to get back to Europe's 'true' roots, which included looking at bloodlines and lineage. Nowadays we would call this looking at the human genome or DNA, but DNA was unknown in the 1930s. There is footage of Nazi researchers in places as far afield as Tibet taking head, nose and eye measurements, looking for racially pure subjects.

Prior to the 1940s, experiments on humans were limited, but experiments on livestock were not. Animal husbandry was then and still is a standard way of creating new breeds of animals for various purposes. The Nazis wanted to breed cows selectively in an attempt to return them to their origins, and the Heck cow was a result of this program. They were specially bred by the German zoologists and brothers Heinz and Lutz Heck to simulate what a racially pure cow would have looked like, according to Nazi theories.

In particular, the Nazis wanted to recreate the long-extinct auroch (a kind of ancient bovine species), but as they also wanted the cows to be aggressive part of the managed breeding programme involved the use of Spanish fighting bulls. So, the Heck cow is a kind of Nazi super cow (a phrase I don't get to use all that often).

As for the Heck cows in Devon, they were, somewhat ironically, turned into rather tasty sausages.

IBM Didn't Think There Was Much of a Future for Computers

Advances in science are always tough to predict, but if a business is centred on a certain type of product, it should do better than IBM did when it comes to predicting the future of that product. In 1943, Thomas Watson, the CEO of IBM, anticipated that in the future,

> The world market for computers would be, maybe, five computers.

That's less than one per continent. The man was the head of a computer manufacturing company, and he wasn't even predicting the need for every capital city in the world to have a computer.

First of all, the statement begs the question, 'If this was the case, why was IBM in business?' And secondly, Watson was stunningly wrong. Today, mobile phones (even old ones) have more processing power than was used to land man on the moon. The modern iPhone (just one of them) has more computer power than the entire globe possessed in 1950. So, shame on Mr Watson for his spectacularly myopic vision.

Modern computers may have changed the world, but it's the internet that's changing history and moulding us as we go on. It's not always a force for good, but we now know far more than we ever did.

But perhaps we shouldn't judge Mr Watson too harshly. Getting the future wrong is not a sign of stupidity, as illustrated by the following quote from 1932:

> There is not the slightest indication that nuclear energy will ever be obtainable. It would mean that the atom would have to be shattered at will.
>
> Albert Einstein

The Nazi Doomsday Device That Could Have Won the War

Nazi experimental weapons are the stuff of legends. While they did not invent the jet engine (that was a Brit), they did have the first jet fighter. But then there were the outlandish prototypes, like the 100-ton Maus tank or the V2 rocket, and other weird inventions that never left the drawing board.

Perhaps their most bizarre idea was one only recently unearthed from a forgotten article in a 1945 issue of 'Life' magazine, which revealed that US Army technical experts came up with the astonishing fact that German scientists had seriously planned to build a "sun gun"'. The design was a mile-wide giant mirror, which could be used to focus the sun on a target, rather like a magnifying glass being able to concentrate sunlight.

The giant orbital mirror would 'focus the sun's rays to a scorching point on the Earth's surface'. The German army hoped to use such a mirror to burn an enemy city or to boil part of an ocean'.

The idea was not exactly new, and pre-dated Hitler. The brain behind the idea was the German rocket scientist Hermann Oberth, who came up with it in 1923. He recognised the potential for rockets to put man-made devices into orbit around the earth, something we now take for granted but which was a revolutionary concept in the 1920s.

Oberth estimated it would take fifteen years and cost 3 million marks to construct such a device. Had his idea been taken up, it would have been ready for the start of the Second World War. But Oberth didn't have war in mind when he dreamed up this idea. No, the original purpose of the space mirror was to provide the people of Earth with sunshine on demand, anywhere on the globe. It was only later that he described this as the 'ultimate weapon'. 'My space mirror,' he wrote, 'is like the hand mirrors that schoolboys use to flash circles of sunlight on the ceiling of their classroom. A sudden beam flashed on the teacher's face may bring unpleasant reactions.'

Had it been constructed, it might well have worked, and it's hard to see how the Allies could have countered such a weapon. Fortunately for the free world, Oberth wasn't given funding.

The Olympic Torch Relay Was a Nazi Invention

It may surprise you to learn that the idea of lighting the Olympic torch in Greece and then relaying it to its destination wasn't original to the first modern Olympics but came more than a generation later. The first modern Olympic Games, held in Athens in 1896, were a small affair, with just fourteen nations and a total of 241 athletes who competed in forty-three events. The first time a torch relay was conducted was for the 1936 Berlin Olympics and was the brain child of Carl Diem, who was the Secretary General of the Organising Committee of the Berlin Olympic Games.

The lighting of the torch itself wasn't new in 1936. The first time it appeared as a centre piece was at the 1928 Summer Olympics in Amsterdam. However, the idea of a relay from a torch lit at the site of the original games and then carried to the location of the new games was an innovation that can be linked directly to 1936. It was so novel that it had no precedent in the ancient version of the games, either.

The list of destinations for the relay was Olympia (Greece) – Athens (Greece) – Thessaloniki (Greece) – Sofia (Bulgaria) – Belgrade (Yugoslavia) – Budapest (Hungary) – Vienna (Austria) – Prague (Czechoslovakia) – Dresden (Germany) – Berlin (Germany). Ironically, in just a very few years, all of these destinations would become either German allies or would be occupied by Axis forces.

The fact that the relay was a Nazi invention led to a dilemma for the first Olympics held after the Second World War (these were the 1948 Games, held in London). The problem was this: it's a good idea, but do we want to copy a Nazi concept? The British Olympic committee decided that it was such a good idea that it should be continued and established as a new tradition (although the situation was further complicated by the fact that Greece was embroiled in a civil war in 1948). The Brits had the torch lit at Mount Olympus, from where it was quickly moved onto a Royal Naval warship, which headed out of the Greek warzone as quickly as possible.

Of course, now the relay is regarded as an essential part of the Olympic Games, and it is hard to imagine them without the build up that this relatively new 'tradition' provides.

The Bravest – and Luckiest – Belgian

The British are immensely proud of their 'stiff upper lip' – the idea that while others flap about or burst into tears or get all emotional, the Brits remain calm and steady under pressure. It's a cliché which seems to be true.

Some claim the Brits are this way because of the Anglo-Saxon DNA that courses through their veins, but it could be it's something from the culture of this island nation. This is, after all, a nation where when somebody steps on our toes, we (the stepped upon) are conditioned to say 'sorry', whereas others are more likely to make a scene.

However, for further evidence that the British stiff upper lip is something that is learnt, rather than something that comes in the blood, you only have to look at Sir Adrian Carton de Wiart, who was the very definition of an English gentleman with a stiff upper lip, except that he didn't have a drop of English blood in him.

Sir Adrian was born in Brussels to an Irish mother and was probably the illegitimate son of the King of Belgium Leopold II, although officially his father was Leon Constant Ghislain Carton de Wiart. He went to an English boarding school and later to Balliol College, Oxford, but left university to join the British Army at the time of the Second Boer War.

He lied about his age (he was nineteen) and enrolled under the false name of 'Trooper Carton'. At the turn of the twentieth century there was something romantic, even glamourous, about fighting for 'king and country', and joining the forces was seen as a noble duty. Whatever it was, it sparked something in this young man, who carried out the most ridiculously brave exploits of any soldier, in any army, ever.

Carton de Wiart never shied away from a fight in his life, and during action in the Boer War he was shot in both the groin and the stomach and was invalided home. It was only then that his father found out that he had left Oxford University to join the army, and he was furious. But young Adrian had found his calling in life, and his father eventually agreed that he should continue in the forces. So after recovering from his wounds, Adrian returned to active service.

As the First World War broke out, de Wiart was fighting with the Somaliland Camel Corps in the Somaliland Campaign. This was a colonial conflict typical of the age, and once more he was in the thick of the fight. During this campaign he was shot twice in the face. Yes, that's correct: the man was shot *twice* in the face and lived. He did, however, lose his eye and also a portion of his ear, and was awarded the DSO (Distinguished

Service Order) for his troubles. De Wiart had now been shot four times and sustained three serious injuries, more than enough battle scarring for any soldier ... so, time for retirement? Not for de Wiart.

Once again he recovered from serious injuries and went to fight on the Western Front, where he lost his left hand in 1915. His hand had been badly wounded, and the doctor refused to amputate his fingers, so Adrian, worried about the potential for infection, pulled off his own fingers. He now had only one eye and one hand, so he was clearly out of the fight, right? Wrong. He fought on in the trenches and suffered further wounds when he was shot (deep breath) in the skull and ankle at the Battle of the Somme, in the hip at the Battle of Passchendaele, in the leg at Cambrai and in the ear (the same one that had previously been damaged) at Arras. It should come as no surprise that he received the Victoria Cross in 1917.

However, we are talking about the 'stiff upper lip' here, and it would have been positively uncouth to brag about receiving the military's highest honour, so in his autobiography there is no mention of his VC, although the publisher added a section to cover the award. Despite all his wounds, de Wiart concluded with,

Frankly, I had enjoyed the war.

After the First World War, he was sent to the newly independent Poland at the time when it was fighting a full-scale war with the new Soviet Union. De Wiart had been despatched by the British government on a peacekeeping mission which was doomed from the start; during his stay, his train was machine-gunned by Ukrainian partisans. On this occasion he survived unscathed. He was later involved in a plane crash that led to his brief imprisonment in a Lithuanian jail, and later still, while on another train, he fought off a Red Army cavalry attack with just his revolver. At one point he fell from the moving train but managed to board it again ... and don't forget that he was doing all of this with only one eye and one hand, so even in the interwar years de Wiart was cheating death.

He became fond of Poland and settled down there to live the life of a gentleman – until 1939. When the Germans invaded Poland, he was made head of the British Military Mission, a role that involved no fighting, except for the part where his convoy was attacked by the Luftwaffe; he survived without a scratch. In 1940 he led the Anglo-French forces in the ill-fated Norwegian campaign, where he came under fire from German naval vessels. He and the troops were evacuated, and he arrived back in Britain to celebrate his sixtieth birthday.

In 1941 he was flown to Yugoslavia on a diplomatic mission, but his plane suffered mechanical failure and crashed in the sea. He was knocked unconscious but was revived by the cold sea water. He and the crew had no option but to swim to the shore, where they were picked up by the Italians and became prisoners of war until 1943.

Following his release, de Wiart was sent on a variety of diplomatic missions to Asia, and it was in Rangoon that he suffered his last major injury. He tripped on a mat, tumbled down a staircase and broke several of his vertebrae. The surgery turned out to be a blessing, as advances in medicine allowed the removal of large amounts of old shrapnel while also setting his vertebrae.

Sir Adrian Carton de Wiart eventually retired to Ireland, where he took up fishing and died peacefully in 1963. By the end of his career he had received twenty-four different awards from Britain, France and Poland.

A Conversation Every Guy Has Had: What's the Biggest Gun?

In terms of artillery pieces (rather than handguns), ladies and gentlemen, 'say hello to my little friend' Schwerer Gustav and Dora. These two colossal artillery pieces were transported exclusively on specially built trains. Designed in the mid-1930s at the famous German Krupp munitions factory, these behemoths were used by the Wehrmacht on the Eastern Front in the Second World War.

Schwerer in German means 'heavy' or 'great', and the fully assembled guns weighed nearly 1,350 tons each. They required crews of 500 to assemble, transport, fire and maintain them, and they fired shells weighing seven tons to a range of twenty-nine miles. The guns were designed for the Battle of France, but were not ready for action when Germany invaded. Because of Germany's blitzkrieg tactics, and because these giant artillery pieces took days to prepare for firing, the frontlines often moved too fast to get them in place. The only time either saw practical service was at the siege of Sevastopol during Operation Barbarossa (the German code name for their invasion of the Soviet Union), where, among other things, they destroyed a Soviet munitions depot buried in the bedrock *under* a bay.

Gustav was later captured by US troops and cut up, while Dora was destroyed by the Wehrmacht near the end of the war in 1945 to avoid its capture by the Red Army and its potential use against Germany in the battle for Berlin. Both guns may have been massive, but they were too large to be of any practical use, and it was the case that even larger weapons were being developed before it was realised that size truly was not everything. A bigger rocket-firing railway gun, called Langer Gustav, was being built when it was damaged in an RAF air raid, and the Landkreuzer P. 1500 'Monster Project' was under consideration as an even larger artillery piece until it was decided that it was a waste of resources.

In a way, these gigantic artillery pieces are symbols of what went wrong with Germany's weapons production during the war. The Tiger Tank may have been better than anything the Allies had, but it was hugely expensive to build, both in terms of time and materials. Meanwhile, the Americans were churning out a dozen Sherman tanks for every Tiger completed. Too often the Germans opted for the impressive or the complex over the efficient, which meant they never had enough of anything. While Gustav and Dora make a good story, the moral of that story may well be 'less is more'.

The Nazis Planned to Kidnap the Pope

In March 1939, Eugenio Pacelli became Pope Pius XII. He was to remain the head of the Roman Catholic Church until his death in 1958. This meant that Pius XII had the unenviable role of pontiff during the Second World War, when he was surrounded by totalitarian regimes largely hostile to Christianity. The Soviets ascribed to Marx's view that 'religion is the opiate of the masses', and Hitler wanted to destroy political Catholicism, which meant the papacy.

As a result of the times in which he found himself, Pope Pius is a controversial figure. His defenders point out that there was precious little a pope could do to stop the Nazi war machine. He did fire off a number of declarations pleading for peace and raising concerns about the Holocaust, and a number of Catholic organisations did help to hide Jews during the war.

Before his papacy, Pacelli created the Reichskonkordat in 1933. This reduced Catholic political power in Germany and, in some ways, helped to legitimise Hitler's quasi-dictatorial powers. However, for a man who was at the helm of moral authority, he never said much against Hitler himself. After the war, Pope Pius was so concerned about reconciliation that there is a question over whether Catholic organisations helped Nazis escape to South America.

So, while Hitler was probably no fan of the papacy, it is not unreasonable to think that he might well have tolerated the Pope. After all, Pius never summoned the Catholic masses (of which there were substantial numbers in Germany at the time) to outright rebellion. Except that Hitler *did* want to be rid of the pontiff, according to SS-Obergruppenführer Karl Wolff, a high-ranking member of the Nazi Waffen SS.

During the Nuremberg trials in 1943, Wolff claimed that he had been ordered to kidnap the Pope and take him to Berlin. According to Wolff, the plan involved putting undercover SS troops in civilian clothes and starting a shootout in front of the Vatican during the Nazi occupation of Rome. In the ensuing confusion, Wolff was meant to step in and whisk the Pope away to 'safety'. It wasn't the most daring plan the Germans might have carried out in Italy. That would be the Gran Sasso raid, when the Nazis sent paratroopers on gliders to free Mussolini, who was being guarded in a mountain resort. It was a daring raid which worked, so the idea of bundling up the Pope and moving him to Germany before anyone could react was well within Nazi capabilities.

There are testimonies to support Wolff's claim, but as the plan was never actually carried out and as there is no clear documentation to support it, historians remain sceptical. It could well just have been that Wolff, as a senior member of the SS, was trying to mitigate his other crimes by claiming to have disobeyed Hitler's order in the matter of the kidnapping. (He said that instead of kidnapping the Pope, he went into the Vatican to warn him.) According to those who knew, Wolff was just the sort of man who would have been entrusted with such a delicate operation, but opinion proves nothing. And although the Nazis were known for their excellent record keeping, they didn't have complete files on all their crimes, so the lack of documentation doesn't prove there was no plan, either.

Historians can only conclude that, while the plan sounds crazy, it isn't implausible, but the truth about the proposed kidnapping will never be known.

Running the Royal Navy Is as Easy as ABC

Trafalgar Square is dominated by a statue of Admiral Nelson, a man of astounding achievements. If you look at the wall behind Nelson, however, there's a row of men not nearly as famous, all of whom have fascinating stories.

Of all the busts, the one that should stand out is that of Andrew Browne Cunningham, known to his contemporaries as 'ABC'. In the Second World War he was the admiral in charge of the British Mediterranean fleet, which, for inexplicable reasons, has never been given the same consideration as other areas of naval conflict during that war.

A commander in the First World War, Cunningham served on multiple ships in multiple engagements and was awarded the Distinguished Service Order (DSO), eventually with two bars. So now we know he was brave, but what did he do that was so clever? Two stories are worth telling.

In the Second World War, the Italian fleet posed a considerable threat in the Mediterranean, but it had several bases that were simply impossible to attack from the sea. In 1940, Cunningham came up with what was then the novel idea of attacking the Italian fleet in port – with torpedo airplanes. The attack on Taranto was the first all-air naval attack in history, and it was a resounding success. The RAF lost two planes but sank one battleship and crippled two others. It was an emphatic victory and showed the Italian navy that there was no safe haven.

What's interesting is that this predated Pearl Harbor by a year, and while the Japanese recognised this as an effective form of surprise attack, it was dismissed by the American High Command as a gimmick. If only they had paid attention to the vulnerability of a stationary fleet, things could have turned out very differently for the US on 7 December 1941.

The second incident occurred when ABC was based in Egypt, a place that was crawling with spies and ambassadors working for the Axis powers. He knew they were watching his every move, so he used this to his advantage. Just when everyone was expecting him to go off with the British fleet, he made sure he was on the golf course at the same time as the Japanese Ambassador (at the time Japan was still, technically, neutral) and played his round in a leisurely fashion. The Japanese ambassador reported to the Italians that Cunningham appeared to be in no hurry about anything, which must mean that he would remain in port for at least a few days more.

However, the moment he finished his round, Cunningham was driven away and set off directly for a secret rendezvous with the fleet. The ploy ensured complete surprise at the Battle of Cape Matapan and resulted in another decisive victory for the Royal Navy against the Italians. The Allies lost three men and sustained light damage to some cruisers, but this time the Italians lost multiple ships, more than 2,000 of their men were killed and over 1,000 were captured.

ABC: what a guy – and every inch a Royal Naval officer. Be sure to look him up the next time you're in Trafalgar Square.

Hitler's 'V' Weapons

The 'V' in V-weapons stood for *Vergeltungswaffen*, which literally means 'retaliatory weapons', but the English 'Vengeance weapons' works too. The V-1 and V-2 are well-known, but not the V-3.

The V-1 was an early pilotless flying bomb that was propelled by a pulse jet engine. It was pointed in the direction of its target (usually London) and fuelled accordingly. When the fuel ran out, it dropped from the sky and exploded. More than 9,000 V-1s were fired at London, with a little over 2,500 hitting the city and killing over 6,000 people.

An early ballistic missile, the V-2 was a huge leap forward in technology and way ahead of its time. It would travel up to the edges of space and descend on its target at supersonic speeds. Once launched, the Allies had no counter measures, and more than 1,000 were fired, killing over 2,750 people. Both of the above weapons were neutralised when their launch areas were captured by the Allies.

Much lower tech, the V-3 was essentially a super artillery piece. It used high-pressure pumps to hurl artillery shells (each had an extra kick from a solid-state rocket at the end) from France to London. The idea had been around for nearly a century, but the Germans took it to a whole new level by building a massive concrete bunker in northern France to house the weapon. Had it been developed as early as planned, it would have fired 300 shells per hour at London, which would have annihilated the city.

The scale of production was massive. In order to accommodate it, the Germans hollowed out a limestone hill, with the core of the base 105 metres deep inside. The concrete roof was five and a half metres thick, and there were multiple shafts with fifty 'guns'. All of this was supported by an underground railway that also had to be tunnelled, and all of this was built with slave labour. It is not known how many died constructing this subterranean cathedral of firepower, but it was likely to have been thousands.

So, compared to the V-1 and the V-2, the V-3 was a step backwards in terms of technology, and the question 'why' arises. It could have been that, by 1944, Hitler felt he had been let down by the complex technologies of the newer weapon types, but as a veteran of the First World War he knew the destructive power of artillery. This is a guess, but it's not entirely wild conjecture. Regardless, a colossal effort was put into preparing this low-tech weapon of mass destruction.

The scale of this gigantic building project had not escaped the notice of the British, but the initial bombing raids couldn't get through the thick concrete defences. So the RAF turned to Barnes Wallis to design something to penetrate the thick outer walls and ceiling. Wallis had previously invented the bouncing bomb, and for this mission he came up with the 'tallboy' – today we would call it a 'bunker buster' munition. This giant ten-ton bomb had a delayed fuse and was able to penetrate the V-3's armoured defences and obliterate its working mechanisms.

However, that wasn't quite the end of it, as the Nazis still had the V-3's high-pressure guns and its ammunition (rather than a base to put them in), so some semblance of it was set up again in late 1944 in an attempt to support a German assault on the city of Luxembourg. The V-3 only fired a little over 180 rounds in a two-month period and, even then, only struck the city a little over forty times. So, the temporarily set up V-3 worked ... just not very well, and it was abandoned as the Allies closed in on the site.

The Great Escape ... in Wales

Most people have heard of the 'Great Escape' and have either watched documentaries or seen the very rousing film of the same name. But we never hear of any German attempts to escape prison. Did it happen? The short answer is yes, but the longer answer is 'the biggest breakout happened in Bridgend, Wales'.

In March 1945, a mix of Wehrmacht and Luftwaffe personnel hatched a plot to tunnel their way out of their prison in Bridgend. They distracted their guards from finding the tunnel entrance by painting a semi-naked lady on the wall directly above it so that the guards were always a little distracted – a brilliant, if lowbrow idea.

In general, German (and other Axis) POWs didn't try to escape from mainland Britain prison camps because it was going to be very hard to get back to Europe, and while conditions weren't great, there was no risk of ending up in a death camp.

However, on this occasion, seventy Germans tunnelled out of their prison before the alarm was raised; after a month-long full-scale manhunt in England and Wales, however, they were all rounded up. Most were found in the nearby countryside, although two got as far as the south coast of England, while a few enterprising escapees grabbed a car and others managed to get on trains.

One key difference between the British and German response to escapees was that all seventy Germans were returned to prison, whereas following the more famous 'Great Escape' fifty of the seventy-six Allied escapees who were recaptured were executed.

Of course, the war was to finish just a few weeks later, but the German POWs had no way of knowing this; they had hoped to get back home and continue the fight. In reality, and with hindsight, they should have stayed in their huts and painted more pictures of nudes as they waited for the bloody endgame of the Third Reich to be over.

The Forgotten Battle of the Rhineland

Picture the scene: tense British, Canadian and US troops sit cramped in metal landing boats under withering machine gun and artillery fire. Not all Allied casualties are from bullets and bombs: some drown, too. Am I talking about D-Day? No, this is Operation Veritable and Operation Grenade, a huge but totally forgotten offensive in February and March 1945, conducted by Field Marshal Montgomery's 21st Army Group. The purpose was to clear and occupy the land between the Rhine and Maas rivers in what was the Allies' big push into Germany.

The offensive had complications: First, the heavily forested terrain between the Rhine and the Maas rivers largely nullified the Anglo-Canadian advantages in manpower and armour, and the situation was exacerbated by soft ground and deliberate flooding of the adjacent land.

This was the heavily fortified northern end of the Siegfried Line, and the point where the Allies believed that a flanking movement around the line was possible. During the two weeks that the river flooded, Hitler would not allow Field Marshal Gerd von Rundstedt to withdraw behind the Rhine. Had the Germans taken full advantage of this formidable barrier, the casualties inflicted on the Allies would have been much higher and might conceivably have stalled the entire Allied advance. Instead, and as usual, Hitler was obsessed with not losing ground, even if it had no strategic merit, and he ordered Rundstedt to fight where his forces stood – a decision which was to cost the Germans dearly.

The fighting was fierce, but the US 9th Army was finally able to cross the river on 23 February, and by then other Allied forces were also close to the Rhine. Rundstedt's divisions, which had remained on the west bank of the Rhine, were cut to pieces in the Battle of the Rhineland. At the end, the Anglo-Canadians had 15,000 casualties and the US had 7,000. Rundstedt's army suffered casualties in excess of 90,000, while 290,000 were taken prisoner. This was one of the bloodiest, but also one of the biggest, Allied victories on the Western Front.

I'm presuming that this is news to most readers, which shows just how selective history is. For example, D-Day doesn't even get into the top five of the biggest battles of the Second World War (they are all on the Eastern Front), and yet it is seared into the Western psyche. It seems some moments just catch the imagination more easily than others.

The History of the Word 'Holocaust'

Say the word 'Holocaust' now and it means only one thing: the annihilation of Jews and other 'undesirables' by the Nazis during the Second World War. However, it didn't always mean that, and it may no longer be considered the appropriate term to use.

'Holocaust' was first used in relation to Hitler's Final Solution in 1942, while the war was still going on. The term is Greek, meaning 'burnt offering to the gods', and dates back to the Hellenic Era, so holocausts happened every day in pagan Europe, but not in the way we now understand. Indeed, making burnt offerings to gods was a fairly standard practice in many societies, including the early Jewish one. Such sacrifices in the Temple in Jerusalem were commonplace, and Leviticus even dictates the way in which these offerings should be delivered. In its origins, the word is neither anti-Semitic nor a crime.

The reason for its initial association with Hitler's acts of genocide was the burning of the corpses in the Nazi death camps, but as time has gone on it has been felt (particularly by the Jewish community) that it's the wrong word for the atrocities of the

1940s. After all, the Nazis put no religious connotation on the acts of burning, they were simply destroying the evidence of perhaps the most loathsome crime in human history.

It must be pointed out that Hitler's Final Solution was not aimed solely at Jews. Romany gypsies, homosexuals, liberal intellectuals and the disabled were all gassed, shot or worse, and all in huge numbers. The figures will be debated for some time, but it's safe to say that between 1940 and 1945 at least 6 million people were murdered in non-combat operations by the Third Reich.

In recent years, the term 'shoah', the Hebrew for 'calamity', has been used more and more often to describe these horrors. This seems to be a much better description of what happened, and the Jewish connection makes it all the more relevant. *Shoah* is also the name of the ten-hour long 1985 French documentary about the Final Solution. Further, the Shoah Foundation was established by Steven Spielberg to preserve the memories of survivors via video interviews, so that future generations can witness, learn and remember.

Do You Know about the British Enigma Machine?

The German Enigma encryption device, able to scramble messages so thoroughly it took the invention of the computer to crack it, is now common knowledge. Breaking the code has been turned into a number of books and movies and quite rightly highlights the incredible ingenuity and extraordinary brains needed to crack a code with more than 158 million million million ways to scramble a message. However, what isn't so well known is that the British took the German Enigma machine one stage further and called it TypeX.

The machine itself existed prior to the Second World War, but it was heavily modified with Enigma-style rotor scrambling and was used into the 1950s. In almost every way, TypeX was better than Enigma. For example, it had five rotor machines (as opposed to three or four in the Enigma) and the rotors contained multiple notches that would turn the neighbouring rotor.

It was also faster, with speeds of up to twenty words per minute, but the cleverest thing that TypeX could do that Enigma couldn't was to occasionally *Not* scramble a letter. This was significant. Those working at Bletchley Park were able to crack the codes because once they understood Enigma's rules of encryption they knew that Enigma would *always* scramble a letter. For example, if an Enigma message showed the letter P, the code breakers knew that the letter had to be anything other than P. With TypeX, you couldn't always be sure, which added a further layer of complexity.

So, why are you unlikely to have heard of it? Well, it was super-secret, and let's not forget that the Enigma story was pretty much unknown until documents began to be declassified in the 1990s. There was no Soviet or Nazi network of boffins trying to crack TypeX because they didn't know it existed. It was used by both the Americans and the British (including imperial and Commonwealth countries) during the Second World War and into the 1950s, when it was eventually phased out by newer encryption technology.

The History of the Bermuda Triangle

The Bermuda Triangle is an undefined (or ill-defined) region in the western part of the North Atlantic Ocean, where a number of aircraft and ships are said to have disappeared under mysterious circumstances.

The fact that you've heard of the triangle is due to a 1952 magazine article by George X. Sand, which highlighted the disappearances. Sand wasn't the first to write about them, but his article was the first to identify the area and to suggest a supernatural element to the Flight 19 incident. The article caused great excitement.

(To explain about Flight 19: this was the code name given to the five US Avenger bomber planes that took off from a naval base in Florida in December 1945. None of the planes returned from what had been a training mission, and official records state that they disappeared for 'reasons unknown'.)

In 1964, Vincent Gaddis's article 'The Deadly Bermuda Triangle' argued that Flight 19 and other disappearances were part of a pattern of strange events in the region. The next year, Gaddis expanded this article into a book, *Invisible Horizons*. It was an instant hit.

An entire section of the book industry has grown up around the seemingly inexplicable: the lost continent of Atlantis, Stonehenge, Nazca Lines; mysterious disappearances and unusual civilisations are popular subjects, explained by conspiracies, aliens and the supernatural. While the theories are fascinating, key evidence is always missing, which the author insists is part of some sinister plot that relies on our ignorance. So the absence of fact becomes a fact to prove the theory; it's genius circular logic.

In the case of the Bermuda Triangle, there is an explanation, and it's pretty mundane. According to the US Navy, the triangle does not exist and the name 'Bermuda Triangle' is not recognised by the US Board of Geographic Names. While people like Sand want to believe in magic or aliens, documented evidence indicates that a significant percentage of the incidents were spurious, inaccurately reported, or embellished by later authors.

A 2013 study by the World Wide Fund for Nature identified the world's ten most dangerous waters for shipping, but the area of the Bermuda Triangle was not among them. Also contrary to popular belief, insurance companies do not charge higher premiums for shipping in this area.

So the history of the Bermuda Triangle is that there is no history. It's just water ... or maybe I'm part of a secret government cover up ...

The Man Who Taught Bruce Lee How to Fight

Ip Man was the Chinese martial artist who tutored Bruce Lee. Any fan of martial arts will probably know that there are now multiple Ip Man movies, as well as a TV series, all of which are glamorised versions of the real man. In reality, Ip spent most of his working life as a police officer, probably quite a kick-ass police officer, but you get the idea.

The real Ip was trained by a martial arts master from a very early age, and he became an expert in Wing Chun, which is a defensive martial art based on grappling or striking an opponent.

In 1917, at the age of twenty-four, Ip joined the police force, where he remained into the late 1940s. During his time in the police, he trained other officers in martial arts, but he was not then a formal tutor. That was to come much later in his life.

Ip lived in turbulent times. He was a child during the Boxer Rebellion and later saw the Japanese invasion of China and the rise of the Communist Party under Mao. Because he had sided with the nationalists, rather than the communists, he feared reprisals and fled to the British colony of Hong Kong, where he reinvented himself as a teacher of Wing Chun. By now he had become a grandmaster of the martial art, but he wasn't a master of any kind in business and had to move his school several times when he failed to make enough to pay the bills. It didn't help that he seems to have become addicted to opium as well, no doubt using business income to fund his habit, but it's impressive that he was able to tutor to the highest standard while also feeding his addiction.

During this era the young Bruce Lee came to Ip to learn Wing Chun, and it was this association that would take Ip Man from obscurity to an international reputation.

Lee found Wing Chun and other traditional Chinese martial arts to be too rigid. He wanted something more practical and studied everything from Japanese martial arts to boxing and fencing before developing his own martial art of Jeet Kune Do.

Ip died aged seventy-nine from throat cancer in 1972, just over six months before Bruce Lee suddenly died. Over the years, Ip's reputation has continued to grow. Despite a difficult life, the fact that he was able to teach into his seventies is testament to the many talents of this extraordinary man.

The History of the War Crime

War is death and destruction, so there is a valid argument that war itself is a crime. But how war has been carried out has changed. Take, for example, a siege: the tactic of surrounding a city and starving it into submission has been used countless times by all nations. It was an accepted tactic for centuries, and there are many famous sieges throughout world history. But the siege of Sarajevo in the 1990s, which was conducted like most sieges, was considered to be a war crime. The death toll wasn't as high as the Prussian siege of Paris in the 1870s, or earlier, bloodier sieges, but the images of civilians dodging sniper fire and families slowly starving was, in our 24/7 media age, witnessed by millions who were horrified and sickened.

Sarajevo showed us two things: that humans can stomach only so much, and that the limit can change. With the advent of rolling news and the technology that feeds it, it sometimes seems like every death is reported and each death is keenly felt. A dozen deaths (or fewer) now constitute a war crime, an idea that was unthinkable even as recently as the end of the Second World War. At first the numbers seem to be too small to worry about ... until you see the footage. Then you care. War crimes used to be about huge numbers of people murdered or abused, but in November 2013 a British sergeant was convicted of a war crime because he shot one wounded Taliban soldier – like that never happened before in war.

The idea of the war crime is, however, probably older than you think. The first war crimes trial, conducted by a tribunal of the Holy Roman Empire, was held in 1474, when the knight Peter von Hagenbach was charged with *not* stopping a massacre. This was the first 'international' recognition of commanders' obligations to act responsibly in the circumstances. Hagenbach argued that he was only following orders (which I would like to call 'the von Hagenbach argument'), an excuse that would be used by countless soldiers of many nations in the future. He was convicted and beheaded.

The tipping point for war crimes was the Second World War, when the actions of the Nazi regime were so extreme as to raise broader questions about the 'standards' of war. This has led to anachronistic ideas, where current social norms are used to judge historic events and accuse past leaders of war crimes. While the judgements may be technically correct (and had any of the generals of historic sieges been tried today in The Hague, most of them would be in prison), it is unhelpful. Perhaps the best way to judge a past event is to think of it in terms of contemporary views. If everyone thought the action was 'business as usual', it wasn't extreme for the time. However, in the case of Peter von Hagenbach, his actions were seen as so outrageous and irresponsible as to put him on trial – so yes, he was a war criminal.

The Hague Conventions, international treaties negotiated in 1899 and 1907, along with the Geneva Conventions, were among the first formal laws of war. In 1945, the Nuremberg trials established other principles not only against genocide, but also against wars of aggression. Finally, in order to prosecute those accused of breaking these established principles, the International Criminal Court in The Hague was inaugurated in 2002.

General George Marshall: Genius or Fool?

George Marshall served in the US Army for over fifty years. He started as a platoon leader in the jungle warfare of the Philippine wars at the very start of the twentieth century and was an important planner in the two world wars.

Let's first consider his greatest achievements. He stayed alive in the Philippines, which was no mean feat, with guerrilla warfare and disease ravaging the relatively small American forces fighting there. Then, in the First World War, he was instrumental in planning the successful Meuse-Argonne offensive in 1918, showing his flair for the logistics of warfare.

However, it's in the Second World War that he becomes a more important figure in military history. In 1939 (when the world went to war again), Marshall was made Chief of Staff and inherited an outmoded, poorly equipped army of about 190,000 men, which he organised and modernised in the largest military expansion in US Army history. Many of the American generals who were given top commands during the war were either picked or recommended by Marshall, including Dwight Eisenhower and Omar Bradley. He may not have been a field commander, but armies need to be organised, and he seemed to be superlative at that.

Perhaps his greatest success came in 1948, when he realised that, because Europe had been destroyed by the Second World War, external help was needed for rebuilding. This would allow normal global economic activity to return sooner rather than later, and all nations would benefit from it. So the Marshall Plan was born, and America put aside $13 billion (at a time when that really was a lot of money) for the reconstruction of Europe. Contrary to popular belief, Britain was not short-changed and, in fact, got more money than Germany.

Marshall's plan worked. Europe did not starve, and the economies recovered remarkably quickly. In 1953, he won the Nobel Peace Prize in recognition of his plan – and it's not often a general wins a peace prize.

So far, so good, but Marshall made three very big mistakes.

His recruitment, training and rotation of troops in the Second World War were fundamentally flawed. Marshall wanted 200 divisions until President Roosevelt pointed out that America could do with a few people at home to produce things like planes, guns and tanks. So his initial proposal was more than halved to 90 divisions.

His second error of judgment was to send raw recruits into battle. When they were shipped over to Europe to fill gaps, inexperienced troops were thrown onto the frontlines, where they often lasted only four or five days before being wounded or killed. This put further strain on the existing veterans and led to growing resentment over the 'useless' new guys. Marshall was great at getting large numbers of men trained up and moved on, and they were also well equipped, but the whole system failed at the last and most important stage: fighting in frontline battles.

The above could be considered a harsh judgment, particularly when compared to brutal Soviet attitudes to training and casualty rates. However, this error pales in comparison to Marshall's worst mistake.

In the late 1940s, as well as the Marshall Plan, America was also putting resources into the civil war in China, and the American-backed forces of Chiang Kai-Shek were winning. In an attempt to broker peace, Marshall put pressure on their allies to pause hostilities. Chiang Kai-Shek was worried about stopping, taking the right lesson from history that if you're winning, keep going and use all the good fortune to your advantage.

The pause gave Mao and his communists exactly what they needed: breathing space to link up with Soviet supply lines. So when hostilities began again, Chiang Kai-Shek's momentum had evaporated. He was also at the end of a very long supply line, compared to Mao who was now getting equipment from just over the Soviet border. In short, in 1949 Mao won a war he should have lost, and the current Chinese communist leadership is the direct result of decisions made by an American general in the 1940s – not that the Chinese give him any credit today.

So in summary, George Marshall was a decent man; he was an excellent administrator who understood global economic recovery and had an eye for talent. It's therefore a shame that, as a general, he sometimes failed in the more 'military' aspects of his job.

The Most Dangerous Movie Ever Made

In the 1950s, epic movies were big business in Hollywood, but once the Bible and the Romans had been done to death, what other great historical stories could they do? The answer was a movie about Genghis Khan. Great idea. He was perfect for a number of reasons: the battles, the conquests, the rise to power – all perfect entertainment for movie-going audiences. Except they couldn't make him too ... y'know ... Mongolian; white America wouldn't accept it. So John Wayne was cast as Genghis Khan. After all, they were both good on a horse, right? Oh, and who even knew what a Mongolian looked like? They used Native Americans as Mongol warriors because, well, they are basically the same thing, right? Also, Mongolia was quite a long way away, and in the 1950s it was part of the Soviet Union, so they just filmed it where all the Westerns were filmed, in the 'badlands' of the American West.

As ridiculous as all of this sounds, *The Conqueror* was unleashed on the world in 1956. Despite the pandering to the imagined tastes of American consumers and the box office draw that was John Wayne, the public didn't like it, and it bombed ... almost literally.

The locations chosen for filming were the same locations where atomic bombs had been tested. So the cast and crew were exposed to dangerous levels of radiation for weeks on end. Worse still, sixty tons of sand and soil from the area were shipped back to the studios so sets could be created to help with continuity. Everyone involved in the studio shoot was walking around in lethal levels of radioactivity. By 1980, ninety-one of the 220 cast and crew members (including John Wayne) had developed cancer. Dozens died from it.

The film ended Howard Hughes' thirty-year career in the movie industry, and he spent millions buying up every available copy of the film because he didn't want anyone to remember it.

John Wayne was honest about the mess, saying that the moral of the film was 'not to make an ass of yourself trying to play parts you're not suited for'.

Racist, toxic and historically incoherent, this is one film that deserves to be forgotten.

Project Orion: Why We Should Nuke Spaceships

The 1950s and 60s in America must have been a golden age for mad scientists. All kinds of ideas were tested, with mixed results. However, Project Orion may win for most ambitious/insane idea. A nuclear bomb produces a huge amount of energy, so what if that could be harnessed as a form of propulsion? To be clear, the suggestion was not to use electrical energy generated by a nuclear power plant (those are being used right now in everything from submarines to satellites); this was using nuclear *bombs* as a form of propulsion to launch vehicles into space.

The idea was simple: detonate a nuclear bomb underneath the vehicle to be launched. Once in the air, gravity would start to pull it down to earth ... unless you detonated another bomb before gravity slowed the acceleration. A second detonation would produce a further burst of speed. Repeat until the vehicle reached escape velocity.

As crazy as this sounds, the theory absolutely works, with the added benefit that the space ship can be of considerable size (with a protective plate underneath to shield the craft from multiple nuclear blasts). For example, a 100-metre-wide ship, weighing 50,000 tons (fully loaded), could carry 300,000 megaton bombs to reach a speed of 10,000 miles per second. This would mean that it was possible to create a ship large enough and fast enough for travel to other planets and solar systems. The theory is counterintuitive, but it is currently one of the best that we have for travel to the stars.

Of course, you would have a blasted radioactive desert underneath the ship ... but hey, no plan is perfect. The Partial Test Ban Treaty of 1963 ended the project in the US. It was revisited as a theory by the British in the 1970s and shelved once again.

Project MKUltra: Why the CIA Invented Conspiracy Theories ... or Did They?

All spy agencies carry out duplicitous acts, whether abductions, assassinations, double-dealing or misinformation. It doesn't matter if we're talking about MI6, Mossad or the KGB/FSB. However, the one that gets all the attention and has the vast majority of conspiracy theories linked to it is the American CIA.

This is in no small part due to its unusual, illegal and absolutely genuine Project MKUltra. The code name is the label for a program of experiments in mind control. These were intended to identify and develop the most effective drugs and procedures to be used in interrogations during the Cold War.

The project was organised through the (now, unsurprisingly, defunct) Scientific Intelligence Division of the CIA, in conjunction with the Special Operations Division of the US Army's Chemical Corps. MKUltra began in the early 1950s and was officially halted in 1973.

The program used unwitting US and Canadian citizens as its test subjects. Carrying out secret drug tests on humans is, of course, illegal, but it gets worse. MKUltra used numerous methodologies to manipulate people's mental states, including the administration of drugs. For instance, completely innocent American citizens were given LSD without their knowledge or consent – and some died. Some CIA operatives knowingly took quantities of government-made LSD and had drug-fuelled parties. It all sounds like a wacky comedy, but one agent thought he could fly and jumped to his death. Other mind control experiments included hypnosis, sensory deprivation, isolation, verbal abuse, as well as more traditional methods of torture. Yes, that's right, torture. As an 'experiment'.

The scope of Project MKUltra was broad, with research undertaken at eighty institutions, including forty-four colleges and universities, as well as hospitals, prisons and pharmaceutical companies. Knowing this, it's easy to see why so many people became paranoid about the CIA, and to see how easily subsequent activities seemed to fit into the whole 'military-industrial complex' mythology, because that's exactly what happened during this project.

In 1973, CIA Director Richard Helms ordered all MKUltra files to be destroyed. However, some 20,000 documents survived the order, thanks to good old-fashioned human incompetence and the misfiling of classified documents. These surviving documents were fully investigated during the US Senate hearings of 1977.

As bad as this was, it was not necessarily the strangest or the creepiest thing the CIA did during the Cold War. 'Acoustic kitty' was the bizarre plan to use a cat as a recording device. It was not the cleverest of many wild ideas.

The Russian embassy regularly swept for bugs (listening devices) but was unlikely to suspect a domestic cat just sitting on the window sill. So the CIA, in its wisdom, decided that a radio transmitter should be planted under a cat's skin, and, of course, its tail was the perfect length for an antenna. (It's just possible that you have already spotted the flaw in this plan, which makes you a whole lot smarter than the CIA agents who dreamed up this nonsense).

When the CIA tried to train the cats to go to specific points, follow people and generally do spy-type stuff, the plan failed because ... well ... they're cats. The only field test was an utter fiasco because when the first cat was released near the Soviet compound in Washington DC it was promptly run over by a taxi.

This entire project is thought to have cost $20 million and was abandoned in 1967.

After the Biggest Gun Conversation, What's the Biggest Bomb in History?

It's got to be a nuclear bomb, right? Well, yes, but here's the thing: a bomb can be larger than a missile's warhead, and an aircraft can carry larger weights than a rocket, so the current crop of nuclear weapons isn't actually the biggest.

Step forward the AN602 hydrogen bomb, also called Tsar Bomba. Its test on 30 October 1961 remains the most powerful man-made explosion in human history. Developed by the Soviet Union, this very large thermonuclear hydrogen bomb had the yield of 50 megatons of TNT, and its mushroom cloud rose over 60 kilometres into the atmosphere.

The Tsar Bomba is the single most physically powerful device ever used by mankind. By comparison, the largest weapon ever produced by the United States, the now-decommissioned B41, had a predicted maximum yield of 25 megatons of TNT. To put this into another context, the 'Little Boy' nuclear bomb dropped on Hiroshima was around 0.15 megatons.

The weight and size of the Tsar Bomba limited the range and speed of the specially modified bomber carrying it and ruled out its delivery by missile. Much of its high-yield destructiveness was inefficiently radiated upwards into space. Quite simply, the Tsar Bomba was an impractically powerful weapon. After the test, it was concluded that a full 100-megaton detonation would create too great a risk of nuclear fallout (hazardous to the citizens of the dropping country, as well as to those on whom it would be dropped, of course), not to mention the near certainty that the release plane and crew would be destroyed before they could escape the blast radius. It looked like no one on the planet was going to go unscathed. It was just too powerful – the ultimate doomsday device.

Only two were ever built: one was detonated, and the other is in a museum in Russia. Let's hope that someone remembered to diffuse it.

Weather Control

Planning, logistics, military strength, training, sanitation, the list of what constitutes a successful military campaign goes on and on. However, one thing that nobody can control is the weather, and there have been many battles when the outcome has been affected by the unpredictability of Mother Nature's whims.

When the USA was facing an apparently never-ending war in Vietnam, it came up with Operation Popeye, the first ever scientific effort to change weather in order to affect the outcome of war. As the earlier article about the CIA demonstrated, during the 1960s the American government was sponsoring some, quite frankly, absurd ideas. To be fair, some of them worked: man landing on the moon was science fiction until it actually happened. At the time, Operation Popeye was classified, because nobody was quite sure if changing the weather was even legal.

Despite all this, it was a brilliant idea. If they could prolong and enhance the amount of rain that fell during the monsoon season, particularly over the Ho Chi Minh Trail that ran through both Vietnam and Cambodia, the Viet Cong and the North Vietnamese Army would have difficulty transporting supplies, tipping the balance to America's advantage. The logic was sound, and there have been plenty of campaigns that failed due to too much rain or lack of supplies.

The plan was to 'seed' clouds. By spraying particles into the clouds they would become heavier, and that would turn the cloud to rain. The aircraft used to do the seeding were three C-130 Hercules airplanes and two F-4C Phantoms.

How well it worked is a matter for conjecture, because it was impossible to know what the weather would have been like if the clouds had not been seeded. Also, it wasn't so much weather control as making clouds denser to trigger precipitation. No clouds, no weather control, so Operation Popeye was really just an attempt to give Mother Nature a helping hand.

As a matter of record, seeding the clouds caused precipitation 82 per cent of the time. But of course, even if it was working, it wasn't enough to win the war.

The US Air Force Dropped Nuclear Bombs on Spain

It's true. The US Air Force dropped nuclear bombs on Spain just once, but they dropped four of them!

In the 1960s the world was in the most intense phase of the Cold War, and the West was in a nuclear standoff with the Soviet Union. Both sides had enough nuclear weapons to ensure MAD (mutually assured destruction). However, contrary to popular belief, for most of the Cold War these nukes were not in missile payloads but in heavy bombers.

It was General Thomas S. Power who initiated a program whereby there would always be B-52 Stratofortresses in the air, flying over friendly airspace, but always within an hour's flight time of targets within the Soviet Union. This constant state of readiness was called Operation Chrome Dome. These B-52s flew thousands of miles, sometimes circling entire continents, and as such needed air-to-air refuelling to ensure they were always up there and always ready to go.

All those aeroplanes, all those bombs, and all that tension; something bad was bound to happen, and in January 1966, it did.

The B-52 in question began its flight from Seymour Johnson Air Force Base in North Carolina. Its payload was four state-of-the-art Type B28RI hydrogen bombs. The flight plan took the B-52 from continental America, across the Atlantic Ocean and on to the European borders of the Soviet Union, before returning home. The lengthy flight required the bomber to have two mid-air refuels – once on its flight out and the other on its return flight home. Both were to be carried out over Spain.

For those who are not weapons nerds, there is the question of how powerful is a Type B28RI hydrogen bomb. These were bombs that were meant to be dropped, not missiles to be fired. They could detonate either on impact or at a certain height above sea level. Together these four bombs had roughly 25 per cent more destructive energy than the total energy of all explosives used in the Second World War (including the Hiroshima and Nagasaki bombs). Forget cities, the payload of this one B-52 could level a small country.

On the morning of 17 January, the B-52 rendezvoused with a Stratotanker from the US run Morón Air Base in Spain. (It's worth noting that the name Morón doesn't mean the same in Spanish as it does in English. It means 'hummock' or 'knoll' in Spanish and is just one of those quirks of language which the locals do not find amusing.) The Stratotanker had the capacity to carry more than 35,000 kilograms of aviation fuel. What happened next is best described by the pilot of the B-52, Major Larry G. Messinger:

> We came in behind the tanker, and we were a little bit fast, and we started to overrun him a little bit. There is a procedure they have in refuelling where if the boom operator feels that you're getting too close and it's a dangerous situation, he will call, 'Break away,

break away, break away.' There was no call for a break away, so we didn't see anything dangerous about the situation. But all of a sudden, all hell seemed to break loose.

Major Messinger is obviously a master of the understatement, because a heavy-laden, flying fuel tanker collided with an airplane carrying four colossal nuclear bombs. The nozzle of the refuelling boom from the Stratotanker tore the top from the B-52's fuselage and snapped off its left wing. The friction from the collision caused the tanker to explode, killing all four men on board. The fireball was so bright, it was witnessed by a second B-52 about a mile away. As the broken B-52 plummeted to earth, surrounded by burning jet fuel and debris, four of the seven crew managed to escape the doomed bomber and parachute to safety.

All of this happened high above the little Spanish fishing village of Palomares, whose inhabitants were completely unaware of the death descending towards them. Three bombs landed near the village: one was relatively intact, and the other two detonated their conventional charges on impact but did not trigger a nuclear chain reaction ... fortunately (though it raises the question 'why'). However, the detonation of the conventional charges caused the spread of plutonium particles over an area of 260 hectares and resulted in a contamination clear up that would last for years. While radioactive contamination is nasty, it's not as nasty as a nuclear explosion, which burns as hot as the surface of the sun. Remarkably, there were no casualties on the ground.

Highly sensitive and dangerous military material was now spread over the Spanish coastline, and the race was on for recovery. The three bombs that didn't vaporise Palomares were quickly found, but where was the fourth?

Days passed and there was no sign. Had it been captured by undercover agents? Soviet spies? Curious locals? The answer was none of these. A fisherman reported seeing something splash down in the Mediterranean, and as there was no sign of the bomb on land it was likely it had sunk to the bottom of the sea. Now the hunt was on to find one lone bomb in the Mediterranean Sea. Using mathematical modelling, twenty-seven ships and submarines scoured the suspect area, but it still took eighty days to find it. As it was slowly brought to the surface, it slipped and was lost to the depths of the sea for another week until it was found again and successfully recovered on the second attempt.

The fisherman who had correctly identified the site where the bomb had landed in the sea technically had salvage rights. The US Air Force settled out of court for an undisclosed sum. The whole debacle is referred to simply as the 'Palomares Incident'.

Fantasy Fight Becomes a Reality

The film *Rocky Balboa* has an unusual premise: after the current heavyweight champion sees a computer-generated match between himself and Rocky, he persuades the former champ to come out of retirement for a final fight. Unbelievably, this somewhat ridiculous scenario has an historic precedent.

In 1967, radio producer Murray Woroner came up with an idea to settle every pub argument about boxing. He said that by putting all the stats and details of each fighter (in his prime) into a computer, it could determine who would win if they ever met. He used the then cutting-edge NCR 315 Data Processing System, a computer with twelve bits of memory (that's not even 1 per cent of a small update for an app today) to crunch the data and deliver a result.

It was a hugely popular publicity stunt, which took place in a series of radio plays broadcast as is these imaginary fights were taking place live.

One of the plays came to the attention of Muhammad Ali. Because he had refused to be drafted to fight in the Vietnam War, he was banned from boxing. Ali was close to bankruptcy; his reputation was pretty much his only remaining asset, so when Woroner claimed Ali would lose in a semi-final to Jim Jeffries, Ali threatened to sue for £1 million. Ever the canny businessman, Woroner offered to pay Ali $10,000 to participate in a filmed version of one of the fantasy fights: Ali against Rocky Marciano, who had retired fourteen years earlier.

Ali needed the money and readily agreed. Marciano also accepted the challenge. The two men, who had never met before, were said to have grown fond of each other as they fought in front of the cameras for days on end in order to get the right footage. The two fighters sparred for something like seventy rounds, which were later edited according to the 'findings' of the computer. As luck would have it, Marciano died in a plane crash three weeks after filming ended.

The fight footage was shown as a one-off event in 1,500 cinemas across America, and it was an enormous success. The estimated takings were $5 million. The 'computer' (really, Woroner, who knew Marciano was more popular) had determined that Marciano would knock out Ali in the thirteenth round, even though, in reality, this was unlikely.

Nazis, Nukes, Nixon and NASA
When Apollo 11 landed on the moon in July 1969, it was widely regarded as the pinnacle of human achievement. There had been numerous great explorers in the past, but the reality of mankind

walking on another world was something humans had dreamed of for millennia.

The Apollo landings were a huge PR coup for the USA, which was then reeling from the Vietnam War – a conflict that was not going well. The space programme was used to show America's technological superiority, wrapped up in a message of peace rather than conquest. The president at the time was Richard Nixon, who was later mired in sinister scandal and forced to resign – the only US President ever to do so. Not even NASA's Apollo programme could salvage his irredeemably tarnished reputation.

But NASA itself was built on sinister foundations. A significant core of the rocket scientists (most notably Werner von Braun) were Nazi engineers who had worked on the 'V' weapons of the Second World War. In the space of twenty-five years, the flying bombs and missiles of the Nazi war machine had been turned into the US rockets of peaceful space exploration. Except that isn't strictly true, either. The vehicles of the NASA Mercury missions in the early 1960s, while they did put men like Alan Shepard into orbit, were essentially intercontinental ballistic missiles with humans in the warhead.

Unfortunately for the Soviets, they had not been able to capture as many notable Nazi scientists as the Americans, but they too had implemented a space programme as a way of refining their ballistic nuclear technology under the banner of space exploration. Indeed, up until Apollo 11 successfully landed on the moon, the Russians had beaten the Americans every step of the way. They had the first artificial satellite to orbit earth, the first human in space, the first space vehicle to carry multiple humans and the first spacewalk – all were victories for the USSR.

The Cold War and the arms race towards MAD (mutually assured destruction) meant that the need for ever longer ranged weapons was essential to both Soviet and US strategies. The colossal Saturn rockets used in the Apollo missions were too large to be used as weapons, but their heritage can be traced directly back to nuclear missile technology.

Fortunately for the USA, von Braun and his team of German scientists didn't openly promote any fascist ideologies, and fortunately for everyone else, the nuclear missiles were only ever used as vehicles for humans.

Office 39: the Story of a Government Out of Control

This is recent history because it is thought that Office (or sometimes Room) 39 was set up in the late 1970s by the then dictator of North Korea, Kim Il-sung. The very existence of such an organisation is an admission by the North Korean regime that its economy doesn't work. The bland name is Orwellian, used to conceal the sinister behind an ordinary façade, because Office 39 is, in essence, a state-run crime syndicate.

The syndicate is designed to generate badly needed foreign currency for North Korea. According to a 2007 report published by the Millennium Project of the World Federation of United Nations Associations, North Korea makes an estimated $500 million to $1 billion annually from criminal enterprises, which are said to emanate from the mysterious Office 39.

As we know, the North Korean regime is highly secretive and trying to peel back the layers of subterfuge on something its government doesn't wish to make public is nigh on impossible, so Fact Alert: this article contains the most conjecture of any in the book, but the speculation is in step with the current thinking of international organisations such as the UN.

Office 39 is suspected of counterfeiting, money laundering and drug smuggling (including synthesising vast quantities of methamphetamine). As it is backed by government resources, it's particularly good at counterfeiting and is the suspected source of the so-called 'superdollar', a high-quality, counterfeited US $100 bill.

The activities of Office 39 are going on today and are under the direct control of Kim Jong-un. Without it, the whole regime would crumble, but its cash flow allows the purchase of prohibited goods as well as the weapons and technology that the Stalinist-style state needs to pursue its ambitions. Office 39 is basically a real-life version of the secret organisations that James Bond takes down.

The Erratic Revolutionary

There's almost always something in the news about elections (democratic or otherwise), wherever they may be, but the coup or armed revolt is still the most common way to change governments in the world. Here is the story of a lesser known 'revolutionary'.

Antonio Tejero was a Spanish military officer who, after the death of Franco, took up a new interest. Antonio tried his hand at a classic military coup, but he wasn't very good at it.

Unfortunately for him (but probably best for Spain), he turned out to be no Fidel Castro or General Franco. His first attempt was in 1978, when Tejero, along with high-ranking members of the police and military, attempted a coup d'état, which they called Operation Galaxia (which makes it sound a lot cooler than it really was). Nobody was interested, and Antonio was sent to prison for mutiny. He was in prison for seven months and seven days, which shows you how harmless the attempt was.

However, Tejero became a lot more famous when, on 23 February 1981, he entered the Congress of Deputies (the lower house of the Spanish Parliament) with 200 Guardia Civil, and held the deputies (MPs) hostage for about a day. This coup became known as the Tejero Coup, and there are some impressive pictures of intimidating-looking armed men in a parliamentary hall.

However, once again, Antonio completely misread the situation, and, more tellingly, he and his 'revolutionaries' were unwilling to fight it out. King Juan Carlos I gave a nationally televised address to denounce the coup, while urging the maintenance of law and the continuance of the democratically elected government. This completely undermined the point of the revolution, and the following day the coup leaders surrendered to the police without a shot being fired.

Tejero was the last of the coup leaders to be released from jail on 2 December 1996, having then served fifteen years in a military prison. He now lives in Torre del Mar in the Province of Malaga, presumably considering whether it would be 'third time lucky'.

Ever Heard of Suharto, Second President of Indonesia (1967–98)?

Suharto was born in 1921 and grew up in humble circumstances at the time of the Dutch occupation of Indonesia. During the Second World War, he joined the occupying Japanese forces and served in their militia, but he saw no military action during the war. After the Japanese departed, the British arrived, and he and his fellow Indonesians formed new battalions and fought the Brits back to the coast. To be fair to the Indonesians, after the Dutch and Japanese, they had had enough of occupying powers; however, had they bothered to pay attention to the terms of peace, they would have understood that the British forces weren't there to colonise them (although they could be forgiven for being suspicious). It was a pointless conflict, which led to the Dutch invading in an attempt to regain their colony. This guerrilla war was to last four years, but resulted in an independent Indonesia and gave Suharto the right freedom-fighter credentials.

In the 1950s and 1960s, he rose up the chain of command in the new Indonesian army. From the mid-1960s, things got complicated, but cutting a long story short, Suharto was smart enough to stay in power without upsetting too many people and without picking a losing side. He was a born survivor. After a period of yet more instability, he finally felt the time had come for him to make his move, and in 1967 he became president, backed by the majority of the military.

Suharto had seen the damage done by political unrest, and at the time the whole of South East Asia was convulsing with communist revolution, insurgencies and wars. Suharto threw in his lot with the West, which meant that from then on the West turned a blind eye to anything he did. Initially he did a good job of developing the economy, at first in terms of its natural resources, and later with cheap labour (Indonesia had plenty of unemployed people). There is no denying that the country's economy grew throughout the 1960s, 70s and 80s. Suharto was a fan of democracy, and he was regularly voted in every five years.

As his popularity and power increased, so did his desire to hold on. He cornered certain commodity markets and put his adult children in charge of them, while also ensuring that no government contracts went ahead without kickbacks. It is estimated that he and his family managed to steal about

$15 billion from the Indonesian economy. To put that into context, you would need to spend over $800,000 every day for your entire adult life to exhaust that amount of money. This is thought to be the largest amount embezzled from one country by one family ever (although some have estimated that Vladimir Putin has accrued a fortune of over $40 billion – something both he and the Russian government strongly deny).

There's only so much corruption any country can sustain, however, and in 1997 the wheels came off the economy. There was only one man to blame, and after thirty-one years in power Suharto was forced to resign in 1998. He lived for a further ten years with the threat of legal action hanging over him, but the deserved prosecution never materialised.

Something Strange Happened on 15 August 1977

Jerry Ehman was using the Big Ear telescope for a SETI (Search for Extraterrestrial Intelligence) project at Ohio State University in the summer of 1977 (the same summer that *Star Wars* came out), when a strong, narrowband radio signal was detected. Okay, that sounds incredibly dull and technical, so let's just say that this signal bore the expected hallmarks of non-terrestrial and non-solar system origins. It lasted for the full seventy-two-second window that Big Ear was able to observe it, but it has not been detected again ... ever.

So what does all that mean? Well, the radio signal could not be explained as a natural phenomenon, but it did come from beyond our solar system. So putting it bluntly, was ET trying to get in touch? The signal bore no relation to any other natural radio signal from space. It was nothing like a pulsar, and nothing like it has ever been picked up since. It is the single best piece of evidence that there may be intelligent life out there.

Except that if it was that intelligent, why send out a radio message just once? Maybe it's not that intelligent. Space is vast, and therefore, a message should be sent out continuously if there is any hope of making contact. But we know this level of stupidity occurs because we humans have been guilty of doing the exact same thing: we sent a message via a radio telescope out into space with the intention to keep repeating it, however it was shut down after sending the message just once because ... well, did we really want a reply? So we have direct evidence of a complex civilisation sending a single message out into space. Did ET do the same thing?

One possible explanation has only recently been proposed. Antonio Paris, of St Petersburg College in Florida, says that the signal originated at the point where two suspect comets – 266/P Christensen and P/2008 Y2 (Gibbs) – would have been passing at the time. As they released hydrogen, they would have generated the signal, but as neither comet was known in 1977, nobody thought to look for them. However, this is still just a theory.

Amazed at how closely this signal matched the expected signature of an interstellar signal, Ehman circled it on the computer printout and wrote 'Wow!' on its side. It is now called the Wow Signal.

How Old Is the World's Oldest Cyberattack?

While this book covers all eras of history, clearly this particular item won't be from ancient Rome. Because the internet has been around since the 1990s, you'd assume the first cyber-attack would be from around then, right?

In fact, the very first cyberattack took place in 1982 and it was catastrophic. It was the height of the Cold War, and the CIA knew the Russians were planning to steal a Canadian programme that, rather mind-numbingly, dealt with pumping systems. So the CIA installed a 'logic bomb' inside the target programme. The idea is that the target programme works normally for a while, but after a certain amount of uses, the programme changes and does something malicious. The amount of uses is, in effect, the fuse before the bomb goes off.

So what happened? Well, the Soviets stole the programme as expected and used it to regulate the flow of oil on their Trans-Siberian oil pipeline (I think you can see where this is going). Months later, the pipeline failed, which sounds like an annoyance but nothing too damaging, however the result was an explosion about one fifth the size of a nuclear explosion and the largest fire seen from space.

The Russians have tried to deny the story, but it seems more likely that the explosion was the result of a cyberattack than just poor Russian engineering. Besides, who wants to admit to being the first country to have experienced malware? If it was possible to do that with 1982 technology, imagine what a bored fifteen-year-old can now do with a laptop.

And so, we started with life on earth before the dinosaurs and end with computerised espionage. History is nothing if not a broad subject.

INDEX

Because the names listed come from so many different cultures I have chosen to make it easy, listing everyone alphabetically by their first name.